Riding Raw

A Journey from Empty to Full

To beautiful
Nadine -
have you
inspiration to
you have
adventure
much love

Sue Hollis

LIONCREST
PUBLISHING

RIDING RAW

A Journey from Empty to Full

ISBN   978-1-5445-1103-0 *Paperback*

        978-1-5445-1102-3 *Ebook*

To Robbie, Jake and Connor

As hard as it was, you let me go...it made no sense but as always,
you were right behind me. I can ask for no more. With all my love.

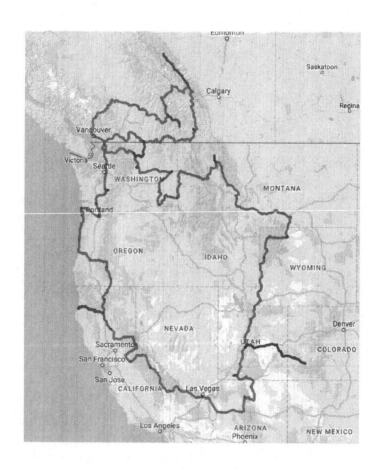

Contents

Prologue

I am so scared, I can barely breathe.

The time has come. I'm packed and ready to roll. I'm about to step onto my beautiful BMW superbike—Voodoo—and embark on a three-month adventure into the complete unknown. That is, if you can call the Pacific Northwest "unknown." It's always been my dream to get on a motorbike, leave everything behind, and just ride off into the sunset. That dream is about to become a reality.

And yet, staring down at my bike, I am terrified.

I'm not a person that scares easily. For most of my life, I have lived on the edge. I've been a serious corporate heavy-hitter for global airlines. I've braved the world of entrepreneurship by starting my own multimillion-dollar company. I've pushed through glass ceilings in male-dominated worlds (and still have the scars to prove it). I've successfully juggled career and motherhood (and no, there is no such thing as "balance"). And for fun—for rest and relaxation—I've injected adrenaline straight into my veins by racing motorbikes, diving with sharks, running marathons, and hurtling down ski runs at breakneck speed. So, no. I don't scare easily.

Why, then, is my heart pounding? Why is fear creating a river of sweat down my back?

Hell, it's not as if I'm heading off solo into the wilds of Mongolia with just a tent, a screwdriver, and a vegan bar. I'm travelling through the US and Canada, for God's sake. Hardly a treacherous environment (although some of the bathrooms I've already seen at gas stations might put that into question). And I'm not pitching a tent every night by myself. I'll be staying in motels (however, staying in a Motel 6 does technically qualify as "camping" for me). So it's not going to be a tough journey devoid of life's critical creature comforts—a comfy bed, a warm shower, and a hot coffee.

Why, then, are my hands trembling and I'm almost at the point of throwing up?

Sure, there are the obvious things that could go wrong—breakdowns, accidents, hitting an elk, getting lost, being lonely, safety scares, hitting a moose (yep, I'm pretty worried about the wildlife). But they're all things I can manage.

I have a very simple mantra in life: "Toughen up, princess." So when things get hard, I know to dig deep. I know that whatever happens, I'm going to be able to figure it out. I've got what it takes to push through, to make it work, to do what needs to be done. I am a warrior through and through. Shield up, sword sharpened. A solo soldier ready to take on the world. There is nothing in life I can't handle.

Except that's all a lie.

The warrior in me is seriously wounded, and I just cannot "toughen up" anymore. I'm standing here in front of my bike—terrified—because my whole world has fallen apart. Everything I believed in, searched for, and strived to achieve feels like an illusion. For so long now, I've looked like a success. But I haven't felt like one. Externally, I've had it all, but internally, a huge hole has been growing bigger by the day.

I am "perfect," but I am broken.

I feel empty and lost and tired. I'm mentally stressed, physically sick, emotionally drained, and spiritually empty. I can't keep living like this. I'm cracking at the "perfect and very successful" seams because it's not enough. I'm not enough. Something big in my life is missing. I have to find out who I really am when I take away all the protective scaffolding I've spent years constructing. And I am hoping above all hope that being alone in my helmet for three months will help me find the answers.

The solution? A 210 kg, 193 bhp, 1000 cc superbike called Voodoo.

But right now, I'm terrified. I've walked away from the life I've known, and I've got no idea where I'm headed or who I'll be when I get there. I guess, like they say, it's all about the journey, not the destination—and in the absence of any other solutions, I breathe, step onto the bike, throttle up...

And ride.

CHAPTER ONE

Having It All

"So, what's the deal? Have you won the lottery or something?"

Sitting astride a spectacular motorbike, cruising through the US with complete freedom at my fingertips, I could understand why the gas station attendant in Oregon had asked me that question.

But if someone had told me as a teenager that someday I'd be "living the dream," I would have laughed. Hard. A full-on belly laugh. *You're kidding, right? How the hell is that ever going to happen?*

Dreaming big was never on our family's radar. My parents were both loving and supportive, but there was never an expectation that life could be bigger than what I saw around me. And what I saw around me was pretty modest. It was a comfortable life, but it wasn't...well...*big*. It wasn't a life where you dreamt enormous dreams for yourself or were hungry to achieve the seemingly impossible. Big lives were for others, right?

My school career advisor obviously thought so. She suggested I'd make a great librarian. *A what?* She obviously hadn't noticed my short attention span or my lack of organisational skills. (They'd still be searching for misfiled books thirty years later!)

Uninspired but undeterred by her prognosis, I headed to university, where I dropped out spectacularly after six months, desperate to discover the world. Surprisingly, the big life was starting to beckon, and being a deckhand on a gunrunner's boat in Antibes was infinitely more exciting than studying Arts Law. (OK, confession: I didn't know he was a gunrunner till much later.)

Eventually, through luck, smoke and mirrors, and a small degree of talent, I managed to bluff my way into a pretty amazing career. After wistfully saying goodbye to a life of intrigue and suspense on the high seas in France (I still flinch when I see men carrying black suitcases), I wandered home to commence life. To get a proper job and become a grown-up.

CAN SHE CUT IT?

And life was good to me. I accidentally fell into travel (I figured if I wanted to keep exploring, I needed someone else to pay for it), where I eventually encountered three amazing mentors who saw more in me than I saw in myself. They nurtured and grew me and, I truly believe, promoted me well beyond my levels of capability.

Somehow, I managed to fake my way from promotion to promotion, although I'm sure I didn't fool everyone, and within a few years, I'd created a pretty heavy-duty career as a senior executive working for major international airlines—a career that allowed me to live and work in amazing countries. (My hunch was right. Stepping into travel did pay off.) However, it was a tough world. It was a confronting, fiercely masculine environment, and to hold your own, you had to be one of the boys. No time for feminine values here—you had to be strong, fearless, and competitive, and you had to play hard.

So I was. And I did. When I was the first woman promoted into a very senior role, the question wasn't, "Has she got what it takes to do the job?" No. The question was, "Yeah, but can she cut it with the boys?" I told them I could piss standing up if I had to. Bring it on.

I was relentless, I was ferocious, and I was driven. I had to be. My survival depended on it.

But that world took its toll. By then, I had two small sons, I was on an aircraft day in, day out, I had zero control over my life, and for the first time ever, my values were becoming more meaningful to me. That was something I'd never seen coming. My career had always been my driving force. Realising that being true to myself had become more important than the next promotion was a shock. But it was a shock I had to respond to. I felt I was losing my soul.

So I quit. Adios. Goodbye. Thanks for having me. I just up and left.

As radical as it sounds, I did have a Plan B. For a long time, I'd been too scared to ask myself the question, "Are you happy?" Because I knew the answer would be, "Hell no," and "Hell no" would need action. "Hell no" couldn't just hang there, unattended, indefinitely. Something would need to be done about it.

But I wasn't happy. I was desperately unhappy in a corporate environment where I had no control, where I was engulfed by an oppressive atmosphere, where my values didn't count, where I felt I couldn't make a difference.

But there was more...deep down inside, I had a hunch.

PLAN B

You know when people tell you to follow your passion? I'm not sure that you do actually follow a passion. Instead, I think you follow a hunch and see where that takes you. For me, I had a hunch that I wanted to create something myself. To build a business based on values, that oozed amazing culture and inspired people to be the very best they could be—and, hopefully, could make money as well. Always important.

And so Plan B was hatched. Together with my fearless business partner, Grant—who was having his own hell-no answer to the "happy" question—we braved the wild world of entrepreneurship and started our own company. A company that, in fifteen years, became a successful, multimillion-dollar travel management business.

Remind me again why I didn't want to become a librarian?

But wow, it was scary. They say you're either a corporate player or an entrepreneur—you're very rarely both. I now know why they say that. Being an entrepreneur is not for the fainthearted. If I'd known the pain, the fear, the sleepless nights, the continual state of panic, the ever-present gnawing in your gut, and the constant pleading with the bank that goes with starting your own company, I'm not sure I would have had the courage to go through with it. Fortunately, my crystal ball was cloudy in those days, so I leapt. What could go wrong, right?

Turns out, everything. At least in the early days.

The first thing you realise when you start your own business is that you run out of money quickly. Very quickly. Within our first year of business, in one week alone, we had a major airline collapse (they owed us money), our biggest client went into bankruptcy (they owed even more money), and then with the tragic events of September 11, everyone stopped travelling.

We were broke with no hope of recuperating the owed cash we so desperately needed. That's never a good position to be in, especially when you're surrounded by smiling faces expecting to be paid (trusting souls). My heart was continually arrested in fear as we begged, borrowed, and probably stole to keep our business—our dream—alive.

As the major breadwinner, the financial security of my family pretty much depended on me. When I decided to leave a high-paying corporate job to go rogue and become a potentially destitute entrepreneur, my very understanding husband, Rob, told me:

"I don't care if we all eat hamburger for the rest of our lives. If it's what you want to do, go do it."

It's just as well he said that. My boys ate hamburger disguised in hundreds of different ways for at least the first two years we were in business, because we were so broke. That was fine for them, but I'm a vegan. Kale's not cheap!

We hung by our fingernails those first few years. More than once, the pendulum could have swung the other way, delivering us a spectacular failure. But slowly, slowly, we clawed our way out and up...and eventually, we broke through. We gained momentum, the business took off, and the dream we'd held to create something incredibly special became a reality. Great people, great clients, great culture—it was worth everything we'd given mentally, physically, and emotionally to bring our baby to life and for it to have a life of its own.

THE FASTER THE BETTER

I was one proud Mumma, in more ways than one. I was proud of what we'd achieved in the business, for sure, but I was also proud of my two sons. Somehow, in all the chaos of me being a corporate heavy hitter and then diving into the precariousness of entrepreneurship, two amazing young men emerged—my sons, Jake and Connor. Despite the craziness I created around them—the bizarre hours, the ruthless work focus, the relentless pushing, the long periods away—somehow, they grew into good, strong, capable men. Men I was proud of.

Truth is, they had an amazing dad. While I was off trying to conquer the world, he was pulling them up with a heavy dose of tough love. I'm sure there were times they thought it was too much "tough" and not enough "love," but hey—they survived! And as a family, we had an intense and powerful bond. We were close, we were connected, and we were a team.

And this team got to live an incredible life.

By now, the banks were courting us instead of threatening us, and we started to breathe a little easier. I don't think you ever completely breathe easily when you have your own business. Somehow, it always feels like there's an asthma attack just waiting to happen. But life certainly became more comfortable. And with "comfortable" came a beautiful home, fast cars, breathtaking adventures around the world, and a financial security I could never have imagined. Wow. How did all this happen?

For me, it was also a life of adrenaline. The faster, the riskier, the more terrifying, the better. (Maybe I *was* meant to be an entrepreneur after all!) Adrenaline was my drug of choice, and I injected it as often as I could. My favourite hit? Fast motorbikes. Apart from a small Husband-Encouraged Hiatus when the boys were little (yep—even I could see the rationale of staying alive until they could make their own lunch), I'd had my butt on a superbike seat my whole life. When I wasn't clocking breathtaking speeds on a track, I was scuba diving with sharks, skiing double-blacks, racing triathlons, and running marathons. Yep, faster, harder, scarier—that was my life!

Without a doubt, I had it all. An amazing career, a thriving business, a loving family, a beautiful home with a garage full of toys, and a life filled with wild, crazy adventures. Despite my inauspicious and almost accidental start (moral: never trust a school career advisor), somehow I'd managed to tick the boxes on just about every possible criterion for success.

To the outside world, I'd made it. I was living the dream. I had absolutely won the lottery of life.

Hmm...really?

CHAPTER TWO

Living the Lie

I was living in a completely divided world—a world where my inner reality and that which I projected on the outside never met. The gap between them was huge, and I never considered closing it, for fear that both worlds would collide violently.

On the outside, I was busy showing the world what I thought it wanted to see. What it wanted me to be—successful, confident, dynamic, invincible. And on the outside, I certainly was all those things. Hell, without blinking, I could secure a $5 million deal with one hand while making a papier-mâché dragon with the other. Don't talk to me about multitasking. I had it nailed! And yep, I balanced it all brilliantly and effortlessly. On the outside.

But on the inside? On the inside, I was a complete mess. A walking disaster. A time bomb ready to explode. Why? Because I was running scared. Deep down, I knew I was a fraud. The life I'd created was only an illusion. I didn't deserve it. At any moment, it could be snatched away from me. Somehow, I'd bluffed my way into this success, but I knew I was a fake. It was only a matter of time before I was found out, and it would all disappear.

THE FRAUD FEAR

My first big career break was when I became the state manager for British Airways in Sydney. I was twenty-five years old, the average age of my team was forty—and you bet they were excited to have me. I had zero man-management experience and even less airline experience. I could barely tell the front of an aircraft from the back. But my boss had "seen something" in me (he's subsequently had his eyes tested) and gave me a shot. Brave and foolish man.

I had absolutely no idea what I was doing, as most of my team would attest to. Every morning, I'd walk into my office thinking, "Today's the day they'll realise I haven't got a clue and they'll fire me." But somehow, I'd survive the day, and every night, I'd leave the office thinking, "Tomorrow's the day they'll realise I haven't got a clue and they'll fire me."

But they didn't. They never figured it out. And although I didn't just survive in the role—I thrived—that feeling never left me. Ever. Throughout my entire career, no matter what the promotion or what the opportunity, I always felt like an imposter. I had no qualifications other than I was street smart, quick on my feet, and could hold my own in a fight—not normally qualities you aspire to as you're making your way up the corporate ladder. Believing I had no real depth terrified me. I lived in constant fear of being found out. That people would realise I was all talk and no substance.

I thought I'd be safe from exposure when we started our own company. But that terror never left me. In fact, it became worse, because this time, I absolutely had nowhere to hide. When the buck stops with you, you'd better have your shit together.

And I didn't. The Fraud Fear that had continually lurked in the pit of my stomach now inhabited my DNA. It had become a living, breathing organism throughout my body. I felt my whole world was held together by a tiny thread that was in imminent danger of shearing. And the real reason behind this fear? No matter what I did, or what I achieved, it was never enough.

I was never enough. And I was running for my life.

To anyone peeking into my life, that statement would have sounded crazy. But despite solid external evidence to the contrary, I didn't believe in myself. That piercing voice was constantly inside my head—that impossibly harsh critic who reminded me that I wasn't good enough, thin enough, successful enough, pretty enough, smart enough.

You know that voice...the one you just can't silence...the one that makes you feel that deep down inside, you're nothing?

I didn't need to worry about other people taking me down. I was more than capable of being my own self-assassin. And to make it worse, I was an assassin who didn't leave an external mark. (I must have picked up some tricks from my gunrunning days!)

LIFE AS A SUPERHERO

The challenge with never believing you're enough is that there are only two other places to find your worth: from other people and from your achievements. When you can't appreciate and accept yourself for being perfect just the way you are—warts and all—you create an emptiness. A void. If you're unable to find love within yourself to fill that gap, you hunt relentlessly for it externally.

My life was a constant search for external validation. My self-worth was inextricably linked to what I achieved and what people thought of me. I needed external success to feel worthwhile, to feel valued, to feel whole. I chased the recognition, praise, and awe in order to feel complete. Inside, I was dying a not-so-slow death, but externally, everything I was achieving was feeding me. I needed the outside world to tell me I was OK, and as long as I kept kicking goals, it did.

But it wasn't just enough to kick goals. If the only value you see in yourself is through others, you'd better make sure what they see is pretty damn spectacular. I couldn't run the risk of revealing my "true" self or of being vulnerable. I couldn't let the outside world see the real me—the fraud, the imposter. And so, enter the superhero, of course! A masked man in costume. What else would I have been?

I have to say, it's not easy being a superhero—having it all together, ticking off life's major success criteria, all while wearing eight-inch stilettos and a skirt so short it was probably more a belt. Not to mention that oh-so-attractive cape, and I'm not even going to discuss the undies on the outside.

But somehow, I managed to pull it off. Big time. I was the ultimate performer. I could nail strategy challenges, win new clients, manage multimillion-dollar budgets, and inspire people to be their very best—all before lunch. I could pull all-nighters and still pitch up bright-eyed and bushy-tailed in the morning. (Black coffee and I have a very intimate relationship.) Sure, I worked hard. Really hard. But the real trick was to make it look effortless. To make it look like I had it under control at all times. No one wants to see a superhero crumpled up in the ladies' bathroom crying with exhaustion and fear, do they?

Then, of course, there was the need to be a perfect mum. I went back to work when both my boys were six months old, and with that came the working-mum's guilt. The guilt that continually seeps through you and sticks a knife of terror into your stomach, wondering if your kids will become axe murderers because you weren't there enough for them. Too extreme? Not for working mums—we all know that guilt!

But I could keep it buried if my execution was flawless. And it was. Most of the time.

I'm not known for my cooking skills (a serious flaw in my superhero persona). More than once, I was found huddled on the kitchen floor in tears, bleating, "I can pull off million-dollar deals, but I can't make a Thomas the Tank Engine cake!" Yet I refused to admit defeat. I ploughed on with my creations, even though Thomas looked like he'd been through a nuclear holocaust. I'd like to think he tasted better than he looked, but I doubt it.

Most of the time, I had it nailed. I was on every school committee. I was a soccer coach and a lifesaving coach. I was up after midnight making beach dioramas (OK, I'd forgotten they were due). I'd sew buttons on school shirts as my boys were running out the door, because they were the only clean shirts they had and I wasn't going to let them wear a dirty one. I'd be up at the crack of dawn making "homemade" cakes for school fundraisers. (Packet mixes were deemed "unacceptable." Are you kidding? With my cooking skills, packet mixes were infinitely safer.) Yep. Flawless execution.

I combined career and motherhood effortlessly. How could I not? Late one night, I went in to check on a tiny Connor, who'd been snuffly at bedtime a few hours earlier. While I stroked him, his breathing became more and more laboured, and I knew he was in trouble. I'm not one to panic, but I'm also a woman of action. (Really?)

We bolted to the hospital, only to have him completely stop breathing in my arms as we arrived. They hit him with adrenaline, and slowly, he came back. Do you have a bigger fear in your life than that of losing your child? With pure terror in my veins, I lay with my small baby, cradling him in my arms, breathing him out of danger. Fortunately, the cocktail of drugs he'd been given quickly kicked in, and within a couple of hours, he was up laughing and being his cheeky, wicked self. Glad one of us was feeling the life and soul of the party! Connor was a million bucks, but I was completely totalled. The shock had taken about everything out of me. I could barely breathe, let alone speak.

They released us from the hospital at 0700—just in time for me to get home, shower, and be at work for a heavy-duty presentation to the airline senior executive board at 0900. I told no one about Connor. I told no one about what I'd been through just hours before—about my small son lying lifeless in my arms. I just fronted up, held it together, and successfully did my job. Because that's what heroes do, right?

IT'S A GIRL

In all of this, I'd love to say that my release was exercise, that it soothed my stress and gave me a place to feel quiet and safe. To a degree, it did. But instead of enjoying sport for the pure joy of it, I had to be a serious athlete. I wasn't content just being a weekend warrior.

I lived in a crazy world of 0430 starts to get maximum training in before the boys woke up, and/or I trained late at night after they were asleep. I raced triathlons, ran marathons, did 100 km walks—the tougher, the more punishing, the meaner, the better. No 5 km Fun Run for me. Give me something that causes misery, pain, and injury. Then I'll know I'm pushing hard.

I got injured. A lot. My trainer once told me, "I don't know why you pay me good money to completely ignore my advice." Why did he need to ask? I always knew best. Add a life of adrenaline to this, and the persona was almost complete.

Well, complete except for one thing: the look, of course. The look had to be impeccable. An amazing wardrobe, the highest of high heels, the shortest of short skirts, makeup perfectly and constantly applied (OK, that part was a necessity). I seriously had it all together. Think "Real Housewives," but without the boobs.

Yep, I had the look, and without a doubt, it was an integral part of my armour. And why the need for armour? Because deep down inside, I was a warrior. The superhero was my face to the outside world, but inside, I was a warrior through and through. I was in full survival mode at all times. Shields up for protection and swords sharpened for attack. Being a warrior kept me safe. Being in a state of constant alert and ready for war meant I always had the upper hand, and no one could harm me—which was often a prerequisite, given many of the places I've worked!

Family folklore tells the story of the day I was born.

It was in the days when fathers weren't present at births. My dad was told he was the proud father of a baby girl.

A girl?...Oh.

Now, I love my dad with everything I have. He would never do anything to hurt me, and he doesn't remember this story. But I do. Very early on, the "son"—the warrior seed—had been planted. Although it lay dormant for many years, all it needed was the right environment to grow. Corporate success created the perfect climate for the warrior seed to not just grow but flourish.

In order to survive, I totally embraced my masculine values. My life was completely goal-orientated and focused on achievement. I was competitive, disciplined, ambitious, and controlling. I led the charge bravely from the front—sometimes forgetting to take my people with me—and I was completely self-reliant. *Get out of my way. I've got this.*

There wasn't a feminine value in sight. Even my boys called me MumDad. I had no time to be soft. I was waging a war out there, and I needed to be tough. To be strong. To be invincible. To be feminine. To be vulnerable. To ask for help meant I was weak. It meant I was less than perfect—and I was never, *ever* going to admit to that.

I mean, who would love me if I wasn't perfect?

CHAPTER THREE

The Warrior Cracks

There's only so long you can keep fooling yourself. You can fool others for a while, but deep inside, you know it's only a matter of time before you self-destruct. I knew this warrior was seriously wounded, and eventually, my injuries would be terminal.

There were so many places I was oozing blood. For starters, I was completely driven by the need to achieve—the next goal, the next target, the next objective. But no matter what I accomplished, it was never enough. No success ever made me feel complete. Success was like a drug. I had to keep doing more, getting more, delivering more—but it always felt empty.

I never had time to enjoy it. When you live in the fear that you're only as good as your last achievement, you don't hang around to celebrate. You've gotta get back out there to bring in the next one, and the next one...and the next one. It was a vicious circle with no end in sight.

HERE'S MY CARD

My work defined me. Completely. My whole identity—my purpose, my reason for being, my value to the world—was inextricably tied to my job. On the inside, I felt like a fraud, but on the outside, my business card told a different story. My title was my validation. It opened doors, gave me credibility, enabled me to be measured and to be recognised. It told a powerful story of success and achievement—of who I desperately needed the world to see me as. I was my business card, and without it, I was nothing.

Here's the thing. When you're looking to others for recognition, you're always fuelled by fear. And fear was jet-propelling me. I was terrified I was going to be found out, and the only way I could protect myself was to keep doing more—to work longer, push harder, stretch further. The need to be perfect in everything I did was exhausting. I felt trapped and cornered. That old superhero suit was getting tight, and I was in grave danger of having my circulation cut off.

And so, I ran.

I ran from everyone around me. If you keep moving fast enough, no one can catch you, right? But the real truth is that I was running from myself. I could feel my world closing in around me, so I needed to up the stakes and push even harder. More work, more committees, more exercise, more adrenaline. Never creating space to breathe, just creating havoc, chaos, and perpetual, manic motion. It was the only way I could stay safe.

Except you're never safe from yourself. In all the noise and confusion, I was desperately trying to keep the silence from seeping into my head. The silence that I knew was clamouring to ask me the toughest of tough questions—a question that had been slowly rising like the tide inside me. It was a simple question, but one that frightened me to the core, because I simply didn't know the answer.

And the question? If I stripped away the facades I'd spent years carefully constructing around myself...who was I? When you pared me back to my bones and exposed my soul, *who was I really?*

How can four small words completely bring you to your knees? I've had political tomahawks buried deep between my shoulder blades that have caused less damage than this simple question.

I had no idea who I was, and eventually that damned deafening silence found its way into my head. The need to know brought the whole house of cards crashing down.

ENOUGH NOW

When the alarm went off at 0430, I didn't move. I couldn't move. Normally, I'm grabbing my running gear as my feet hit the ground. I'm changed, laced up, and out the door in minutes. I may not be awake, but I'm moving. But not that day. Nope. That day, I just lay there—willing myself to get up but unable to shake the ache in my bones, the pain in my head, and the fog in my brain.

As I slid out of bed and made my way to the bathroom, everything felt like it was in slow motion. I knew I was moving, but my legs didn't feel like they belonged to me. I knew I was shaking, but it didn't feel like my body. When I finally made it to the mirror, I knew I was looking at me, but it sure as hell wasn't a face I recognised. (OK, who does recognise themselves at 4:30 in the morning?)

My eyes were dull and lifeless. It was as if my soul had completely drained away. I closed my eyes and tried to get my body to move. But it refused. I managed to get my shorts on, but my arms didn't have the energy to pull my way-too-tight shirt on over my head. So there it stayed—half on, half off—as I slowly but surely began to melt down.

There'd been a number of things that had conspired to get me to this point. There were serious challenges at work, pneumonia and assorted illnesses, tough relationships, and chronic insomnia. But I'd battled on, convinced if I just put my head down, I'd be able to plough through. If I just toughened up, I could get everything back on track again.

Really? What was I smoking?

Today, there was no toughening up. I had nothing left to give. I gave up the battle of trying to get the shirt either up or down and ungraciously slid to the floor where tears of frustration streamed down my face. I knew I was beaten. I couldn't do this anymore. I was done. The life I'd so carefully crafted was over. I didn't have the energy to hold it all together anymore. It literally disappeared in front of me. I was so very tired.

I cried. Hard. I cried for everything I wasn't, I cried for everything I was, and I cried for everything I'd held onto so tightly, desperately thinking it would make me happy. But it hadn't. Far from it. Despite everything I'd worked so hard to achieve, to be, and to accomplish, I was empty, lost, and exhausted. I had nothing more to give. On the cold bathroom floor, I was cracked wide open. Unable to move, unable to breathe, and unable to stop myself from smacking my head on the tiles.

Where to from here? There's only up, right?

Eventually, the tears stopped. There's only so much a girl can cry. Drawing breath, I surveyed the scene. It wasn't pretty. I stopped struggling and managed to extricate myself from the shirt that had completely brought me undone. If my eyes were bad before, they were disastrous now—red, ugly, and shrunken. But they were the least of my problems. My heart was beating almost uncontrollably. I was close to throwing up, and in my head was rolling one long word: *whatthefuckdoIdonowwhatthefuckdoIdonowwhatthefuckdoIdonow.*

With complete clarity, a voice from the bottom of my soul smacked me hard: "Enough. Enough now. Just quit."

Just quit what? Quit crying, quit feeling sorry for myself, quit smacking my head on the tiles? Can you be more specific? And while you're at it, who the hell are you to tell me what to do? It's only a momentary lapse of not having my shit together, if you don't mind! Back off!

But it wouldn't. Those words kept coming at me, harder and harder, stronger and stronger. It's amazing how you can be in such a place of compete devastation—so overwhelmed and horrifically broken—but at the same time have crystal clarity on the way forward. I knew what I had to do.

THE WAY FORWARD

My whole life had been focused on building *head success*, but my heart success was completely missing. Despite everything I'd accomplished, I felt empty. My joy for living had evaporated. There was a giant hole inside me, and somehow, I needed to fill it. I needed to find what made me whole, what gave me joy, what set my soul on fire. I needed to find *me*.

At that moment, with my head still aching from the tears and the tiles, I was clear. If I had the courage to ask the questions, I would find the solutions. And if I was brave enough to follow through on the solutions, the hole would be filled. I didn't have the final plan sorted, but I was clear on the first step. I needed to slow down, to drift, to float, to be free, to just *be*.

I got up off the floor, brushed away the tears, put on a very short skirt, and for the second time in my career, I quit my job. That same day. I had to quit while the tile marks were still on my forehead, otherwise I'd have chickened out. I knew I had to make changes, and I knew I had to start today.

Now, it's one thing to quit your job in the land of the corporate. It's very much another to quit when it's your own business. But quit I did. I loved my company, and I loved our people, but I didn't love my job. I'm a great starter—I love the thrill and the pure panic of starting something from scratch (it's easy to say that now!)—but maintenance? Not my strength. I was tired, stale, and restless.

The real kicker? Deep down inside, although I refused to admit it, I was struggling. I was the front man of the company—the leader, the inspirer, the instigator. No matter what the challenge, it was my job to raise the flag. To rally the troops and to help drive us forward. But not anymore. Things were tough in the business, and I couldn't find the energy to shake us by our bootstraps and take us to the next level. For the first time ever,

I didn't have the answers. I didn't even know where to start looking for them. I knew I wasn't cutting it, and to stay would not have been the right thing for my company, for my people, or for me. It needed and deserved more than I now had to give.

None of that made for an easy conversation with my business partner. You can imagine how well that went, when I called him on vacation in Italy and blurted out, "I'm gone. I'm outta here. We need to find a replacement for me."

Next time I quit my business (and given my attention span, I know there will be a next time), I'm going to plan that conversation with a little more grace, empathy, and consideration.

Sadly, that wasn't the way I played it. I had to get the words out quickly or they'd dissolve in my mouth and stay inside me forever. But imagine waking up in stunning Italy—a double espresso in hand—and getting a crazed call from your business partner. Something along the lines of, "I haven't given this any thought, and I have no idea how it's going to work, but I just have to go. I have to leave the business. And soon."

Certainly not my finest moment! My partner is an amazing man. Together, we'd created an incredibly successful, powerful company. But a business partnership is like a marriage, and sometimes even good marriages struggle. We'd reached the point where we both wanted different things for the company. We both had different needs and expectations for the business, and that naturally caused tension. Sometimes good tension, sometimes not so good. Not being unified in our vision wasn't good for the company, and it wasn't good for us. It was time.

That conversation caused a lot of pain. He was shocked, angry, frustrated, and seriously pissed off. Rightfully so. I get it. I deserved that reaction. I'd given zero thought to the consequences of my "announcement" for either of us or the business, but I was so driven to act. I had no choice. It was impetuous but intuitive. Right down to my DNA, I knew that quitting was the first step to my recovery. To me reclaiming myself.

If a kickass career and heavy-duty business card were what defined me, it was time to let them go and really find out who I was.

SPACE TO BE

As tough as that call was, I knew I'd started to take control of my out-of-control life. For the first time ever, I'd listened to the voice in my head (the one I usually dismissed as being schizophrenic), and I'd stopped fighting. No hesitation, no second guessing, no thinking, "If I just work harder, everything will be OK." I put my shield down, and I walked away. Peacefully, calmly, confidently.

That is, for all of about thirty-two seconds before the "Holy shit, what now?!" panic kicked in. You know that moment—when it seems like such a great idea at first but then reality hits? I'd made this grand gesture and was courageously stepping away from the life I knew, but now what? It's one thing to realise you have to heal yourself, but it's another to know how to do it. I had no idea where to start. What do I do, where do I go, what do I learn, what do I change? How do I fill this enormous hole in my heart that's threatening to engulf me?

Innately, I knew the solution had to be in doing something completely opposite to everything I'd ever done. I hadn't found the answers in action, achievement, or adrenaline, so I figured maybe it was about having space and stillness. Maybe I just needed to be by myself. There were so many things I needed to work through, and I knew I needed to work through them alone. I'd gotten myself into this mess, so it was up to me to find a way out. (Still a solo player.)

So, what were my options? Meditation? Nope. I'd rather watch paint dry than sit in silence. Yoga? Not enough colour and movement. (I've always thought if you sped yoga up, you could get it over and done with in twenty minutes.) Retreats? Nope. I'm not big on navel-gazing in Bali. Spiritual advisors? Well, they were only going to tell me to meditate. Ashrams in India, walking the North Pole, climbing Everest, learning to base jump—they were all on the list. But nothing felt right. For a couple of weeks, I wandered aimlessly, drowning in confusion.

Where was that damn "enough now" voice when I needed it to help me know what to do?

Turns out, it was right there all along.

In the middle of the night, I bolted upright in bed. There, finally, were just two words: *go ride*. Of course! How had I not known? That's where my heart is. That's where my soul is alive. I need to ride. I've got questions to answer and wounds to heal. I've got armour to drop and spears to lay down. I've got layers to unpeel and truths to reveal.

I have to slow down, to drift, to float, to be free. To be able to follow my feelings, to connect, to create space. To just be. I need space, I need to breathe, I need to be alone.

I need the silence of my helmet.

I need to ride.

And what do I want to ride? A beautiful, 1000 cc superbike called Voodoo. So much for slowing down, finding peace, and letting go of adrenaline.

Oh, well. I can't break all my old habits at once.

CHAPTER FOUR

The Escape

If you think having a conversation with your business partner about leaving your company is tough, imagine how challenging it is to tell your family—your husband and your two sons—that you're going to "find yourself" by riding a motorbike around North America solo.

"No, you're not."

Excuse me? Think again, people. I'm going.

"No, you're not. This is not going to happen. It's insane. It's not safe. It's dangerous. You could be in the wrong place at the wrong time. You've got no support. It's not safe. (Did we mention that?) You're absolutely not going. We're putting our collective feet down."

Oh, that was the wrong card to play. You can tell me lots of things, but you can't tell me what I can or can't do. (That selfish, self-propelled warrior was still alive and kicking.)

I'm going. End of conversation. Just get over it.

Eventually, they came around. I understood they were worried. They knew I was a capable rider and could handle a bike in just about any situation. But they were deeply concerned about me being in situations where I had no control, personally or physically. Secretly, I think they were also worried I might not want to come back!

But for all their fears, they knew I needed to go. They'd seen the dark place I'd been in. They'd watched me slowly implode over the past few years, and they knew it was something I just had to do. They didn't like it. They didn't really understand it. They weren't sure how it would help, but they loved me enough to support me—or they knew better than to get in my way!

And so, what to ride? Who would be my partner in crime on this wild adventure?

SOMETHING SENSIBLE

The smart, general consensus was for me to ride a proper touring bike—something sensible. Something that had a big fuel tank so I didn't need to worry about running out of gas. Something that allowed me to carry a lot of gear so I wasn't limited to just taking two pair of undies. Something that had a comfortable upright riding position to save my back, hands, and assorted body parts after hours on the road. Yep, that made sense. I test-rode a few touring bike options, and they were good. Very good, and very sensible.

But since when had I ever chosen sensible over wild, crazy, and reckless?

Instead, I wanted a rocket. I wanted something dangerous and fast. A weapon. I wanted a bike that looked as if it were going 100 kph even when it was standing still. I wanted something sexy and beautiful—something that had the potential to scare me. I knew what I wanted. I wanted a BMW S1000RR. The fastest production bike in the world.

Despite being told by a bike dealer that he'd never heard the words "touring" and "S1000RR" together, despite knowing that the hours I'd spend hunched over a tank would paralyse my hands and arms and my legs would look like pretzels up around my ears, despite knowing I'd often be riding on fumes, that she was so tall that only my toes would ever touch the ground and that there would be a serious question about having enough space to carry heels—that's exactly what I wanted. I wanted a BMW S1000RR, and no amount of sensibility was going to change my mind. Looking good is all that counts, right? Why spoil the habit of a lifetime?

The boys and I had previously lived in Vancouver, and Jakey had recently moved a couple of hours away to Whistler, British Columbia, to work as a cinematographer. Whistler felt like home, and it seemed the logical place to start my journey.

But first, I had to find my bike. A friend in Vancouver went on the hunt, and within a couple of weeks, the purchase had been made. I was the proud owner of a spectacular, breathtaking, state-of-the-art machine, and it was love at first sight.

She was like a shark. She was sleek, moody, and menacing (a bit like her new owner, really!). She was dark and mysterious, and I knew she'd bite me hard if I wasn't careful. Her name? Voodoo. My mistress of magic. She would be my home for the next three months. It would just be the two of us together taking on the world, and I knew we'd be inseparable. Well, I hoped we'd *really* be inseparable. (It never ends well when you separate from your bike!)

While Voodoo waited impatiently for me to arrive, I tidied up the remaining ends of my life.

LOOSENING THE GRIP

I bought the maps, I packed and repacked my minuscule gear bags—having to decide between essential wet-weather gear or enough toiletries to set up a Sephora flagship. (It was a tough call. A girl has to look her best, even when wet.) I practiced with the GPS tracker I'd reluctantly agreed to take to appease my boys. And of course, I left my whole reason for being—my complete validation to the world: I left my job and my company.

After not-so-graciously breaking the news of my abdication to my business partner, and once we'd both stopped reeling from the shock and the pain, we luckily and very irritatingly found a sensational CEO almost straight away. (Damn, how did that happen? How could I be replaced so easily and so quickly?)

And it hurt. It *really* hurt. Letting go of my role was hard. My company had been my driving passion for over fifteen years. It was tough on my ego to hand over my role to a new and very capable CEO who grabbed the opportunity with a vengeance and instantly started doing amazing things, damn her. Things I just didn't have the fire or energy to do anymore.

But I couldn't have my cake and eat it too. I couldn't head out into the great unknown looking for answers and still hold on manically to my business. As painful as it was, I had to acknowledge that I was infinitely replaceable, and very slowly, I let go. It was absolutely what I needed to do, but it wasn't pretty. During our handover, there were times when I kicked and screamed and behaved very unattractively, but eventually, I loosened the grip on my fifteen-year-old baby.

Quitting was much more than letting go of the reins. Quitting was terrifying. Walking out of my company on the last day filled me with deep terror. What was my value to the world if the things I'd been recognised for didn't exist anymore?

And the real killer? Who would love me now after my superhero had crashed and burned? Who was I if I wasn't perfect? More to the point, deep down inside, *who was I really?*

They say that pain is the only motivator for change. Now, how lucky was that? I had a lifetime of change to make, and I figured the torment of riding 400+ kilometres a day on a superbike would certainly be painful enough to force me to make that change—and fast. I was in for a wild ride.

CHAPTER FIVE

Whistler to Osoyoos, BC

DAY 1: WHISTLER TO SPENCES BRIDGE

I looked at my bags sitting unceremoniously on the floor. Everything neatly and efficiently packed. I checked and rechecked—maps, tracking device, passport, gear—yep, all good. I circled round and round the apartment. The circles didn't take long—it was a very small apartment. Nothing forgotten, nothing to fix, nothing to add. It was all there. I was good to go.

Except I wasn't.

The more I looked at my bags, the more terrified I became. What the hell was I doing, embarking on this crazy journey? Was I insane? What was I trying to solve that couldn't simply be discovered in a couple of therapy sessions and learning to meditate here in Whistler? I was seriously pissed at the "enough now" voice! How and why had it brought me here?

I was scared. For once, I couldn't bluff my way out. There were the obvious challenges—a solo girl (OK, a grown woman) on the road, wandering through the great unknown on a motorbike. But that was well within the realm of "I've got this." There was a deeper fear that had me completely paralysed as I surveyed the detritus of my gear.

What happens if this trip doesn't give me the answers?

FREEDOM'S A FUNNY THING

I'd put a lot of pressure on this trip to "solve" the things that were causing me pain. To show me what I needed to do to heal the hole in my heart. But what would I do if the answers didn't come, if I didn't get any insights, if there was no growth, no big revelation? I knew I couldn't go back, but I had no idea how to go forward.

Letting go frightened me. This journey needed to be about letting go of belonging, of being needed, of control, of not achieving. Releasing *doing* and stepping into *being*. It meant letting go of having an anchor, then just following my heart and my intuition. Letting the superhero fly off into the distance and having the warrior take off her armour.

Damn—how come I couldn't just get on my bike and ride? Nothing like high impossible expectations to leave you unhinged.

I was also scared of the freedom. Freedom's a funny thing. We all seek it, but when it's suddenly given to you, it can be daunting. It's kinda like being given the keys to the Ferrari you've always wanted, and then being too frightened to drive it. Too scared of the power. Freedom means choice, and choice means conscious action. Sometimes that level of accountability can be terrifying.

Looking at my gear piled carefully on the floor, I had the ultimate accountability. This journey would be what I made it. The lessons that came from it would be the ones I opened up to. Healing and insight would only come if I surrendered.

Seriously? No wonder I was paralysed. But the more I stalled, the worse it got. In the end, the fear of not going became stronger than the fear of staying. Well, that and the fact that I was about to run out of daylight. Having wisely chosen to pack "dress-up clothes" instead of a tent, I knew I had to leave and find a hotel or risk spending the night on the side of the road. Always a good incentive!

When all else fails, you fake it till you make it. I stood up, juggled my bags—two side bags, a roll bag, and a tank bag—jammed my helmet on my arm and, taking a deep breath, stepped out of the apartment and into my grand adventure. I was on my way.

Well, kind of. What I hadn't realised was how impossible it was to pack all this gear onto Voodoo. If I'd had more than a couple of days between picking her up and going, I would have done a trial run with the gear. That would have been infinitely sensible. Truth be known, even if I'd had two weeks, it wouldn't have been any different.

"It'll be fine. It'll all fit. I'll make it fit!" Keep pushing, keep forcing—that always works! After putting the gear on, taking it off, and putting it all on again, forty minutes later, I thought I'd finally nailed it.

I stood back to survey my handiwork and came to two sobering conclusions. First, my gear looked like the Leaning Tower of Pisa. It would only be a matter of time before I lost the sum of my worldly possessions all over the road. Second, my beautiful thoroughbred race horse—my breathtaking race machine— now looked like a cart horse. I leaned into her closely, and in a whisper, apologised profusely for making her look like she should be pulling a plough. I knew she was embarrassed—she was a purebred after all—but there was nothing I could do. This was going to be our life for the next few months, so she'd better get used to it.

I had one last call to make before we hit the open road. I needed to say goodbye to my beautiful son. As I pulled up to his office, Jakey wandered out—the ultimate creative: black shirt, black jeans, black boots, his hair tied up in a bun. I got off my bike and looked at him in wonder. Where had he come from, this precious man-child? Surely not me. I was so proud of him. He'd overcome incredible obstacles to be standing here in Whistler, creating his dreams. He was so independent, but we were still so linked. Mother and son: an unbreakable bond.

He hugged me tight—I'm not sure which one of us didn't want to let go—and as he eventually pulled away, he looked at me and whispered, "I'm so proud of you, Mum...but do you really want to do this?"

I brushed a wayward strand of hair from his face—there were always rogue strands escaping from the bun. What should I tell him? That I'm scared beyond belief? That I'm frightened? That I absolutely don't want to do this? But that I need to—I have to.

Desperate for a last touch and with all the confidence I could muster, I held him tight and whispered, "It's OK, baby. I'll be fine. I've got this."

With tears flooding into my helmet, I got onto my wild, crazy big girl—my Voodoo—and together we headed off down the road.

DATE WITH VOODOO

OK, truth be known—we wobbled off down the road. In the movies, I'd have been riding smoothly and effortlessly off into the sunset. In reality, I couldn't get this girl under control. I'd never ridden with gear before. The weight distribution was all wrong, and she would just not behave. She wouldn't lean, and it felt like she had the aerodynamics of a brick. We were all over the road. And despite my brilliant efforts at packing, at the first big bump, my roll bag that had been perched precariously behind me flew out of position and smacked me hard in the back.

I learnt two very important lessons within the first ten minutes of my journey. Number one: no matter how tightly you think you've got things tied down, tighten it again and repeat three times. Number two: always pack your heels to the rear of your roll bag so they don't spear you in the back when it catapults out of position.

But eventually I started to breathe into being on Voodoo. We were only just starting to get used to each other—getting used to a new bike is just like dating. You start by taking it easy. You get to know each other gently before the gloves come off and you go at it full tilt, so to speak. Right now, we were still in the early relationship stage, when you're on your best behaviour, not pushing the boundaries—dancing around each other. At this point, I wasn't sure who was leading who, but I knew deep down in my soul we were going to be invincible—that together, our partnership would be amazing.

Or, we would be, after I stopped for gas. Had I chosen a touring bike, I would have had a big gas tank and would never have had to worry about fuel. Sensible option, remember? But Voodoo was a race bike and designed to be as light as possible, which meant she had a very small gas tank. I was paranoid about running out of fuel, so a mere 30 km out of Whistler, I pulled into a gas station and squeezed a pathetic two dollars of gas into her.

The old guy behind the counter looked out at Voodoo. There she was, shining proudly in the sun, looking more than a little menacing.

With a smile, he said, "Nice bike. Where ya headed?"

"Not sure," I shrugged.

"So...how will you know when you get there?"

"I'll just know."

He squinted, looking at me quizzically. "What will you do when you get there?"

"I'll come home."

"Sounds like a plan," he nodded.

JUST GET STARTED

Sounds like a plan? Really? What part of this was a plan? I had no idea what I was doing, I had no idea where I was going, and I had no idea when enough would be enough. I just knew I had to keep moving forward. So we rode, and it was glorious. Breathtaking. Heart-stopping. Up through Duffey Lake and into huge mountains sprinkled with fresh snow. Past aqua green rivers with sunlight bouncing off rocks and impossibly beautiful glaciers.

For once, I ignored my usual, "Stay on the bike, keep going till you get to your destination" impulse—the predictable, goal-achieving warrior impulse—and pulled over to breathe in the beauty. I parked next to an enormous RV—more an apartment block than a vehicle—and before I'd even eased myself off Voodoo, an elderly gentleman, wizened and grey, stepped out of the van and sidled up to question me about Voodoo and my journey.

Despite the fact that I was well behind schedule and nervous about riding over the mountains and into the desert in the dark, we sat. By the side of the river, we talked about life, about journeys, about regrets.

As I eventually stood to leave, he took my hand and mentioned he'd just harvested some fresh sage—would I like to take some with me? As he opened the door to the RV, the smell was unbelievable. I'm sure he must have been harvesting a few other "herbs" along the way, but hey—good on him! It made me laugh. This beautiful, gnarly gentleman, out there on the road—cruising, seeing the world, smoking joints, and harvesting sage. Too cool.

With my fresh sage (no really, it was sage) carefully tucked in my roll bag, and a smile in my helmet, Voodoo and I pushed on through treacherous passes where the roads were literally carved into the side of the mountain. Passes where I hung on by my fingernails for fear of going over the side. *Seriously—have these guys never heard of guardrails?* We passed through moonscaped deserts, huge ravines, breathtaking lakes, and dry, hot flatlands. Not bad for the first day on the road.

With exhaustion slowly seeping into my bones, I found my first home—a quirky little dot of a town called Spences Bridge. The infamous bridge had washed away years ago, but the town remained, as did its one and only hotel—an old inn built in 1852, which might have been the last time the bathrooms were remodelled.

But it was full of character, with a meandering river in the backyard and a railway line in the front. It was, however, sadly lacking a restaurant. As was the town. But all was not lost. Along the road leading to the inn were wild fruit trees—apples, peaches, apricots. With a bucket in hand, I wandered outside and picked plump, fresh fruit for dinner.

With the juice of a fat, pink peach running down my arm, I sat on my balcony overlooking the train track and smiled. What a day. The fears that had almost engulfed me in the morning had disappeared—for the moment, anyway. By the time I'd stopped fighting Voodoo and started to dance with her—after I'd dropped her into a few corners and felt her pull underneath me, I was home. I was breathing. And in the middle of nowhere with this whole crazy journey ahead of me, I was happy.

And those fears? Today, I realised that the more you think about things, the worse they get. The answer was to just do it. To just get started, get rolling, and get on with it.

I remember reading that the brave are still fearful—they just take a deep breath and step into their fears anyway. Good to know.

DAY 2: SPENCES BRIDGE TO VERNON

Another thing that would have been good to know was the true meaning behind my romantically named *Zen Suite*. My hotel room, described as being "superb for train enthusiasts" was shorthand for, "Beware: enormous Canadian Pacific express trains will hammer right past your window all night and blast their horn every hour, on the hour." *Really? Was that necessary?*

Come five o'clock, I was so wired and rattled that sleep was a distant hope. Putting on my running shoes—what else are you supposed to do at five in the morning?—I crept downstairs, let myself out the back door, and went to check on Voodoo.

Fortunately, the trains hadn't disturbed her. She was right where I'd left her the night before, which was a surprise. The owner of the inn had kindly told me to bring her in off the road and park her behind the hotel. Beautiful. I'd been nervous about her being on the road her first night out, and in theory, the offer sounded great. Except, "behind the hotel" was all gravel.

Now, Voodoo is a superbike. Anything other than tarmac makes her impossible to control. She doesn't do dirt. She doesn't do sand. And she sure as hell doesn't do gravel. Funnily enough, nor do I. I'm vertically challenged...OK, I'm short—162 cm without heels—which means when I'm on her, the only part of my feet that touch the ground are my big toes. And she's heavy—close to 210 kgs loaded—which is OK when we're moving, but manoeuvring her? If she falls, she falls. There's nothing I can do to stop her once she gets past a certain point, and there's no way I can pick her up.

I figured at some stage on the trip that would happen—it was only a matter of time because she was so big. But damn it, it was not going to happen my first night out!

It took me twenty-five minutes, a lot of bargaining with Voodoo—who'd already started to gain the upper hand in this relationship—and more sweat than I thought humanly possible to get her parked up. We didn't know each other well enough at this point to trust each other, and I was damn sure that despite everything I'd done to secure her, she'd be on her side in the morning.

But there she was in the early morning light: proud, gleaming, and upright. After planting a kiss of thanks on her tank, I headed off, following a windy, dusty road that led into town—with "town" being a few small streets and a handful of dwellings just off the highway.

MY FIRST GIFT OF THE JOURNEY

This small, quirky place was bursting with colour. Houses, trucks, fences—anything that stood still long enough had been painted all the colours of the rainbow. I noticed the dogs kept moving, as did I—just in case.

Grabbing fresh apricots from a tree for breakfast, I wound my way back to the inn where I immediately bumped into the resident "guest," Vincent. Vincent looked like he'd lived life to the fullest. He was in his early sixties, but he looked about eighty. I'm guessing booze, cigarettes, wild women, and very hard living will do that to you, but what a life.

With the fifth cigarette of the day dangling from his fingertips at eight o'clock in the morning, and a glass of "something medicinal" in his hand, he talked about his life—a life that had taken him all through Europe chasing success and women. I'm not sure in which order.

He was a writer with a handful of books to his name, a musician, and an artist. His watercolour paintings were breathtaking. But life had broken him beyond belief. Yet here, in this quirky inn with the river in the back and the trains in the front, he'd found his place of healing. We shared the back veranda—sometimes saying nothing, sometimes saying everything.

As I readied to leave and headed towards Voodoo—bags in hand and happy to see she was still upright—I noticed something sitting on her. There on my seat, held down by a couple of stones, was a small, beautiful watercolour that Vincent had left me. I'm not sure that any other gift would have been more precious at that moment. I didn't need to say goodbye or thanks. He knew. As did I. Tucking it carefully into my tank bag, I took a deep breath, kicked Voodoo into gear, and pointed her towards Vernon.

STARTING TO FEEL ALIVE

One of the brilliant things about riding a bike is that, in your helmet, no one can hear you scream. On the Coquihalla Pass—the main highway into Kelowna—I got to scream in pure, unadulterated joy.

It's a high mountain pass—close to 1300 metres—and it's cold. (OK, not so much fun.) And it's *fast*—so fast! Before I left, I'd been told by a number of people that I needed to slow down, literally and figuratively. That had seemed like great advice, until I hit the Coquihalla.

By this stage, Voodoo and I had stopped waltzing and had moved on to a tango. We'd started to feel like one body, one entity, moulded together. There's nothing like flying at 200 kph down a breathtaking highway to kick you into the next stage of your relationship. My big girl and I were hauling. We were at speed, adrenaline-fuelled, frozen, and screaming—Voodoo in her engine and me in my helmet—both spine-tinglingly alive.

I was laughing as I dropped down the side of Okanagan Lake with its colour unlike anything I'd ever seen—a stunning translucent blue caused by clay in the lake that reflects and scatters light in unusual ways.

And I was still laughing as I made my way into Vernon, despite the fact that I'd spent ninety minutes on a tense, tight, and infinitely scary mountain pass along Kalamalka Lake, only to be told near the end of it that the rest of the road was "closed for repairs." *Really? How long?* "Oh, about five hours." *Five hours? Ya think a sign at the beginning of the pass might have been a good idea?* Obviously not!

But what the hell—back I went, clinging along the side of the mountain, holding my breath and trying not to close my eyes in the scary bits (never a good idea on a bike). What's a three-hour detour between friends? It didn't matter anyway. Where else was I supposed to be but on an adventure?

DAY 3: VERNON TO AINSWORTH

Before I'd left Australia, I'd bought every map of the Pacific Northwest known to man. I had a rough idea of where I wanted to go—circle through British Columbia and Alberta, then head down to Montana, Washington, and California before winding my way back through Colorado and Wyoming. Every weekend before I left, I spread the maps out on the dining room table, looked at them for about five minutes, then carefully folded them up and put them away. The more I looked at them, the more daunting they became, and the more daunting they became, the less I wanted to go.

So I stopped looking.

I stopped planning. I carefully folded my maps (OK, confession: it took me two months on the road before I could fold a map properly), packed them all away, and decided I would just make it up as I went along. I would bluff—the story of my life!

THE FIRST LESSONS

Instead of choosing my route by destination, I chose it by

"Spectacular Bike Roads" deciding to only travel on wild, brilliant bike roads and cross-country backroads wherever humanly possible. Freeways, highways, and main roads were limited. Through most states in the US, that meant squinting over my maps at night, building routes to the squiggliest, squirmiest-looking roads, because tight, twisty roads meant spectacular riding.

Today I rode what's considered to be the seventh best bike road in BC, and if this is the seventh, I don't know if I can handle the excitement of the first. What a ride!

You have to hand it to the Canadians—they sure know how to build a brilliant bike road. Big sweeping bends and corners that light you up with excitement, all surrounded by breathtaking, heart-stopping scenery.

And if that weren't enough, they also throw in wildlife! Like deer. Standing right in the middle of a corner.

Now if you don't know much about bikes, your most vulnerable position is when you're in a corner—when you're leaning over hard and you're just about to hit the gas to pull through. No surprise—that's exactly where I was when, out of nowhere, two deer ran in front of me. I had three seconds to make a choice. Braking wasn't an option (if you brake in a corner when you're leaning, chances are you and your bike are going to go in two very different directions) so you make a call—*go left or right?* I called right, and fortunately, they ran left. *Holy shit! How did I make it through that?*

I was still hyperventilating about an hour later when I made it to the Needles Ferry, which would take me over the Columbia River. But I started to breathe once we were on the water. It was the first time Voodoo had been on a ferry, and both she and I loved it. The sun keeping us warm, the gentle lapping of the water to help us relax, spectacular scenery to keep us in awe—in fact, we loved that ferry trip so much, we did it three times that day. But not by choice.

ARE WE EVER REALLY SAFE?

Remember my potential gas challenge given the size of my fuel tank? Because it's such an issue, as part of my planning every night, I also made route decisions depending on where I could get gas. In the wilds of BC, sometimes that was difficult. But I knew today there would be a gas station just as I got off the ferry. I'd be safe.

Gas Lesson One: Nothing is ever as safe as you think.

We rode off the ferry and straight into the gas station—the only one for miles—and it looked suspiciously closed. But I didn't panic. There was someone out front. An elderly lady in an enormous pink robe sat rocking in her chair, a beer in her hand at eleven in the morning.

I didn't even get the chance to shut Voodoo down.

"Don't bother getting off your bike. We're closed," she shouted. "We were robbed last week, and I've been robbed so many times, that's it. We're empty, and I'm closed for good."

Oh. Breathe. I looked at the sign: 55 km to the next town. I looked at Voodoo's fuel gauge: 40 km till she's empty. *Oh. That's not good.* Do I ignore the precision of BMW technology and risk it? (Voodoo is German—she knows within a centilitre how much fuel is in her tank.) Or, do I go back on the ferry and take a side trip to where I know there's gas?

Since I'd already cheated fate once that day, I played it safe. I went back on the ferry, cut inland, gassed up, and then returned— much to the amusement of the crew, who I became great friends with as we sat in the sun together for two hours waiting for the broken-down ferry to be repaired. Never a dull moment on a ferry.

While we waited, I struck up a conversation with a fearless woman in her late fifties who was riding a Harley with a suitcase perched precariously behind her. Both she and the bag were barely hanging on. Her husband of thirty years had come home one day and demanded a divorce, completely out of the blue. Their separation had been horrific, and she'd been left with nothing except enough money to buy a Harley.

Incredibly, she'd never ridden a bike—or even been on the

back of one—but she'd taught herself to ride, put her suitcase on the back, and had taken off. Destination unknown. Time frame unspecified. She was just going to cruise until she'd had enough. And I thought I was brave.

Late in the afternoon, fuel tank satisfied, I pulled into the whimsical little town of Ainsworth Hot Springs, nestled gently alongside Kootenay Lake. I was in heaven. I'd checked into the cutest of cute little cabins right by the water where the room was so narrow I could touch both walls with my arms. My landlady—a beautiful Scottish lady with the accent, boobs, and hair to be a complete double for Mrs. Doubtfire—had upgraded me to the "suite," because I looked tired. (Really? This is how I look all the time!)

I sat on a tiny balcony overlooking the blue-green lake for hours—watching the water, unable to move, just breathing. As the sun went down and the stars came out—despite my "tired" appearance—I felt the weight I'd been carrying starting to melt. There was such a confidence in my heart and soul that I'd made the right decision by getting on the bike. I was so sure that I was doing the right thing, and that whatever came my way was meant to come my way.

I smiled. *I'm doing it! I'm actually doing it! And...I'm happy.*

DAY 4: AINSWORTH HOT SPRINGS TO RADIUM HOT SPRINGS

I was so happy, in fact, that as I headed out for my sunrise run along the river the next day, I just had to belt out a few tunes. The sun was on my shoulder, the air was crisp, the lake was sparkling. I was so in awe of everything—just buzzing to be alive. How could I not sing my lungs out as I ran? Embarrassing for sure, but only the deer could hear me.

Turning the corner for home, I passed two RVs parked in a pullout, where they'd enjoyed a spectacular view of the lake overnight. Their owners were sitting peacefully in fold-out chairs, breathing in the view and the morning, their hands wrapped around huge steaming mugs of coffee. Sucker that I am for coffee first thing in the morning, I slowed down to a trot on the off chance they had a fresh pot brewing.

The plan worked. Within minutes, they'd pulled up a chair, and I was sitting—coffee in hand—sharing the world with three beautiful fellow gypsies.

For nearly two hours, we sat in the sun together—trading stories, trading lives, trading dreams. I was stunned by their openness and their willingness to let a complete stranger into their world. They didn't know anything about me. We didn't talk about my "history." I wasn't my achievements, I was just me—at that point in time, a wild, smelly Aussie out running on the banks of Kootenay Lake who happened to drop in for coffee and a chat. I didn't need to be anything or anyone else. Just me. And it was perfect.

FIGHT OR FLIGHT MODE

I ran back busting with bliss and gratitude for the incredible morning I'd just shared. It'd had a huge impact on me, and my heart was bursting as I headed back to my cabin. But as I stepped into my room, the air was instantly sucked out of my lungs. There on my bed sat an enormous plastic bag—a plastic bag filled with all the colours of the rainbow. A plastic bag filled with my medication.

The truth was, I'd been pushing life pretty hard before my "enough now" wake-up call. I wasn't taking care of myself, and my body was slowly starting to fall apart with injury after injury. It got to the stage where my trainer pulled me aside one day and asked me what the hell was going on—reminding me that an injury was always your body's way of telling you that something's not working in your life.

Yeah, yeah—whatever. Life's perfect, thanks. Increase the training, please.

But the real downhill spiral started when an annoying cough turned into pneumonia, which is what happens when you ignore your body and try to push through. Despite being on some pretty heavy drugs, I just couldn't kick it. By the time I'd finally gotten my breath back, debilitating back pains took over, followed by bad stomach problems. Ulcers. Of course. Add to this chronic insomnia, where at best I was getting three hours of sleep a night, and things started to spiral out of control.

The doctor's diagnosis? "Your level of stress is dangerously high. Your body is constantly in flight or fight mode, which is impacting your ability to sleep, your ability to function, and your ability to heal. You've gotten yourself into a shocking state, and you're not capable of getting on top of this. You need help, and I'm going to give you something to start calming you down."

Something to calm me down? Are you kidding? I'm a bloody super-hero! I don't need help from you or anyone else. Out of my way, please. I've got this!

But I didn't have it at all. I was a disaster—a screwed up, stressed out sleepwalker desperately trying to get through each day. After storming out of the doctor's office, I sat in my car for about fifteen minutes. Admitting I needed help was excruciating. When had I become someone who needed medication to cope with life? But he was right. I slunk back to his office, and after trying to negotiate the dosage (how was it that I still thought I knew best?), I walked away with boxes and boxes of brightly coloured pills to help me "relax."

And there they now were, emptied out of their foil packs, sitting neatly in a giant plastic bag on my bed. Three months—enough to last me my whole trip. No one knew about them. Just me and the doc. I'd been so embarrassed about needing help that I hadn't even told my family. Even to them, I couldn't admit the truth: that I'd slowly but surely been disintegrating right in front of their eyes. So much for being a superhero.

No matter where I moved in the room, that plastic bag stared at me. I picked it up. I put it down. I picked it up. I put it down. It was taunting me—the bag of pills that told me I needed help. That I was damaged. That I was broken.

And then it came to me. If this road trip was going to heal my spirit, then it was damn well going to heal my body. Before I could change my mind, I tipped everything into the toilet and flushed—twice, just to make sure.

OK, so that's settled then. No more medication. That was easy!

Sometimes, there's a fine line between bravery and stupidity, but I've never worked in half measures. I knew the two were linked—curing my heart would also cure my body. I couldn't work on one and not the other. If I was going to do the work to fix my soul, then let's throw in the body as well. Simple!

I'd recently read Louise Hay's book *You Can Heal Your Life*, which suggested that what happens to us externally—illness, in particular—is caused by what we think and believe internally. Based on her philosophy, when I looked up the causes of ulcers, stomach, back, and my other assorted ailments, it always came back to the same issue: fear of not being good enough. (Really? Now that's an interesting concept!) The fear that had kept me running, hiding, and jumping for years was now the cause of my illnesses? Could it be that simple?

Well, without medication now, there was only one way to find out. I wrote a few positive affirmations aimed at addressing my fear of not being enough, taped them to my tank bag so I could see them all day, and joined the queue for the Balfour Ferry.

It was quite the queue. On the other side of the river, they were holding a hippy festival, and they'd obviously decided to start the fun at the ferry. It was a chaos of colour, mysticism, and marijuana. Tie-dyed T-shirts, clairvoyants, interesting "incense," sitars, tarot card readers, gypsies—everything was rainbows and psychedelics. (Shame—if I'd known earlier, I could probably have sold my medication. *Just kidding!*)

I'm not sure if it was the smoke or the naked joy at having liberated myself from my daily pill-popping performance, but as I leaned against my bike in the ferry line—a box of organic blueberries in my hand, watching the riot of confusion around me—I smiled. Deep inside, I felt free. I felt me.

TODAY'S GIFT

But I also felt the desperate need to ride, and what a road we'd chosen. The number one bike-riding road in BC—the road from Crawford Bay to Creston along the shores of the stunning Kootenay Lake. The most perfect bike road planted right in the middle of the most perfect scenery. Gorgeous, deep bends; tight, torturous turns—breathe. Fly. And breathe again. What insightful bike-god had given us that? I had no idea, but I was thankful.

However, it was a rider's paradise that was filled with back-to-back RVs—and let me tell you, these babies own the road. They stick together like glue. Lumbering, wallowing, drifting all over the road. Rented RVs are the worst. The drivers are usually inexperienced, and it's impossible to know just how they're going to try to kill you as you pass. Frequently, they travel in packs. Get three of them in a row, and no matter what your 0–100 kph speed is, it's precarious getting past them—safely, anyway—and on my first day without pills, I was in no mood for heroics.

But the RV graveyard was meant to be. As much as I wanted to hit this breathtaking road at speed, being forced to slow down was perfect. It was just what I needed. Instead of hyperventilating through corners, I got to breathe. To be present and truly experience the majesty of everything around me. What a novel concept—slowing down and appreciating. Funny how the Universe works sometimes.

Eventually, we shook off the posse, and after sliding through valleys and winding through mountains, Voodoo and I finally shut down for the night in the peaceful alpine village of Radium Hot Springs.

I sat under the shade of an enormous, gnarled tree outside my very Swiss-looking cabin. I felt just like Heidi. (Now, where are those lederhosen?) The owner of the hotel—a graceful woman in her early forties with a welcoming face and smiling eyes—joined me. She'd just picked bright red, juicy tomatoes from her garden, and together we ate and talked. Instantaneous friends, immediate confidantes.

She asked me what I'd learnt on this day. What had this day given me?

The answer was simple. It had been a day of small things. Nothing big or momentous (unless you count the pill-dumping exercise), but a day of many small things that had made my heart sing. My early morning run, connecting with wonderful people, coffee by the roadside, small boys on the ferry who sat on Voodoo the whole crossing, stunning scenery, the sun on my back, fresh organic fruit, the haze of mystics, piloting such an amazing machine, and eating fresh, ripe tomatoes in the shade of an aged and gnarly tree.

Appreciating the simple. That was the gift the day had given me.

DAY 5: RADIUM TO JASPER

The next morning, I figured the route to Jasper would be an easy 360 km—should be a breeze. But as I sat over coffee, all packed up and ready to go, an uneasy question squirrelled its way into my head. There are gas stations between Radium and Jasper, right? Voodoo is good for about 200 km. It's a popular road. Surely there's gas in between?

The general consensus in the coffee shop was "Mmm...no idea... but I doubt it. It's a national park." *You're kidding me, right? How the hell am I supposed to get to Jasper? Push Voodoo the last 160 km?* OK, Plan B: take a side trip via Lake Louise. If I gassed up there, put Voodoo in rain mode and stayed under 100 kph, I'd probably breathe her in. Probably.

There are three different riding modes to choose from on Voodoo: rain, sport, and "holy shit this is terrifying" race mode. Normally, I'm in sport mode. Rain mode, funnily enough, is for rain. In bad weather, it stops the bike from disappearing out from under you—always useful. But it also uses less fuel.

Rain mode it is. Let's give it a shot.

HARLEY BOYS

I headed up through the mountains of the stunning Kootenay National Park, and at Lake Louise, I squeezed every single ounce of gas I could into Voodoo. With rain mode selected, we slowly started the climb to Jasper. And I do mean slowly. Having to keep her under 100 kph was a nightmare. There's nothing more embarrassing than being overtaken by RVs. But I decided I'd rather be embarrassed by being slow than run out of gas. Besides, I was on the Icefields Parkway—one of the most spectacular roads in Canada. I just needed to chill out and enjoy the scenery.

About 70 km from Lake Louise, I decide to stop and take a photo. Despite the incredible beauty around me, I'd resisted snapping to conserve gas. But the lakes were so beautiful, a stop was called for. Into the tank bag and out with the phone. OK, out with the maps, the wallet, the sunnies, the vegan bars...but the phone? No phone. Gone. Missing in action. *Shit, shit, shit!* My phone was my whole world out there! There were only two places I could have left it: the gas station at Lake Louise or all the way back at Radium. None of the options were brilliant, but I had no choice. Back I went, with my heart—or probably my foot—in my mouth.

I was begging the Universe as I pulled back into the gas station. *Please let it be there.* It was bad enough to have added an extra 140 km to the day. I didn't want to make it an extra 260 km if I had to head back to Radium.

Sitting right where I'd parked Voodoo previously were two enormous Harley riders. They were the real deal. Big, ugly, scary, the occasional tooth missing, covered in tattoos and leather, hands like bananas, and bandannas to cover the scars. But as intimidating as they were—I had to man up and ask them the question: *Have you seen my phone?*

Now, under normal circumstances, I would have crossed the road to avoid these guys. They would have scared the hell out of me.

That just goes to show what an amazing connection I would have missed. Sure enough, my phone was on the counter at the gas station, right where I'd left it. When I came back to Voodoo, phone in hand, the Harley boys got off their bikes and hugged me with excitement. (At least, I think it was excitement!)

We had such a laugh. They told me they had to look mean because they couldn't look pretty. I could vouch for that. But despite all their gruffness, they were just pussycats. Cheeky pussycats who gave me their number and told me that if ever I came through again, I was welcome to stay at their apartment. Just let them know and they'd send me the door combination, as long as I didn't bring any men back. They didn't like men coming back. *Seriously? Who were these cuties?* Well, those mean-looking, badass boys were now my besties. The road does that for you.

After a kiss and a hug goodbye to the boys, I was back onto Voodoo, back onto the road to Jasper for a second time. And for the record, there *is* a gas station between Lake Louise and Jasper. With her belly full of gas, I switched out of rain mode and gave Voodoo the beans.

Despite the beauty around me, I was desperate to get inside. I'd had enough. It'd been a long riding day and it was cold now—really cold. No surprises on the Icefields Parkway, I guess. I stopped and put on my heated vest, which worked a treat on my core initially, but eventually I felt like a defrosting chicken. The middle bits were warm, but the outside bits were still frozen.

I was shaking with cold, and I was in pain. Five hundred kilometres on a sports bike is exhausting. My riding position was so contorted that, after about 400 km, everything started to hurt. I spent my time moving body bits around in rotation to ease sore feet, sore knees, sore bum, sore back, sore neck.

I lost the feeling in my fingers. My arms stiffened up from leaning on my wrists, and my knees ached from being up round my ears for hours. The trick I found when I was tired on Voodoo was to lie on my tank bag—although I think I would have had more support if I'd had bigger boobs or a bigger belly. And I had to be careful not to nod off.

But speed and cold keep you awake—well, that, and the vigilant police who, just outside of Jasper, decided I was *doing* too much of one (speeding) and that I'd *had* too much of the other (cold). I guess being blue was a giveaway. In an act of generosity—or it could have been because it was the end of their shift and they didn't want to do the paperwork—they let me off with a warning. But their wisdom rang in my ears:

"You know what? You might want to slow down and enjoy the view."

The story of my life, accurately and succinctly summed up by the Jasper Police Department. Who would have thought?

DAY 6: JASPER TO BANFF

And the view certainly was amazing. The next morning, I ran to the top of the world—or at least the top of a peak in Jasper—where I stood, breathless, looking down at the hamlet below me. An embracing little town, full of character and sleepy energy, was stirring below me. The sun hit the mountains, creating a beautiful golden glow. All I needed to do right now was breathe and be thankful for everything I was experiencing—the cool crisp air, the sun on my face, the silence in the wind, and the beauty stirring my soul.

It felt amazing to run for the pure joy of it. To not be training for anything, to not have a running schedule. To throw away the heart rate monitor and just run like a crazy, wild kid through moss-covered trees with laser beams of sunlight streaming through their branches. Along twisting mountain trails, undulating and unpredictable.

Over coffee later that morning, it started to dawn on me that for the first time in years, I was actually starting to feel calm. I would like to have pushed my status to "relaxed," but calm was a great start—anything other than my usual manic. The months before the trip had been tough—my health, stepping out of work, replacing myself in my own company...life had taken a toll on my heart and my spirit. But here, I felt soothed. I was loving the space to breathe, the space to play, the space to create.

IS THERE A TRICK TO THIS?

Already, I could feel myself starting to slow down. Goals, tasks, and checklists had always driven my life—achievement being my highest god. But today? Without a goal in sight, I decided it was time. It was time to step into one of my darkest fears. Time to scare myself senseless. Time to stop running...Yes. It was time to meditate.

I've always had a very interesting relationship with meditation: I refused to do it. Full stop. I was always insulted when some well-meaning person would quip, "You really need to relax. You should try meditation." Only the brave had made that suggestion, and they'd usually only made it once. I was never destined to meditate. I would rather have root canal therapy than sit silently in a lotus position—even for five minutes. Meditation was never going to happen.

Until it did.

Grabbing another coffee (probably not a good thing to have three coffees before trying to meditate, but I had to get through it somehow!), I picked my way along a tree-lined river bank and found the perfect spot: a large, flat rock on the edge of the water. So far, so good. Now what? Just close my eyes? Is there a trick to this?

Once I stopped fighting, I sat peacefully—eyes closed, ignoring the mosquitoes—for about twenty incredible minutes. (OK, I probably dozed off for about fifteen of those minutes.) But for the first time ever, I got it. And yes, at best I only had two consecutive silent breaths before my mind found shiny new thoughts to play with, but those two breaths were amazing.

I'd fought meditation for years, not wanting to surrender to it, because it was a sign that I needed something. That I was weak. That it was a prop. And look where that had gotten me: a bag full of pills and a numb butt from sitting on a bathroom floor, crying my eyes out. Yep, that'd worked well.

It was early days—OK, it was one day—but if I'd crossed the bridge with meditation, what else could I let go of? What else had I been holding onto that made no sense or created zero value in my life? The possibilities were endless! Luckily, I had a good four hours on Voodoo to work that all out in my helmet.

But first, I needed to load up. I had a very complicated bag set-up on the bike. To be frank, you needed a degree in origami to put it all together—stowed, strapped, and set up every morning. The first few mornings, gearing up had been disastrous. I had equipment going everywhere, bags continually put on out of sequence, the wrong straps tying the right bags down, bags moving and flying all over the bike. I couldn't get it right. I was losing an hour every morning—not to mention losing my sense of humour.

This morning, in my newly acquired state of calm, I remembered a beautiful quote from Zen master WuDe: "How you do anything is how you do everything." Made sense. Gearing up had assumed enormous proportions in my head—it was seriously a big thing. What would happen if I broke it up into a series of small things and did them all really well?

So I gave it a try. Step one, stop struggling. Step two, slow down. Step three, turn it into a slow, mindful ritual.

"OK, gently put this bag on first, calmly secure this bag. Pause. Carefully put this bag on second, slowly bring the loops across. And rest. Step across to the side of the bike, peacefully tighten the straps. Continue to breathe."

This was how I turned loading into a real art form, where getting the process right was actually beautiful. I stepped back and looked at the Leaning Tower of Pisa in amazement. A zen masterpiece. *Look at me!* Let's just hope the bloody thing holds as brilliantly as it looks.

And it did, but only just.

BRING MY BAGS UP

Heading south through the Icefields Parkway again towards Banff should have been a ride from heaven. Jaw-dropping scenery, ancient glaciers, cascading waterfalls, pristine lakes, sweeping valleys—this road had it all. Yet, I saw none of it. For two reasons.

Firstly, about 3.2 minutes after leaving Jasper, I was hit with an almighty crosswind, which lasted the entire four hours it took me to reach Banff. Crosswinds are interesting on a bike. Being hit with a crosswind necessitates riding at a forty-five-degree angle to stop the bike from becoming a kite—from being picked up and deposited unceremoniously on the other side of the road or, as is sometimes the case, completely off the road. Never a good look.

Remember, Voodoo is a heavy girl, so you'd think she'd weigh enough to stay firmly fixed on the road. You'd think. The challenge is that I'm not heavy enough to hold her down. So the only way I can control her is to hang off the side of the bike with my knee virtually on the ground to counter the wind pushing me the other way. That's usually fun and exciting for about ten minutes. For four hours, it's a nightmare. It also means you see nothing but the yellow line on the centre of the road. Even lifting your head a little throws you off balance.

Not that it was too much of an issue, because I couldn't see anything anyway. It appeared there was a bug convention between

Jasper and Banff, and every bug in the known world was attending—at least half of them dying a horrible death on either my visor or my body. My jacket looked like a graveyard. The thing I can't work out with bugs is that, when they die on your visor, they never kill themselves on the side, where you'd still have vision. No. They always die smack bang in the middle—right in front of your eyes so you're completely blinded.

And that was my excuse for nearly hitting a caribou that wandered right out in front of me. Guess I was too busy concentrating on the small stuff to see the big stuff!

Looking and feeling decidedly worse for wear—covered in dead bugs, dust, dirt, and slush from head to toe—I pulled up to the front of my "Great Extravagance" for the journey: the inimitable Banff Springs Hotel. (OK, I'm embarrassed to admit I wanted to stay there. After all, it hardly fits the "riding through the wilds with just a tent, freeze dried lentils, and a g-string" concept. But hey—once, maybe twice, a trip could be excused.)

The look on the face of the immaculately attired valet was priceless. Wearing a flawlessly tailored, long, dove-grey jacket, he took one look at me (OK, he probably smelt me as well) and advised, "Deliveries are round the back."

I don't think so. Sweeping my leg over Voodoo as elegantly as I could, I got off, handed him the keys, and in my best "tally-ho" voice, said, "I'm checking in. Could you please park this and bring my bags up?"

I have always wanted to do that! To bring a bike into a five-star hotel and ask them to park it (sad, I know!). To his credit, he recovered brilliantly. I know he desperately wanted to hose me down and dip me in disinfectant before he'd let me in, but by that stage, we were laughing. There was no way he could park Voodoo, and there was no way I was going to let him, but I'd had my three minutes of fun.

I'd created complete chaos and confusion. So much for zen.

DAY 7: BANFF TO LAKE LOUISE

You know that feeling when you wake up knowing exactly how you want your day to go? I had a perfect picture in my head. It was going to be an easy riding day, so I had space and time to create the perfect morning. A slow, loping run on a beautiful trail I'd discovered a couple of years ago, finding a quiet place for a compulsory coffee and to write, and then sitting in glorious nature to see if I could get this meditation thing to work two days in a row. Bliss.

Or not.

Straight off, my run was nixed. The valet, still in his immaculate dove-grey tails, "strongly advised" me not to run where

I'd planned. There'd been bears in the area recently, and it wasn't safe. I'm not usually one to heed "strong advice," but given I didn't have capsicum spray—and I'd been told that bears actually eat the spray before they eat you—for once, I listened and rerouted. But damn! Not happy.

I grabbed my coffee—which just tasted like black hot water, a pretty unpardonable sin for me—and was about to find a seat when a guy backed into me, spilling his latte everywhere, but mainly all over me. There's nothing like the smell of wearing a milk latte—especially for a vegan!

Breathe. It's fine. Just find a beautiful spot to meditate.

But that wasn't going to happen either. It had started to rain, so I couldn't head into the forests, and in the only covered areas protected from the rain, smokers were huddled together desperately sneaking clandestine cigarettes.

The serenity I'd experienced yesterday had been like trying to hold custard. I'd had it, but it was gone. I was restless, disoriented, and more than a little petulant. I'd designed the perfect morning in my head, and absolutely nothing had gone to plan. What the hell?

ANONYMOUS GRATITUDE

Here I was, sitting in one of the most awe-inspiring places in the world, and I was agitated. *Really?* I couldn't run where I'd wanted, my coffee was crap, I smelt like a cow, and my meditation hadn't been perfect. Actually, with that list, it's no wonder I was cranky! But seriously—get a grip!

Nursing another cup of black hot water, I flicked through the random quotes and affirmations I'd written before I'd left, hoping they'd inspire me on my journey of change. My journal fell open to just what I needed to see (how does that happen?)— another gem I had heard from WuDe:

"A lot of suffering comes from wanting to be what is not, and wanting not to be what is."

Now that was a slap, and it was just what this miserable, grouchy diva needed to hear—although I had to read it a few times to really work it out. To me, it meant that we spend so much of our lives wanting things to be different instead of truly appreciating the joy and beauty we already have.

The message struck me to my core, as did the realisation that my frustration had mainly been caused by my inability to control situations. It was a shock to realise I actually couldn't control everything that happened around me. However, I could control how I reacted to it. I could choose to be bad tempered in the face of first-world adversity, or I could choose to accept the situation and still find joy in the day.

There are lightning-bolt moments in your life where messages are shocked into you, and there are other moments where the knowledge just seeps in. Like an intravenous drip, the lessons were slowly starting to trickle through. About time!

In this place of incredible beauty, I thought about gratitude. Instead of complaining, how about being thankful? I'd heard that even your worst day changes with gratitude. It was worth a shot. So I started to write.

It was hard at first, but after about ten minutes—once I'd been grateful for the obvious—the faucet opened and everything flowed out. I couldn't stop with just writing. The power and emotion was so strong that I texted my family and friends, thanking them for being in my life and telling them how much they meant to me. I poured my heart out and got beautiful messages back from all of them—including one from my business coach. His reply was, "Thanks. That's great...but who is this?" I'd forgotten I was unidentifiable on my cheap Canadian SIM card. Even better! There's nothing like the power of anonymous gratitude.

In an unusual place of deep peace, I loaded a feisty Voodoo, and together we made the short, lazy 60 km hop to Lake Louise, which was perfectly timed for me to squeeze in a hike up into the glacier before nightfall.

Without a doubt, Lake Louise is one of the most beautiful places in the world. With its impossibly serene turquoise lake encased by proud, imposing mountains and spectacular glaciers, it literally takes your breath away. And that was just what I needed—to be completely immersed in spectacular nature so my happy heart could continue singing.

That was the plan, anyway. Sadly, the old competitive warrior in me had other ideas. Despite hiking amidst incredible forest beauty—crystal blue waterfalls, sparkling streams, tiny, brightly coloured wildflowers—I saw virtually none of it.

Not content with a peaceful, gentle walk, I needed to turn my hike into a speed march where the biggest competition was myself, and I wasn't taking prisoners. I powered up the side of the glacier—never missing a beat, pushing at breakneck speed, overtaking everyone in my way to get to the top as fast as I could. I saw nothing but my own feet all the way up.

With a lemongrass tea warming my hands, I sat in the sun on the veranda of a tiny wooden tea house perched at the top of the ridge. I'd annihilated everything and everyone in my path. As the cool breeze started to dry the sweat on my back and chill my bones, I sat in bewilderment. *What the hell was that all about? What is wrong with me?* I couldn't even hike in one of the most beautiful places in the world without it becoming a competition. It's bad enough that I need validation from other people to feel good. But why the continual need to compete with myself? What was I trying to prove?

I had no answers. I decided I wasn't going to leave the tea house until I'd found them—but eventually, the cold and the realisation that mentally smacking myself wasn't a good option either, forced me back down the glacier.

Still, five cups of tea had shown me something: I might not have the answers, but the first step in finding them was to see myself as I truly was. I didn't necessarily like who I saw at that tea house. But in seeing that competitive warrior, I knew I could change her. Eventually, and with time, patience, and kindness.

I had plenty of time left in my helmet to make those changes, but today, the self-judgement had to stop. Heading down the glacier was a very different story. I slowed to a crawl. I stood mesmerised by the intricate beauty of tiny flowers. I smelt the richness of the damp, moist earth. I felt the cool breeze on my skin. I listened to the gurgling of a small stream as I walked slowly beside it. And I remembered—as I'd forgotten so many times already on this trip—it's about the journey, not the destination, right?

DAY 8: LAKE LOUISE TO WYCLIFFE

It was raining. Correction: it was absolutely bucketing down. And it was cold, cold, cold. When I poked one eye open and saw the torrential downpour the next morning, I remembered to be grateful—grateful I wasn't in a tent—and then I immediately retreated to the warmth of my covers. Nah, this isn't happening. I'm staying right here.

What should have been happening was me running to the top of Victoria Glacier—one of the most soul-soothing runs I'd ever done, and one I'd been busting to do again, since I'd first done it a few years earlier. But in this rain and cold? You're insane. Forget it.

But I couldn't forget it. Regret is a strange thing. Logic and sense completely evaporate when regret starts creeping into your mind. The more I looked at the glacier, the more it taunted me, and eventually I caved. I knew I wouldn't forgive myself if I missed the chance to run it. Regret having had a spectacular victory, I layered up and headed out into the elements.

It was truly miserable.

THE POWER OF REGRET

I have a deal on the days I don't want to run. I give myself twenty minutes, and if I still feel like crap, then I can turn around and come home. I never come home. But it was pretty damn close today. I was soaked, frozen, and grumbling—remember gratitude, gratitude—but without feeling it, I kept climbing, head down to keep the stinging rain off my face, higher and higher.

I tried to remind myself that experiences were only good or bad depending on the perspective we give them, but I failed miserably. From this perspective, the experience was *worse* than bad.

There's an old saying that "above the clouds, it's always sunny."

Funnily enough, it was. As I ran higher, the clouds began to evaporate around me. Suddenly, out I popped, right into warm, golden sunlight. It felt like I'd wandered into heaven—standing high above the clouds, enveloped by glorious, imposing mountains, with the startling white snow of the glacier almost blinding me in the sunshine. Even more beautiful than I'd remembered. I just love the power of regret!

Or I did, until I started the run home.

A FEAR TO RUN FROM AND A FEAR TO FACE

As I dropped back into the clouds and into the rain, to the side of me I suddenly heard something large and lumbering making its way not-so-gently through the trees. Then came the noise. A deep growling, grumbling, rumbling sound that made me stop for all of about ten seconds.

Here's the thing. I was scared of bears. Few things in the wild scared me, but bears? Running on the trails in the very early morning light certainly made me potential bear fodder, and I had just one plan if I met one: to run downhill. I'd heard that bears can't run downhill because they've got short front legs. Not that I wanted to get close enough to find out.

Now, I've never heard a bear growl, but it's a sound you don't need a degree in Animal Science to work out. *Shit!* Time for the plan. Run downhill as fast as you can! I bolted. I ran as fast as my sturdy tabletop legs could carry me. I'm not sure whether the plan worked or the bear decided my vegan ass wasn't all that interesting, but either way, I made it back to the hotel—alive, and in record time!

But the rain continued, and no amount of positive or wishful thinking stopped it. OK, there was something else that frightened the life out of me: rain. I hate riding in the rain. It's cold, dangerous, hairy, and just plain miserable. I'm a complete wimp in the rain. There. I've admitted it. I hated having my heavy Voodoo slide out from underneath me, never knowing what she was going to do next, slipping all over the road, and feeling like I was just seconds away from sliding unceremoniously down the road on my butt. Understandable, really. Add to that debilitating cold? This was not going to end well.

I hid in my hotel room for as long as I could, just "giving it another hour," but eventually I realised I needed to man up and get out in it. With that "Mmm...I think I want to vomit" fear in my stomach, I headed to the underground car park to load Voodoo up. *Think zen, think zen, breathe, you'll be fine.*

Alongside me, a young guy packing his warm, cosy, and very dry sports car, turned to me in pure amazement and said, "You're going out in that? Are you nuts?"

He certainly wasn't the first person to have asked me that. And he was right. I was absolutely nuts. But sometimes you just have to do what has to be done. Sure, it was cold and wet, but I had to keep moving. I'd checked the weather forecast every three minutes for the last two hours, and it wasn't going to get any better for days. I couldn't keep hiding in the car park all day, so I had to get moving. *Toughen up, princess.*

That's easy to say when you're dry and under cover. So much harder to do when the minute you leave the safety of your concrete castle, the rain stings, the wind whips, and your bike bites. Big time. For about 130 km, Voodoo went for the ride of her life—most of it without me, while I tried to hang on for grim death. A superbike in the rain is a thing of beauty, so long as you're not on her. She slips, she slides, she won't lean, and she has a propensity to go sideways when you least expect it. But she's elegant in her execution—like a ballerina without the tutu.

I, on the other hand, was anything but elegant. It's one of the great mysteries of life. No matter how good your waterproof gear is, eventually water will find its way right down to your undies. By this stage, water was actually filling my boots. It was oozing out of my gloves, and my heated vest had the consistency of a wet duvet. At least I knew that if I came off, the landing would be soft.

Breathe, breathe, breathe...this is all part of the experience. Enjoy the ride!

But the Universe has an amazing way of knowing the exact

moment when you're about to completely lose it. About two minutes before that happened, the sun came out and the whole world changed. Sure, I was steaming as if I'd just stepped into a dry cleaners, but is there any problem in the world that brilliant sunshine doesn't cure? Certainly not when you're looking like you've just swum the English Channel, boots and all.

In the literal middle of nowhere, I pulled in for gas. For once, I wasn't "gas critical," but I had an important rule of survival on the bike: never pass a gas station. As I struggled to get off Voodoo, water pouring from every orifice, an old guy bounded from the office, busting with energy and fire.

"The bad news is that I've got no gas," he said, a smile lighting up his face. "The good news is that I love your bike. Have you got time for a chat?"

The second important rule of survival on Voodoo was to never pass a bathroom. By that stage, I'd worked out that the size of Voodoo's tank was directly proportionate to the size of my bladder. So, do I have time? Sure, once I've struggled off this baby and found the restroom. Where else do I have to be right now?

Together, we sat in the sun. With steam pouring off my body, Dan the Gas Station Owner and I set the world right. In our friendship, I discovered a marathon runner, a soccer player, a running coach, a Porsche racer, a yoga teacher—a man of many talents with a pure joy for life and adventure. Every ounce of water that my body had absorbed had been worth it just to sit in the sun, connecting with this beautiful soul.

Taking Dan's suggestion for a place to stay found me in a glorious B&B by the river, just outside the town of Wycliffe. It was isolated, but I wanted for nothing. Taking fresh avocados and salad down to the river, two deer joined me as dinner companions. They were short on conversation but long on attitude, and I could feel their resentment at my intrusion. I told them I was plant-based, but I'm not sure it helped.

There I sat, the lazy flowing river slowly washing away the stress and tension of the day. From my rickety, paint-peeled chair at the water's edge, I let it all go. The rain, the cold, the fear—already distant memories.

DAY 9: WYCLIFFE

I decided to take the following day off from riding. My excuse was that I needed to dry everything out. My boots *were* still leaking all over the floor, but the real reason was that I knew I still had a lot to learn about slowing down. On a journey where I had nowhere to be and no time to be there, I was still pushing hard, ploughing through the miles, moving, moving, moving. The fact that I needed an excuse was telling. But I'd had a message from a close friend the night before, reminding me, "Less miles, more smiles." More smiles it is, then!

There were some amazing characters staying at the B&B, including a Dutch theology professor, a family on a rafting holiday, and a wealthy dude who flew his own seaplane to all the top fishing spots in the world—quite an eclectic crowd. Over breakfast, while they ploughed their way through sausage, eggs, and hash browns, the obvious questions were posed to me: "Why are you a vegan? How do you get your protein? Isn't it boring eating kale every day?"

FOOD AND ME

I've always had a crazy relationship with food. Even as a kid, I hated the taste of meat. I used to sneak it off my plate and slide it under the table where my grateful (and very fat) dog would devour it. Despite my traditional "meat and three veg" background, my mum eventually gave up the fight, and I became a vegetarian. At that point, it certainly was a taste, not a conscious decision.

As a runner, I was concerned about protein. I was worried that my body wasn't getting the fuel it needed to rebuild and repair. You need a bucket load of protein, right? So as much as I hated the taste, I continually loaded up with protein shakes, egg whites, egg whites, more egg whites, and fish...yet I still felt tired, I was still getting injured, and I had no zing. But hey—I was doing what everyone recommended, so it had to be good for me, right?

Wrong. Living in Vancouver, I came across a great book, *The*

Thrive Diet, written by Brendan Brazier, a world-class triathlete who'd dramatically improved his health and triathlon success by becoming plant-based. Interesting. If it worked for him as a professional athlete, maybe it would work for me?

At the same time, I crossed paths with a book that also had a huge impact on me, *Finding Ultra*, by Rich Roll, who'd gone from being an overweight thirty-nine-year-old couch potato living on fast foods and heading for a certain heart attack, to becoming one of the world's top endurance athletes. Oh, and he achieved that after moving completely to a plant-based diet.

That was it for me. I flushed all the protein shakes down the toilet (you can see there's a pattern here, and you might also see a lot of muscular fish swimming out there now). I banished the eggs from the fridge, I let the fish swim free, and I became plant-based. And it worked for me. I felt healthier, stronger, and so much better within myself. Go kale!

After breakfast, I headed down to the river to find my rickety chair and to contemplate. The story I'd told as to why I'd moved to plant-based had been true—I'd done it to improve my health, my fitness, my overall well-being. But there'd been a deeper reason behind the move. I'd moved to being plant-based because it's almost impossible to put on weight when you're eating carrots, kale, and cucumber.

As an anorexic, that had been a key but silent driver for me.

YOU HAVE TO MAKE A CHOICE

My first bout of anorexia was at fourteen. I was the perfect child, the perfect student, the perfect athlete. I was doing everything at such a high level that a fear slowly crept into me—a fear that everything I was achieving could be taken away from me in a heartbeat (and so, the pattern began). Stepping into anorexia gave me a degree of control in a life that I felt was out of control. It was the drug that fed my need for perfection.

I dabbled around the edges of anorexia until it kicked in big time at nineteen. I simply stopped eating. My life consisted of one apple eaten very slowly at lunchtime, and Diet Coke to fill the hunger pangs. Ah, the control! When everything around you is going crazy, controlling your weight and appearance feels amazing!

The thing with anorexia was that, once it was in my head, it never left me. I may have gotten the symptoms under control from time to time, but never the disease. Even in periods where I wasn't "technically" suffering from anorexia, my whole thought process was anorexic. I could never walk past a mirror without telling myself I was fat. It was a complete process of self-loathing—there's no other way to describe it. I was continually viewing myself as imperfect. There wasn't an ounce of self-love in there anywhere.

At twenty-five, I had a bout that pushed me over the edge. I'd gotten so thin that my gym had suspended my membership (no problem—I just found another one.), my parents and friends were distraught, and finally, weighing in at 32 kilos, the doctor made the call that I had to be hospitalised.

Just before the entrance of the hospital, my then-fiancé Rob pulled the car over, switched off the engine, and with tears pouring down his face said, "Look, I love you. And I'll lose you to another man, but I won't lose you to this disease. Now you have to make a choice, and you have to make it right now: me or anorexia."

He's a good man. I made the right choice. But that need for perfection never left me. It consumed me, it exhausted me, and it completely controlled my life. It was a terrifying place. A place so dark...a place I was incapable of escaping. The energy it took to sustain "perfection" took a staggering toll.

And that was part of the reason I was here—on this journey, sitting by a river, watching it flow by. Amazingly, the river didn't have a single worry about whether it was fat or thin, weak or strong, beautiful or ugly. It was perfect just as it was. As was I.

In my hard, wooden chair, I reflected on my day of exploration, confrontation, hard truths, and being honest with myself. After all these years, I had another choice to make: to let anorexia go once and for all, or to hold on tightly to a story that just didn't serve me anymore.

By the side of the river, I found the perfect boulder. It was rounded and flat—a beautiful blue-grey colour. Struggling to hold it above my head, I tossed it into the river with a grunt and all my might. And there it sat—containing all my fears, my expectations, my paranoia and my perfection—as the water slowly washed around it and over it.

"See ya, Anorexia. It's been fun!"

With a toss of my head and a quiet smile, I walked my numb, droopy butt, my not-so-skinny thighs, my little pot belly...my perfect self back to the house.

DAY 10: WYCLIFFE TO NELSON

Sitting on my gnarly old chair by the river the next morning—the sun glistening on the water and a gentle breeze playing on my body—I closed my eyes to meditate and tried to silence my mind.

But my mind was having none of it. Every time I achieved one silent breath, my mind instantly bounced into, "So, all this wandering around aimlessly is cool, but what's the next step?"

Ahh, there she was. The old warrior demanding answers, demanding to know where all of this was headed. Not content with just being, it needed to know exactly what the future held when I finally shut down Voodoo at the end of the journey. Having stepped out of the security of a controlled life, it was pressing for answers. "So what's next? What's the big goal? What's the big plan?" The warrior was hanging on tight.

ENJOY THE SUN WITH ME

If you can't beat it, join it! Instead of trying to shut that voice out, I leaned into it. Sitting in meditation, I asked a simple question: "OK, Universe, what's the way forward for me?" A reasonable question, but I didn't get a reasonable answer.

"Be patient."

What? Can you repeat that? Be patient? No, no, no. You don't get it. I need answers, and I need them right now. I don't have time to be patient. Patience isn't one of my strengths. Just tell me now, and I'll be OK. I'll let it go once I have the answer.

But no. "Be patient." *You're kidding me, right?* What the hell did that mean? How long did I have to be patient—and patient for what? Should I be expecting a lightning bolt at some stage?

I'd resisted spiritual counsel when trying to work out the next steps in my life, but as luck or the Universe would have it, I'd met two incredible teachers—Michelle Capper-Fay in Sydney and Ross Kerr in Vancouver—prior to my departure. Although I'd only had a couple of sessions with them, their impact on me had been profound.

With the benefit of their wisdom, I sat with the next question: "What does being patient actually mean?" *Breathe. You can do this. You can work it out.* After circling the question round and round in my head, slowly the answers came. My old self wanted to know the destination. It needed to know the objectives, goals, and definitives. It demanded clarity.

But my new self had to be patient. To surrender and trust the process. To be OK with not knowing, and to just let go. Right now, there was no other definitive for me than to get on Voodoo every day and ride. The rest would unfold if I was open and just trusted.

That demanded more of me than I thought I could give. Letting go was such a terrifying concept. And as for surrender, wasn't that admitting defeat? That was like asking me to stand naked in front of a football team. I couldn't let myself be that exposed.

Damn. Really? Just surrender and be patient?

It's funny how the Universe consolidates its lessons. The plan that morning was to head to Montana and the exquisite Going-to-the-Sun Road—one I was itching to ride. It was a long ride, so I was anxious to get going. I was packed and ready to roll, when Dale, the owner of the B&B—a serene woman in her early sixties, with deep crow's feet around her eyes from a lifetime of smiling—patted the chair alongside her in the garden and said, "Sit. Slow down. Come and enjoy the sun with me. I'll make a fresh pot of coffee."

I can't...I have to go...I need to ride...This has been lovely, but I have to hit the road.

But those two words came back to me—*be patient.* So, pulling up a chair, I surrendered and sat in the garden with Dale, as the deer wandered around us. We sat in the sun together—sometimes talking, sometimes just being—and it was precious beyond words.

In this case, it seemed patience really was a virtue. A fire had just closed the Going-to-the-Sun Road, and it wouldn't be open for days. Had I left earlier, I would have ridden for hours only to be sidelined by fires. Glad I'd listened to the Universe!

EXPECT THE UNEXPECTED

A reroute was necessary. After poring over the maps and reviewing logistics, a new destination was selected: Nelson, BC. It would mean some backtracking, but it was backtracking on some of the best riding roads in BC, so I figured I could manage that.

Heading back to the Kootenay Ferry, Voodoo and I were seriously pumped. Instead of the straights of the past few days, today we were treated to huge sweeping corners and flowing bends where Voodoo dropped and rolled with serious attitude. While I hung on for dear life—my senses screaming—Voodoo took command and just nailed it. What a performance.

Within hours, I'd left the harsh starkness of the Rockies and was surrounded by massive pine forests and crystal lakes. It was just perfect...except.

Except I had my first really terrifying moment, if you don't count deer, caribou, and riding side saddle in crosswinds. Today, I discovered logging trucks, and it wasn't a pretty encounter.

Two massive trucks were hightailing it together, and there wasn't room between them to overtake them separately. I had to wait for just the right moment, and in all the curves, that moment was a long time coming.

The wind whipping off the back of the trucks created a huge vortex, which sucked me up and threw me all over the road, making Voodoo impossible to control. It felt like I was in a giant washing machine as I sat behind them, and I knew I had to get out of there before it reached the spin cycle. At the same time, I was being blasted by detritus from the load—wood chips, sand, dust, and other unidentifiable flying objects made it impossible to see. I had a couple of attempts at passing them but had been in grave danger of being concertinaed. *Be patient. Be patient.*

I had to force myself to breathe. These suckers really scared me. Eventually, the perfect moment opened up, and taking a deep breath, I dropped Voodoo back a gear and gunned it. As I careered alongside them, they both started to move over. I had visions of their chains breaking and the logs falling on top of me.

Yep, I'd been watching too many movies. But the worst part was riding through the flying debris. At one stage, I automatically closed my eyes to stop the dross from getting into them. Not a good thing to do when you're overtaking a truck.

But Nelson was worth the adrenaline. After a day of drama, I walked into town to relax and catch the Friday-night markets. Instantly, I was surrounded by colour, craziness, and chaos— typical street-stall markets mixed with people dancing, bands playing, very large ladies blowing even larger bubbles, guys doing tricks on mountain bikes, dogs biting small children, people hugging and then crying into their beers simultaneously. You know—the usual Friday-night entertainment.

Life on the road. Expect the unexpected!

DAY 11: NELSON TO CASTLEGAR

What I hadn't expected the next day was the weather. Each night, in addition to reviewing routes, distances, roads, and gas stations to determine my next port of call, I'd now added "fires" to the checklist, as much of the Pacific Northwest was ablaze. The one thing I hadn't added was weather. And why would I? This was summer. It was never going to rain! Hold that thought.

I woke up the next morning to black, overcast skies. It had rained hard all night. I know this for a fact, because I'd been up every hour on the hour as Canadian-Pacific trains blasted by my window with full horn engagement at two in the morning... and three...and four...gotta love a cheap hotel!

Despite the rain in Nelson, fires overnight had closed my planned route. So it was back to the maps at six in the morning for new destinations—up to Revelstoke, down to Osoyoos, and then a flyby in Whistler to see Jakey for his twenty-first birthday. Done. Looking good.

But there was a fatal flaw in my plan. I hadn't bothered to check the weather forecast going north—which, given the amount of rain we'd had overnight and the ominous blackness of the skies overhead, might have been a good thing to do. But nah. A quick check on the iPhone showed a 50 percent chance of rain, which also meant a 50 percent chance of sunshine, right? Always the optimist. Let's go with the sunshine version!

Two important lessons were learnt that morning. Number one: remember that a 50 percent chance of rain actually means you're going to get rain, no doubt about it. Number two: never trust the weather forecast on an iPhone.

A NEW DEFINITION OF SURRENDER

Full of sunshine and confidence, we headed out. I seriously believed that my power of positive thinking would keep the rain away. Surprisingly, it didn't. About fifteen minutes out of

Nelson, it started. The amazing thing about being on a bike is that you actually get to smell the rain before it hits. Although that sounds romantic, you don't ever smell it in time to do anything about it. It literally went from ugly and overcast to a horrendous downpour in minutes.

In the middle of nowhere, I had a choice: to keep going in my summer riding gear and hope the rain would stop (that was never going to happen) or pull over on the side of the road, unpack (yes, dismantle the Leaning Tower of Pisa), pull out my wet-weather gear, and get changed in public. Given it was already bucketing down, option two was the only way forward. Without a skerrick of shelter in sight, that meant unpacking in the pouring rain. Why is it when you urgently need something, it's always at the bottom of your bag?

And the worst was yet to come. I had to get changed. At that point, I was so wet I almost dropped my pants and changed them right in the middle of the highway. Figuring that my bare butt might cause a few accidents, I decided to run for the protection of a distant bush. Next time, I'll change on the highway. (Who would have thought a blackberry bush could have done so much damage?) But a girl has to do what a girl has to do.

Finally all kitted out, off I went. I think my wets probably held together for all of about six minutes before the hurricane (I'm sure it was more than just your average torrential rain!) managed to find every crease and crevice on my body. Within minutes of the deluge, my wets gave up their feeble attempt at absorption and water started pouring in. Everywhere. When I moved my neck, water cascaded down my back. When I lifted my hands, water gushed out of my gloves. When I moved my foot, water flooded out of my boots.

Just when I thought things couldn't get worse, I rounded a corner to discover construction work—of course—which meant two things. First, I had to sit in the rain for fifteen minutes waiting for my side of the road to be open, and second, when I did get to proceed, they'd ripped all the tar off the road to re-lay it. For 25 km, I got to ride on pure road base mesh.

On a bike, base mesh is breathtakingly slippery at the best of times. Put it together with torrential rain and the odd side of gravel for extra interest, and suddenly life became way too exciting to handle.

For twenty-five torturous kilometres, I held on for dear life. Voodoo slipped and slid all over the road, with every second so intensely scary that I realised I was forgetting to breathe. I was in serious danger of blacking out due to lack of oxygen. As my big, heavy girl continually skated from underneath me, I forced myself to whisper out loud, "Breathe, breathe, breathe." *Hold it together. Stay focused. Stay confident.*

I also had a mantra running 'round in my head: "Whatever comes next, I can handle it. Whatever comes next, I can handle it," which was pretty easy to say given whatever came next couldn't have gotten much worse.

Reaching New Denver, I pulled into a gas station and tucked Voodoo under an awning for shelter. I didn't need gas, but I needed to regroup. I was cold, wet, and overloaded with adrenaline. I still had another 150 km to do, and I needed to stop shaking. Was it cold or fear that was making my hands look as if they were completely disconnected from my arms as they flailed wildly?

Yet the warrior was snapping at my heels.

Get it together. It's OK. You've come this far. You're through the worst of it. Just keep going. Just keep going. Just keep going. Schedules, deadlines, time frames. Stick to the plan. Stop grizzling. Get going.

Get going? I trailed a torrent of water into the bathroom, where I unsuccessfully tried to warm my body by rotating it like a contortionist under the hand dryer. What on earth made me think that was going to work? I was overwrought enough at that stage to ask myself the inevitable question, "What's wrong with you? You're frozen to the point of not being able to function, Voodoo is like a giraffe on marbles all over the road, and this incessant rain is making conditions insanely dangerous. But you want to keep going? For another 150 km?"

OK, fair point. For the first time in a long time, common sense kicked in, and I decided to surrender—having found a new definition of surrender: *accepting what is*. Over coffee with a very understanding barista who forgave me for leaking all over his carpet, a new plan was formulated.

ALL FOR NOTHING

The rain was socked in for at least another three days heading north, so Revelstoke was out of the question. The east was also being hammered, and to the west, it was just mountains. In the end, I had just one option: head back south towards Nelson again. *You're kidding. I've done all this for nothing?* Such are the lessons on a bike journey.

If it were humanly possible, the second lesson of the day was harder than the first. By now, the rain had set in with vigorous determination, and I was getting wetter, colder, and even more scared than I'd been in the morning. My visor decided to fog up, and I had no choice but to ride with it open—or be completely blind.

The stinging, freezing rain poured into my helmet in such great volume that I almost needed a snorkel to save myself from drowning.

With ice cold water pouring into my gloves, I'd lost all feeling in both hands. The challenge with being unable to feel your right hand is that it controls both the throttle and the brake—two critical pieces of bike equipment. When you can't feel your fingers, you have no idea how much pressure you're applying to either, and that's the kiss of death on a treacherous, wet, mountain road. Every ten minutes, I was forced to stop by the side of the road and shake my hands vigorously to get the blood and feeling back into my fingers. Then we'd do it all again.

Eventually, we found our way to a beautiful Shangri-La: a stunning B&B on the outskirts of Castlegar, where the owner—an ex-firefighter from Toronto—welcomed us both with open arms, fresh towels, a washing machine, plus a hot tub big enough to host a small village for me, and a warm, heated garage for Voodoo.

Six horrific hours on the bike, and we'd moved a mere 45 km. Such is life. At least I can honestly say there wasn't a second of that 45 km when I hadn't been present. Not for a minute did my mind drift to sadness of the past or fears of the future.

OK, maybe that's not strictly true. There were a couple of times where I foresaw a scary accident and/or dreamt of a warm bath and dry clothes. But for most of the day, I was completely in the moment. I had to be.

Later that night, I snuck back to the garage to wipe Voodoo down and to kiss her tank. To thank my amazing Big Girl for having done so brilliantly, and to promise her that tomorrow would be easy. Compared to today, tomorrow would be a breeze.

DAY 12: CASTLEGAR TO OSOYOOS

I lied.

The morning was beautiful. Heading out for a run along the glorious Columbia River—where I found wild apples and raspberries for breakfast—I laughed about our adventures the day before. It's funny how a warm bed and dry clothes can give you a whole new perspective on life. I was raring to go. Until the rain started.

It rained and it rained and it rained. It was *worse* than yesterday. How was that possible? I did seriously consider bunkering in at my beautiful B&B and spending the day in my hot tub—coffee and book in hand. Now how good did that sound? It was incredibly tempting, but my time was being squeezed. I had to keep moving or I wouldn't make it back to Whistler in time for Jakey's birthday.

So...onwards. I geared up, gritted my teeth, kicked an ever-so-slightly grumbling Voodoo into life, and stepped into the torrential rain.

It was horrific. Within minutes, water was past my ankles in my boots and everything that I'd so carefully nursed back to life the night before was completely waterlogged. *Sorry, Voodoo. The forecast said "dry!"*

BRING IT ON

In the belting rain, I turned Voodoo west, and together we started the climb through Gladstone Provincial Park, which took us through mountain passes over 2,000 metres high, and through treacherous, icy switchbacks, where the water was either incredibly deep on the road, or it cascaded like a river around me. Rockslides and gravel on the road scored extra excitement points for the morning!

The climbing continued, along with the challenges. In the deep water, I'd aquaplane round corners and would just get Voodoo under control in time to hit gravel and slide sideways. It was "interesting" to say the least.

And damn, it was cold. It was colder than I'd ever experienced, and within about fifteen minutes, I'd completely lost the feeling in most parts of my anatomy—particularly the extremities, which is a bugger, because they're the ones you really need on a bike.

The challenge when you're cold on a bike is that you don't flow. You're stiff, choppy, and uncoordinated when you're frozen, and that makes the bike twitch and jerk disturbingly beneath you. There's no rhythm or fluidity. You tend to force the bike, rather than flow with it.

Voodoo was no exception. When we hit deep water troughs that sent us sideways, I had to have the courage just to go with her—to ride it out through the deluge rather than fight her and try to stand her up. Time after time, I had to remind myself, "Go with the bike, go with the bike, go with the bike. Be soft, be soft, be soft."

The thing is, the bike knows. Voodoo certainly did. She knew when I was frightened. She could tell if I'd lost confidence, if I hesitated, if I wasn't strong enough in controlling her. And she would misbehave. She would try to get the better of me. No matter what, I had to be in control of my powerful, feisty girl. I had to remind myself it would all be OK. I just had to keep it together. To focus on what I needed to do, and ride it out. Be in control. Be confident. (The things we tell ourselves when we're scared shitless!)

At the top of a mountain pass, I pulled into a viewing area, shut a heaving Voodoo down, and in the pouring rain, I lifted my visor up and just...laughed. I sat there and just *laughed*. (OK, there was probably a touch of hysteria there, as well.)

"Bring it on! What else can I have today other than lightning? I'm frozen, I'm sliding on ice and gravel, I've got torrential rain, I'm drowning, I've got frostbite in my fingers, the roads are flooded...OK, Universe. Is there anything else you can throw at me? Bring it on! Bring it on!"

REWRITING MY STORY

One of the most inspirational people I've ever encountered is Dr. Michael Gervais, an amazing psychologist who explores the bounds of human potential with elite athletes. He has a philosophy that has become a powerful driver in my life: "Every day, we have the opportunity to create a living masterpiece."

Every day, we have the opportunity to create, to build, to make something special of our lives. To be outstanding in whatever we're doing. And at the end of every day, we get to ask ourselves, "Did we really go for it today? Did we really use the day to build a living masterpiece?"

My living masterpiece today was rewriting my story. That morning, knowing Voodoo and I would be in torrential rain and riding treacherous roads for more than three hours was seriously daunting. The story I started telling myself as we pulled out of Castlegar was one of fear and doubt, not to mention being miserable at the thought of where all that water was going to end up. And I'd just gotten my undies dry!

Eventually, I looked at it as an opportunity to create a living masterpiece. My masterpiece for the day would be about being confident, making the most out of this crazy situation, learning, getting better at riding in tough situations, and keeping my sense of humour, no matter how much water was in the bottom of my boots. That was my focus, and I was determined to come through the other side soaked but stoked. It might not have been a masterpiece for everyone, but it was for me.

A situation like that also helped me appreciate the small things. It was amazing how my appreciation progressed through relativity.

Torrential rain to heavy rain: Yay!

Heavy rain to rain: *So* good!

Rain to drizzle: Outstanding!

Drizzle to 60 percent visibility: Heaven!

Low visibility to overcast: Too easy.

Overcast to a hint of sunlight: Stop the bus! This is too good to be true!

I eventually made it out of the rain, off the pass, and into Christina Lake—a sleepy little town with huge, bright geranium pots lining the sidewalk. Still dripping from my eyeballs, I floated into a coffee shop to warm up. The sun was out now. I was starting to steam, and miraculously, the thawing process had begun. As I dripped water all over the foot of a quiet, elderly man standing in the queue next to me, he gently leaned over and, patting my frostbitten hand, said, "You look like you've had a hard day. Let me buy you a coffee." I must have looked as bad as I felt, but I was incredibly touched by his kind gesture. It was the start of a beautiful day of connections.

One of the things I reflected on while deep in the waters of my hot tub in Castlegar was that I never really made connections in my old life. Sure, I had plenty of friends, but I never really went out of my way to connect with people I didn't know in day-to-day life. I was always too busy. Head down, eyes averted, running from task to experience.

This was now my new life. Time to do things differently. I made the decision that every day I would shine my light brightly. That I would go out of my way to connect through a smile and a conversation with everyone who came into my life.

Be careful what you wish for! My light was so illuminated today that I traded horror stories of the rain with a bunch of BMW riders, and I chatted to a man whose dog would only eat dough-nuts (he lived at Tim Hortons!). I was given a bag of organic cherries by a couple at a gas station (it ended up more like cherry juice by the time I got to my hotel, but it was still delicious). A bunch of Harley riders invited me to lunch with them at the pub (they still scare me), and I had an amazing conversation with a supermarket checkout girl about life and running away (in which I'm an expert). It's amazing how the whole world opens up when you, too, are open.

As I sat by the side of the road, about to head down the desert pass to drop into Osoyoos for the night—dirty, damp, and disgusting—I asked myself one question: "Did I really go for it today?"

Hell yes! Now, get me a bath!

DAY 13: OSOYOOS

We both needed a bath. After three days in rain, grime, and grit, Voodoo had things growing on her and was in desperate need of some mechanical TLC. The decision was made to bunker for the day and regroup.

After leaving Christina Lake, we'd traversed alongside the Kettle River through the plains and flatlands, skirting through small towns and villages dotted along the river bank. For infinitesimal moments, I caught snatches of rural life as we rode close enough to tiny houses to peek into their windows. For the briefest of moments, I stepped into the lives of others—seeing tables laid for lunch, drying clothes flapping in the breeze, smoke billowing from chimneys. Such a beautiful, gentle snapshot of the real world.

Leaving the flats, we started to climb higher and higher into a breathtaking mountain vista, the air crisp and invigorating. We flew over the top of the pass, and instantly the world started to change yet again. Beneath the bracing pine switchbacks, we twisted through the hot, harsh, dry desert with its ferocious beauty, rugged and wild. Despite the arid environment, vineyards and fruit trees flourished boldly on the outskirts of Osoyoos Lake.

It was such a place of stunning contrasts, and the perfect spot to wash, dry, degrease, and oil. After engaging in hand-to-hand combat with the giant hose at the car wash, both Voodoo and I ended up clean, shiny, and waxed. She looked like a million bucks. I, on the other hand, had not scrubbed up so well.

Time for her chain lube—not something I'm used to doing. Usually, my "pit crew" at home managed the technicalities of bike maintenance, so for me, it was time to learn. And the lesson? Yes, you can over-lube a chain. Voodoo will be spitting grease all over me now for the next 100 km. Ah, well. Practice, not perfection.

I do, however, manage the air pressure in my tires by myself (look at me). In Australia, it's a really simple process. First, it's free, and second, you simply dial in the amount of air you need, connect the pump to your tire, and it adds the correct pressure automatically. Simple. No wonder I can do that myself.

Tire pressure management in North America, however, is a completely different beast. First, you have to pay for it (Really? You pay for air?), and second, the process is gobsmackingly convoluted.

The air valve on a bike is located in the middle of the mags, which makes it conveniently impossible to access, given the location of the brakes in the middle of the wheel. For fifteen minutes, I struggled trying to get my arm underneath the brakes and through the mag wheels to get the air hose attached. I laid on the ground. I sat up. I laid on my back. I laid on my stomach. I tried my left arm. I tried my right arm. *Bloody hell! You've got to be a contortionist to do this!* It was sizzling hot. Sweat was pouring off me, and I was covered in more grease than my uncleaned oven.

After watching me for a few minutes from the luxury of his air-conditioned truck, a young guy in cowboy boots sauntered over to me. Trying not to smile, he asked, "So, little lady, do you need a hand?"

No, this little lady did not need a hand!

"No, thanks. Appreciate the offer, but no. I've got this. All under control. Thanks."

As if! There was no way I was going to admit defeat, let alone ask for help.

Shaking his head just ever so slightly (but enough for me to see it), he returned to his truck and started to gas up. Luckily for me, it takes a long time to fill a truck, and after another ten minutes of being spread-eagle on the ground with my arm at a forty-five-degree angle, I had to admit I was failing spectacularly. More to the point, I'd actually managed to let all of the air out of Voodoo's tires. They were completely flat. Great!

I had no choice but to ask for help. Damn. I don't *do* "ask for help." More than a little mortified, I faced my potential saviour.

"You know what? I'm really sorry, but actually I don't have a clue what I'm doing. Do you think you could give me a hand?"

To his absolute credit, he didn't laugh—not in front of me, anyway. After just thirty seconds in front of Voodoo, he asked a bizarre question: "Where's your tire pressure gauge?"

"My what?"

"Your tire pressure gauge. You've gotta have a tire pressure gauge."

"Mmm...and that would be...?"

"Oh my God, how long have you been riding this bike?"

"Well, about twelve days, but it's..."

"Come with me."

After buying me a gauge, and with infinite patience, he taught me the fine art of adding air to tires in North America. A new skill acquired, a new friend made, and importantly, a new step taken forward on my journey. Asking for help had been such an anathema to me, but I'd allowed myself to be vulnerable and—amazingly—had survived.

It was either that or ride back to Whistler with two flat tires, but I learnt an even bigger lesson that morning. As my cowboy friend and I worked together—him coaching and me failing—I realised that asking for help was more than one-sided. It was actually a gift.

Letting myself be vulnerable had allowed my new friend to feel valued. I'd never seen asking for help in that light. I'd always been so focused on me—on not wanting to look weak or out of control. Amazing the lessons you get at a gas station.

"You keep that pressure gauge close now, you hear, little lady?"

Oh, I will. You can bet on that. Every time I look at it, I'll remember that I'm safe being vulnerable—which is handy, because I know I'm going to need just as much help next time I have to use the damn thing!

BREATHE AND PUT THE COFFEE DOWN

By lunchtime, all my maintenance chores were done, and it was time to grab a coffee and find a spot in the sun. To chill and to just enjoy being still for a while. It should have been a welcome relief after the carnage and adrenaline of the past few days, but no. I was restless, disoriented by not being in perpetual motion and struggling to just *be*. How on earth was I going to create a living masterpiece on a recovery day—on a "not in the saddle exploding all over the road" day?

My days had been nothing but full-on from the minute my feet hit the ground in the morning to the minute I curled up my toes in bed at night, completely exhausted and spent. I'd been driven by a process—a set of rituals that kept me focused, absorbed, and in constant action. Up, run, meditate, set intentions, decide on the masterpiece, write, check maps, load up, on the bike, ride, off the bike, off-load, check maps, pull routes. Objectives, destinations, and achievement.

It's easy to create a masterpiece when you're running hard towards something, but how do you do that when you're sitting still?

I felt itchy and agitated. I couldn't just sit here. I needed to be doing wild, crazy things—things that, at the end of the day, made me feel like I'd really gone for it. I should have been on the road. I should have been exploring, I should have been riding hard. I should, I should, I should...I *should* have smacked myself. That's what I *should* have done! Has there ever been a word more effective at creating guilt and pressure than "should"?

OK, breathe. Always a good thing to do when I'm antsy enough to bust out of my skin. Breathe and put the coffee down. Eventually, having finally let go of equating the fear of stillness to lack of achievement, it dawned on me that creating a living masterpiece wasn't all about action. It was knowing you'd been true to yourself, you'd grown, and in some way, you'd added value to the world.

After breathing deeply to calm myself, I made the call. On this day of recovery, my living masterpiece would be created by *me* committing to *me*. By taking care of myself, by doing a long meditation, and by being truly focused on being present—right here, right now.

As my favourite Zen master WuDe says, "If you can't be happy right here in this moment, nothing you do, nothing you achieve, nothing you become will give you happiness." In that moment, in that stillness, with the struggle for achievement for once overcome, I was finally *more* than happy.

CHAPTER SIX

Osoyoos to Winthrop, WA

DAY 14: OSOYOOS TO HOPE

Just before I left on this crazy journey, I came across the concept of setting an intention every day. Putting it simply, an intention is a guiding principle for how you want to show up in the world. It's an aim or a purpose you want to align yourself with. As I hit the road with Voodoo, I decided to put it to the test, and I committed to setting an intention with the Universe every day.

Before I left Osoyoos, I set my intention for the day: to live with a completely open heart—to be open to every connection, every opportunity, every person who came my way. I'd barely gotten off Voodoo at my favourite coffee shop when the Universe decided to get the ball rolling.

Sitting outside in the sun, steaming cup of black coffee in hand, I was joined by two spritely gentlemen who offered to keep me company. They were local vineyard owners in their early eighties with a lifetime of friendship and laughter between them. They were competitors in business but compatriots in life, and tears of laughter streamed down my face as they told one wicked story after another—usually at the expense of the other one.

As they left, they insisted on buying me another coffee. How could a girl refuse such charmers? But their seat was instantly filled by a chopper pilot—a handsome kid who looked young enough to still be learning to use a fork. He had an amazing job: flying over cherry trees after the rain so that the down draft from the chopper blades would disperse the water and stop the cherries from splitting. *Seriously? That was a real job?*

Turned out, it was, and it also turned out he was just as funny as the two gentlemen he'd hot-seated it with. Between the three of them, it was a deep belly-laugh day. Hanging with the boys had put me about two hours behind schedule, but it was worth every second to have shared their stories, laughed with them, and stepped into their lives for even a small moment.

On this trip, I was learning how breathtakingly open people were capable of being with me. I'm not sure why. Maybe it was because I was transient—I mean, who was I going to tell their dreams, their regrets, or their fears to? Conversations at the gas station or a coffee shop generally started with questions about the bike but very quickly became intense discussions, where they revealed more about themselves than sometimes I needed to know.

Funnily enough, it became a real source of joy for me to have people open up and share their world with a wild girl on an even wilder motorbike. The connections I made each and every day were completely fuelling my soul. In fact, they were *healing* my soul. I could feel it.

But my soul had to get a wriggle on, or I'd be travelling in the dark. Not something I liked doing on Voodoo.

The road from Osoyoos to Hope was a gift. Harsh, desolate red desert one minute, lush green and purple valleys the next. Blink your eyes, and the lush valleys turned into Wild West gold country, where craggy, angry peaks of yellow lined the road. Look again, and you were in a glorious pine-covered forest, winding alongside a sparkling blue-green river. It was like journeying through five different countries, all in the space of 150 km.

STEP OUTSIDE, PLEASE

Lunch was in Princeton—a quirky little town, full of character and attitude. Leaving Voodoo languishing outside in the sun, I headed inside, dropped all my gear on the nearest table and hightailed it to the bathroom. I'd spoken to a biker at a gas station the day before and asked him how big his gas tank was. His reply? "About twice the size of my bladder." Good for him. When one of mine hit empty, the other one hit full. And I was busting.

On my return, standing alongside my table was the biggest bear of a policeman I've ever seen in my life, and he did not look happy.

"Are you the registered owner of that BMW parked out front?" he asked. I nodded fearfully.

"Step outside, please. Right now."

At that point, I figured that the U-turn I'd done ten minutes earlier over double-yellow lines right outside the police station had caught his attention. How could it not have? But no—my "plates didn't add up." *My what?*

For twenty minutes, I tried to explain the unexplainable. A nonresident Aussie travelling through North America on a Sydney license, owning a Canadian-registered bike out of Whistler. He peppered me with questions. Was the bike really mine? Where was I living? How long was I staying? Did I have a work permit? The barrage went on and on—without a smile, without drawing a breath. It was a hardcore interrogation.

Finally, *finally* he understood, and the minute he got it, it was like a light being turned on. Instantly, we became mates, and had (of course) the most amazing conversation.

He'd been a motorcycle cop in the Vancouver Police Force for many years, and as we stood on the footpath together, I was treated to incredible stories of riding Harleys on the force. It was amazing—as was his transformation. In a matter of minutes, he'd gone from stony-faced hard guy to being completely lit up. It was beautiful.

He warned me about my next stretch. It was one of the most treacherous roads in BC for bike-rider fatalities. And I knew why. The road was a biker's dream—dropping corners, tight twisties, flowing bends, and a beautiful fresh surface that almost encouraged you to speed. Almost.

"Do me a favour," he asked. "Take it easy out there?"

"You bet, officer."

I was sufficiently sobered by this time and still relieved he'd missed the U-turn.

"Well, I'll make sure of that."

OK, you do that.

Lunch was had, Voodoo was gassed and raring to go, and together, we powered out of town—the warning completely forgotten in the excitement of such a brilliant bike road. Just as I flew over the top of a crest, I spotted him. There, parked on the side of the road was my new best friend, waiting for me. Like a shark, he pulled in behind me and sat on my tail, and together we did the speed limit for about 25 km. There's nothing quite like a police escort out of town. I'm not sure whether he wanted to make sure I was safe or to make sure I left town, but either way, it made for a very slow, sensible, and infinitely safe ride out.

Slow was good. It gave me a chance to appreciate the beauty around me. Rich green pine forests, tight mountain passes, high peaks, and small ravines surrounded us as we climbed up, up, up. Tight hairpin bends, huge fast descents, swift flowing rivers. I was cold, hot, cold, hot depending on whether I was going up or down, and all the way, Voodoo and I were completely encased by glorious, bold, majestic mountains.

PULLING INTO HOPE

I was almost on an emotional overload. It had been a day of beauty, adventure, and genuine heart opening. I was tired and looking forward to finding a bed, pulling my boots off, and sitting quietly. Very quietly. But the Harley rider on Pump 7 at the gas station had other ideas.

He was the real deal. (Aren't they all? I'm always terrified to ask what they really do. I've got a huge suspicion that most of these hairy, scary guys are actually accountants in drag.) Covered in tats from head to foot—well, the bits that I could see anyway—bandanna, fists like meat grinders. Yep, scary to the max. Normally, I would have made myself as inconspicuous as possible, but this was open heart day, remember? I knew I had to live my intent.

Looking over at him while Van Halen pumped from his speakers, I shouted nervously, "Cool song." And it was.

He wandered over. *Oh no.* "Ya like that song?"

I nodded bravely.

"Do you like to dance, Baby Doll?"

Who? Baby Doll? And do I what? I don't think so!

But there, surrounded by grey-power retirees in RVs, cool bikers, families in four-wheel drives, and just about everything that moved, a huge, scary Harley dude and a wimpy BMW chick did a turn at the gas station.

I'm not sure Van Halen would have approved. I think we both murdered "Jump" as we sang and danced, but it was quite the performance. It's not often you get called Baby Doll by a Harley rider, and I'm not sure anyone else could have gotten away with it. But I guess anything is possible on an open heart day.

As I left the gas station, smiling in my helmet at the power of intention, the thought did occur to me: tomorrow I might just want to intend to "Ride to Whistler quietly without causing any commotion." That would probably be a nice change.

DAYS 15–19: HOPE AND WHISTLER

It felt strange riding back into Whistler, knowing I was going to be off the road for a few days. My heart was torn. I'd been riding for over two weeks now and was just settling into this astonishing journey. Nothing had prepared me for the life I'd led over the past two weeks. I was still shaking my head in amazement at the rich adventures, intimate connections—usually over a gas pump—and the unexpected joy of letting go of control and embracing the complete unknown each day. It was starting to feel like a comfortable pair of slippers (not that I've ever worn slippers), and I wasn't ready to put on my hard, uncomfortable, real-life boots yet—even for a few days.

But as much as I'd embraced surrendering to the unpredictable, I also loved the structure of my routine. Wake, run, meditate, write, load, ride—and then doing most of it in reverse again at the end of the day. It had become a meditative practice, and there was a gentle comfort and security in the process. It was soothing, and in the soothing, it was healing.

Then, there was me. Astride the incredible Voodoo was a woman I was starting not to know. Bit by bit, chinks were appearing in her armour. She was letting go and releasing, questioning and discovering, changing and growing. Who was this woman, this warrior who appeared to have put down her sword? I wasn't sure, but I liked how she was evolving, and I didn't want to lose her. If she stepped off Voodoo, would she disappear?

But Jakey was only going to be twenty-one once, and I wanted to be with him. To tell him how proud I was of the man he'd become, how blown away I was by the amazing life he'd created all on his own, and how awed I was at everything he'd overcome to get to this place in the world.

Jakey had done it hard.

As a small child, learning did not come easily to him. One of the most important lessons I've learnt as a parent is not to have expectations for your children or to hold onto dreams for them that are yours and yours alone. It's an easy thing to do. I remember holding both of my boys in my arms when they were tiny babies, wondering what the world would hold for them, wondering what they'd achieve. Would they cure cancer? Would they save lives? Would they broker peace in the world? My dreams. Not theirs.

CELEBRATING JAKEY

Very early on, I realised Jakey's path would be unlike anything I'd ever envisioned for him. School was hard. It was difficult for him to grasp concepts, to understand what he was being taught, and to keep pace with his peers academically. As I watched him struggle more and more every day, I released those expectations, understanding that whatever happened, his journey was his journey. It wasn't mine. He would be whoever he was meant to be, and no matter what his learning challenges, he would find his place in this world. And he would be fine. (I kept telling myself that!)

At primary school, he'd held it together through rote learning, but high school presented a whole new challenge. In an environment that required comprehension, cognitive thought, and the ability to reason, the gap between what was expected and what Jakey could deliver grew exponentially. And my beautiful boy started to drown. It wasn't a slow descent—it was straight to the bottom of the pool.

We threw everything at it that we could. Tutors, therapists, counsellors. I was continually scouring the world for brain breakthroughs. If I had even the slightest sniff that "something had worked" in addressing learning challenges, we subjected Jakey to it in the vain hope we could find a solution.

But nothing worked, and bit by bit, I lost my child. My beautiful, funny, cheeky child slid into a very dark, black place. He'd lost all his belief and confidence in himself. There's only so many times a parent can say, "You are smart, baby—you just learn differently to everyone else." Because no matter what you say or no matter how many times you say it, they know. And they just don't believe you.

By the time he was fifteen, the whole family was exhausted, overwrought, and in such a place of helplessness. Assignments, homework, study, and exams became a full-time commitment for Rob and me. After a long day at work, we'd spend the whole evening working on schoolwork with Jakey. And yes—full confession—there were times it was easier to write assignments myself. It was either spend six hours helping him do them or punch them out myself in an hour. (Let me tell you, I wasn't happy if I didn't get a good mark.)

It was slowly killing us. Every waking moment was devoted to getting Jakey through the nightmare. And man, did that boy work. He was putting in three times the effort of his friends for a quarter of the result. Holidays, weekends, late at night, Jakey just put his head down and worked relentlessly to try to keep up. He never questioned it; he never fought it. He knew that's what he had to do, and so he just kept working harder than any kid should have to.

But it wasn't sustainable. Late one night, he came into the laundry as I was folding washing. Sitting up on the bench alongside me, my precious son leaned over, put his arms around my neck and in a small, tearful voice whispered, "I can't keep doing this. I just can't go on. You have to find a way out for me. I can't do this anymore. I'm done."

Never had I heard more terrifying words. I tucked him back into bed, telling him everything would be OK—and then promptly sat on the bathroom floor, my head buried in my arms as I wept uncontrollably. I had no idea what to do next. How to help him. How to find a way through this heartbreaking hell. I knew I couldn't bandage the situation anymore. I had to find a permanent solution.

The following morning, I went out for coffee and literally fell over a huge display of a book by Norman Doidge, *The Brain That Changes Itself*. It was meant to be! Within ten minutes, I'd read about a school in Canada that specialised in addressing cognitive learning issues, and within two hours, I'd secured Jakey the last spot in their school in Vancouver for the new school term starting in seven weeks. I figured I'd better meet Rob for lunch and break the news to him—we were moving to Canada.

And move we did. Within seven weeks, the boys and I were

living in Vancouver while Rob stayed in Sydney. I ran the business operation remotely, and crazily, we cross-commuted for two years.

It was a tough yet amazing time. And it worked. Jakey's brain rewired itself following some incredibly hard work on his behalf, and his whole world took off. He discovered he had an amazing talent in film and photography, and after finishing film school in Sydney, at the age of nineteen, he nailed a role in an award-winning production company based in Whistler, BC. Now, he was truly living the dream—living and filming a life of action, adrenaline, and adventure. He had found his place in this world, like I knew he would. He was more than fine.

And now he was turning twenty-one. I had twenty-one incredible years to celebrate, and there was no way I was going to miss that!

And celebrate we did. It was a buzz to spend a couple of days just hanging with my boy. We have always been close, and even though he'd only been in Whistler by himself nine months, he'd grown and changed so much.

Although, some things never change. Is there ever a point in a parent-child relationship when they pay for dinner?

DAY 20: WHISTLER TO MANNING PARK

Preparation for departure a few days later was chaos—frantically packing, plotting routes, checking Voodoo's vital signs, making sure she was fired up and ready to growl, checking my passport (OK, finding my passport), renewing visas, cleaning the dead bugs off my jacket, repacking, cutting the first packing in half and repacking again. (*Seriously?* Was I ever going to need the black off-the-shoulder number I'd been lumping all over Canada?) Toss it. The heels, however, stayed. Zen and the art of high heels—a girl still has to have her priorities!

After kissing a sleepy Jakey goodbye, I headed out early, back along a familiar route. North to Lillooet and then east back towards Osoyoos heading to the US border at the tiny town of Nighthawk. I loved that name. *Nighthawk.* It sounded like a covert CIA mission. The 100 km road was divine—still one of my favourites in the whole world. Stunning mountain passes, sparkling rivers, and scrappy roads hanging off the side of a cliff. This baby had it all, and I was glad to be riding it again.

In the silence of my helmet (OK, there's really no such thing as silence in your helmet when you ride without earplugs), I thought back to how differently I'd felt leaving Whistler for the first time just two weeks ago. Had it only been two weeks? Already, it felt like a lifetime.

The girl who'd wobbled out of Whistler then had been terrified—of what lay ahead, of what had been left behind, and of who and what she might discover on this journey. A deep fear had nestled into the pit of my stomach then. I had so many hopes and goals for this journey, and I was desperate to achieve them. I needed answers and solutions, and I was petrified I wouldn't get them.

But as I rode through the heat of the desert—out into the dry, unforgiving rocks of red, orange, and ochre—it was a shock to realise that fear had been replaced by something completely unexpected: the thrill of anticipation. The biggest difference for me this time around was I now had no expectation for this journey other than to experience joy every day and to be present with my emotions. I was beginning to understand I didn't need this journey to "achieve" or "fix" anything. I just needed to be. Not do. *Be.*

No goals, no expectations, no hopes. Just the experience.

By the time I'd reached Manning Park for the night, I could barely string a sentence together. The ride in had been gruelling—hot, hard, and harrowing. But the Universe had an amazing reward for me after braving the elements: Lightning Lake.

As I sat alongside this picturesque azure blue lake, surrounded by obligatory bright-green pine trees and craggy mountain peaks, I took a deep breath and slowly exhaled, trusting completely that whatever this incredible journey gave me, it would be perfect.

DAY 21: MANNING PARK TO WINTHROP

Manning Park was soothing as I ran at the break of dawn. Trickling streams, crooked bridges, tough hills, rocky declines, dense thick trees forming a thick canopy above my head with the sun straining to push its beams through the tangled branches. I laughed hard as I ran, completely immersed in the sheer beauty around me and the joy of movement.

Before rolling out, I decided to grab a coffee and just sit, readying myself for the next leg of my journey. I was apprehensive about crossing the border into the US. Canada was home. I loved the gentleness, the warmth, the slower pace of life. The US was—well, it was not Canada. What challenges awaited me as I crossed that thin white border line?

SIPPING, NOT GULPING

I nursed an Americano that an automatic coffee machine had given birth to (what was I thinking—coffee from a machine? At least it was warm!) and set my intention for the day: to stay present. To focus on every small detail, like enjoying my coffee (taste excluded). Today, I enjoyed feeling the cup in my hands, holding the warmth, smelling the aroma, watching the steam rise, feeling every sip as it flowed through my body. It's amazing how all your senses are energised when you choose to be present. (Normally, I would have experienced just one sense: a burnt throat from trying to drink it too quickly!)

I also set an intention to be brave. A wave of anxiety was starting to wash over me. I'd learnt so much on this journey already about trusting the process—about surrendering to the experience and being patient that the answers would come. But what if they didn't? What happens at the end of this if I still don't know what's next? What happens at the end of three months if I still don't know the way forward? What if, what if, what if...

Breathing deeply, I remembered to step back into being grateful. Being grateful for a breathtaking run this morning, grateful that the bears had left me alone, grateful for the sun filtering through the trees, the fresh raspberries on the track, the smell of damp earth, and the bliss of movement.

I was also grateful for the freedom and space I'd created and for the amazing piece of machinery that was sitting in front of my cabin waiting for me—who just might go without me if I didn't get a wriggle on. Sipping (not gulping) the last of my coffee, I reminded myself I'd be fine. It was going to be OK.

Pointing ourselves west towards the border, we headed out—back through Princeton and on through the Similkameen Valley, which is pretty damn up there in the Awe Rating Scale. We rode through flats and alongside a river, passing along the bottom of one stunning valley after another. In some places, the terrain was harsh with yellow rocks and landslides, and then suddenly a reprieve of lush green pastures. I'd describe it as breathtaking, but that was more my next encounter.

DUDE, SO SHAKEN

Traffic had been heavy along a four-lane highway, and I'd been sitting in the fast lane for about ten minutes, picking off the dawdlers in the slow lane. A huge, black pickup truck hugged my butt—sitting in my slip stream and letting me be the fall guy if there were police ahead.

There were two more cars to overtake before I was clear of traffic. As I came alongside the first car, I realised he was coming in so fast on the car in front that he was going to run out of room. Instantly, I got a flash: *He's coming in way too hot. He hasn't seen me. He's going to pull straight over onto me.* A second later, that's exactly what he did, and in that same second, I planned and executed an escape route.

I pulled into the oncoming lane to create a gap for him. Luckily for both of us, there was nothing coming the other way. The look on his face as he glanced left and suddenly saw me right alongside him on the wrong side of the road was one of pure terror. If I hadn't had the space to move over, he would have completely pulverised me.

Avoiding crazies is a critical skill when you ride a bike. It's never (well, not usually) you who causes the problem. It's someone else who just doesn't think. I have a very simple survival rule: ride like everyone around me is trying to kill me, and therefore, expect the unexpected. That's exactly what happened here. I had a second sense about what was going to happen and planned an exit strategy. Despite the adrenaline rush, I was still relatively calm.

But the guy in the truck behind me wasn't. A couple hundred metres down the road, I pulled into a fruit stand to get some fresh cherries, and the truck raced in behind me. Before I'd even had time to get off Voodoo, the owner—a handsome guy in his early twenties—came flying out of his truck, raced over to Voodoo, and hugged me hard.

"Dude, dude!" *Dude?* "Oh my god, oh my god, oh my god. That guy nearly hit you! I was right behind you. I thought you were gone. I had to come and check to make sure you were all right!"

I was fine, but he wasn't. After insisting on buying me a box of cherries and a bottle of water, we sat in the shade next to Voodoo while he chanted, "I'm so shaken, I'm so shaken, dude, I'm so shaken." Luckily, *this* dude—the one who had almost been smeared down the road—was managing to hold it together.

GIVE THE UNIVERSE A BREAK

Convincing the US border guards to let me in—an Aussie girl on a Canadian-registered bike with no fixed address in the US—was a tough sell. "You're travelling through the US on a bike for three months on your own? Sure, sure. Off your bike, please. Unload your bags. Are you carrying weapons? Is there anything you might want to tell us about before we find it?"

Are you serious? Look at me! I'm a plant-based, green-juice-drinking woman of a "certain age!" Do you think I'd be carrying weapons or "anything else?" (I did have a quick worry about the sage, just for a second!)

Eventually, the bags were unpacked and repacked, the passport stamped, and we crossed the thin white line into Washington. Yay! Fresh tracks. A new country. Even riding through 35 km of gravel I encountered about three minutes after crossing the border couldn't deter my enthusiasm—although, in some of the hairier moments, I could hear this strange voice coming from my helmet: "Today is not the day you drop your bike. Today is *not* the day you drop your bike!" The power of positive thinking. (It did dawn on me later that within this affirmation was the assumption that someday I would actually drop my bike. Just not today!)

Staying upright was a vital thought to keep in my head. Late in the day, as I came through Omak, tailgated by an enormous logging truck with only a credit card width between us, a deer suddenly bolted out from a parking lot—yep, a parking lot—and straight across my path.

Another big decision moment. Do I hit the deer, or do I jam my brakes on, miss the deer, but get run over by the truck that was right up my butt? Decisions, decisions. I have no idea how I missed the deer or the truck—probably closing my eyes helped—but somehow, we all skated through. I decided the Universe must definitely be watching out for me—and that I must be trying its patience big time today. It was time to call it quits.

DAY 22: WINTHROP

Nothing prepared me for Winthrop. It was like being in a John Wayne movie, down to the wooden sidewalks. The town had been settled in 1883 when gold was discovered in the hills, and not much had changed since then. Maybe the addition of the gas station. It was serious cowboy territory. I kept waiting for the sheriff to come riding through town, for cowpokes to be thrown through the swinging saloon doors, and for the gun-slinging showdown at noon. Ah, those were the days!

I fell in love with it. After my harrowing day in the saddle the day before, I decided to bunker in and enjoy the town for an extra day. Two hours in the hot tub always makes that decision easy.

I'VE GOT THIS

I headed out at first light for a gentle run through the countryside. It was exactly as I'd pictured small town, rural America. Pastel yellow wheat fields, fat cattle grazing, big hay rolls stacked to perfection, and a cute, tiny town with a river running right through the middle of it.

As I ran, I listened to one of my favourite songs, which has a beautiful line about being lucky enough to count the ones you love on both hands. It touched my soul as I hit rewind about ten times, soaking up the emotion and the sentiment, realising I needed more than both hands and both feet to count the ones I loved.

Yet, the ones I loved had been vocal. The night before, I'd given a watered-down version of the day's adventures on my blog, and I'd woken to a barrage of emails from my team, all questioning the wisdom of this crazy journey. They didn't doubt my ability, but they were fearful that if I spent enough time on the road on a bike, sooner or later the odds were not going to be in my favour. The day before had been a good example of that.

What was hard for me to explain—because at the time I didn't understand it myself—was my growing relationship with the Universe. For the first time, I was starting to embrace an undefinable connection with a power greater than myself. At the beginning of the trip, I'd begun a daily pre-engine start-up routine where I'd ask the Universe to protect Voodoo and me as we rode. It started off as a safety net—an insurance policy. What have you got to lose by asking?

About ten days into the practice, as I sat on Voodoo one morning and asked for protection before firing her up, a very loud voice came through in my helmet: "Sure, but you've gotta do your job."

Well, that threw me. What did that actually mean—doing my job? I guessed it meant not taking unnecessary risks, not riding at crazy speeds (Mmm...might need to think that one through), and being ride-ready—having mind, body, and soul together every day. And probably watching out for wildlife.

Fair call. Can do. It's a partnership here. You do your job, Universe, and I'll do mine.

As difficult as it was to explain my baby-steps connection with the Universe, I had—perhaps naively—a confidence that I was being taken care of. I was being protected, and I'd be safe on this journey. It was a risk for sure, but it was a manageable risk that came with the territory. I knew I'd be fine.

I've always believed in, "Never live a porridge life." For me, that means never settling for grey, boring oatmeal. Make your life granola with nuts, fruit, and berries (no yoghurt—I'm plant-based!). Full of colour, texture, and taste explosion.

Don't be average. Don't settle for second best. Don't accept the safe and easy, the predictable, and comfortable. Take risks. Grab life and experiences that are vibrant and joyous, that scare you, that inspire you, that keep you guessing, that truly bring out the best in you.

That's never living a porridge life. It's a lot to put into a cereal bowl, but it's worth it!

Without a doubt, I was fortunate enough to be creating granola right now. I'd worked through enough porridge in my life to know I never wanted to settle for bland, grey oatmeal. I never wanted to settle for the easy or the safe option (although it probably wouldn't hurt once in a while). At this point in my life, I only ever wanted to be in a place of passion and joy.

In the past, I'd taken this analogy to its extreme—having pushed too hard and too far, becoming overwrought, exhausted, my adrenals shot. But it's why I rode. Sure, it kicked in the adrenaline (some days more than others), but when I'm on the bike, in control of a feisty machine that will bite me if I get it wrong, the pure adventure gives me joy.

Since my track record here had not been good, trying to explain that *now* I knew what "too close to the edge" looked like was tricky. I had zero credibility. It was way too early in the journey for anyone to have faith that I knew what I was doing, and they expressed that lack of trust in no uncertain terms.

When I'd started my run, steam came out of my ears. How did they not see that I needed to do this as much as I needed to breathe? How could they doubt my ability to pull this off?

Then, purely by coincidence (is there such a thing?), on came that beautiful song. With a shock, it suddenly hit me. I let go of my belligerence and my need to defend, and I finally got it: I was that "lucky man," surrounded by people who loved and cared for me. Their emotion and fear came purely from a place of love, and that was about as good as it got. I was blessed to have the love, support, and concern of so many people.

I silently whispered to them all: *I have to keep doing this, but I promise I'll do my job, OK?*

CHAPTER SEVEN

Winthrop to Portland, OR

DAY 23: WINTHROP TO EVERSON

Freedom is a funny thing. It can be both liberating and scary. It means choice, and choice means action. Sometimes the responsibility of taking action can be even more scary than not having any options at all. On this trip, I had the ultimate freedom. Where I went, how I went, and when I went—but that freedom was daunting.

It was also a little scary. Maps, roads, directions, and the difference between west and east had always been like a foreign language to me. Even after three weeks on the road, when I came to a sign that gave me an option of Highway 57-N and 57-S, I had to quickly draw a compass in my head to remember which way to go—and road choices need to be instantaneous at 120 kph!

Part of me wanted structure—to have a route, a journey, a plan all mapped out well ahead. You've gotta love the security of a good plan. Don't you hate it when you get back from holidays and someone says, "Did you see the temple in Ubud?" *The temple? Oh, there was a temple?* I wanted to squeeze this journey to the max. I didn't want to miss a thing.

But given the enormous fires raging through Washington, a plan wasn't feasible. I was literally making it up as I went along each night, usually starting from scratch again when I awoke to find fires had shut down yet another planned route. For someone who loved control, structure, and objectives, this was either a nightmare or the perfect learning opportunity. I was still debating which!

Sitting beneath a huge peach tree in Winthrop, I sipped coffee and spread my maps out under the watchful eye of a doe and a tiny spotted fawn. I stared at the maps hopefully. Willing them, begging them to tell me the most amazing route for the day—the one that would set my hair on fire with adrenaline and excitement, and spectacular scenery as well, please. But no matter which way I turned my reticent maps, they refused to reveal any secrets or even give me a hint.

Damn. It was up to me to decide the best route. *Pressure on.* I looked up at the tiny fawn bouncing and jumping all over the grass—never taking a straight line, experiencing life in a random series of leaps—and it dawned on me. *Every* day was the perfect day. No matter what route I took, which leap I made, I would always get an amazing adventure. I had the freedom to change my location and my plans, and if one day didn't turn out exactly as I'd envisaged it, it would still be special. No matter where I ended up, I would experience what I was destined to experience. And it would be perfect. Always.

Amazing—letting go really does take the pressure off. Kinda wonder why I hadn't been doing that more often.

LESS IS MORE

I'd met the owner of the local bookshop in town the day before, and he'd invited me for coffee before I left town. He was fascinated with Australian authors and wanted me to share my favourite writers and their works. After staying up half the night to research who my favourite authors might just be (!), I headed into town.

We spent an hour together. While I talked about Australia, he pulled out maps and gave me recommendations for bike routes. (See what happens when you let go and just open yourself completely to the unknown?)

I had to laugh at the synchronicity of life as we pulled out of town. No such thing as coincidences, right? Another example of an experience I was destined to have.

However, there was one experience I was sure I didn't need to have. I'd sacrificed seven matching sets of bras and undies in order to make space in my roll bag for half a dozen aromatherapy oils that I used every morning, depending on how my body and soul were feeling.

That morning, I'd chosen lavender—and I'd had a brain wave. *How about I put it in my helmet and breathe relaxing oils while I'm on the road?* The idea was perfect. The execution was a nightmare. True to form, I figured if two drops were recommended, surely ten would be better. I always knew best!

Ten drops were definitely not better. The smell in my helmet was so intense, I had no choice but to ride with my visor open to stop my eyes from blistering. I was, however, very, *very* relaxed!

SENSORY OVERLOAD

Highway 20 from Winthrop to Concrete had a huge reputation to live up to. It was considered one of the very best bike roads in Washington, both for riding adrenaline and for spectacular scenery. I had big expectations as I left town—visor up, eyes still watering.

The first 10 km were nice. Big pine trees, gentle forests, pretty scenery. Very nice. But "nice" is, well...just *nice*. Your Aunty Beryl is nice. Doing yoga is nice. Eating tofu is nice. (OK, maybe not so nice.) But nice is not drop-dead exhilarating, spine-tinglingly spectacular, breathtakingly awesome or scream-in-your-helmet sensational.

Oh, how wrong I was. After those first 10 km, and for 100 more, the whole world revealed itself at once. We traversed high mountain passes, climbing thousands of metres in elevation where I could look down and see the road snaking below me. We flew through terrifying ravines—tight, narrow, and twisty— where it seemed like Voodoo just dropped left, right, left, for hours. I never thought we'd be upright again.

Our world was full of big, black tunnels burrowed deep into the sides of mountains that gave me vertigo in the dark as I hurtled towards the tiny pinprick of light at the end. (Lesson learnt: take your sunglasses off when you go through tunnels!)

The smell of pine was so strong it actually overtook the lavender in my helmet (which was still burning holes in my eyeballs), and the colours were beyond description. Dams, rivers, impossibly blue lakes, tiny towns surrounded by pastures—Highway 20 had it all. The road swept, turned, dropped, dipped, and curled over steep inclines with trees desperately trying to hold on. Complete sensory overload.

I was laughing so hard inside my helmet that I actually had to pull over at Ross Lake and breathe. A rider on a big touring Beemer who'd been on my tail for about fifteen minutes followed me in. As we took off our helmets, not a word was said. We just looked down at the incredible crystal blue water below us and laughed in awe and pure joy.

Eventually, we talked. A seriously cool dude from Vancouver, he was out touring solo for a few months on a bike fully kitted out with everything but a breadmaking machine. He did scoff at Voodoo, the bastard. She might look like a refugee boat, but she still handled like a thoroughbred!

We rode together for about 100 km, and it was a buzz to have a companion. Not that you get to talk much when you ride with someone, but there's a silent camaraderie that brings you together. Plus, just the teensiest bit of competition. Seeing who could take the best line in corners and come out fastest reminded me that the warrior was still alive and kicking.

Oh, I was supposed to have given that up when I put my shield down, right? OK, work in progress. I'll start again tomorrow.

When I'd decided on this journey, a lot of riding friends volunteered to join me for all or part of the adventure. As tempting as it had been to have company, I knew I had to do this by myself. The lessons I needed to learn would only be found if I were solo. I also knew that riding by myself would open up connections that just wouldn't reveal themselves if I were riding with a friend. Solo it was.

But for today, having a playmate had been a real buzz. We rode together most of the way to Everson—the closest town I could find to Mt. Baker, which I was planning to hike. As I cruised through town looking for a place to stay, I came across the most perfect B&B called—wait for it—Kale Cottage. Now, as a plant-based aficionado, could there have been anywhere more perfect?

A quick U-turn and fifteen minutes later, I found myself encased in my own private cocoon, luxuriating in a serene cottage garden under the boughs of drooping willow. The garden was a riot of intoxicating pinks, oranges, reds, and yellows, and a lavender scent mixed with orange, lemon, and mandarin.

With the last of the day's warmth on my shoulder and the gentle humming of bees in the background, I shook my head in amazement. Could it get any better than this?

DAY 24: EVERSON TO MT. BAKER

I woke up the next morning, and before my head had even left the pillow, all hell broke loose.

A tsunami of homesickness hit me. I had no idea where it had come from, but the emotion completely consumed me. I missed my boys, my family, my friends. I missed my life. What the hell was I doing here in a strange bed, in a strange house, in a strange country? Why wasn't I home with all the people who loved me?

The sadness seeped through my whole body. It was a deep, painful ache, and I just wanted to pack up and come home. To forget this absurd ride—*enough now*—and head back home to be held by those who loved me. For all my flaws, I was still loved.

I wasn't just homesick. I was seriously disoriented and overwhelmed. I'd been on the road for over three weeks now, and the experience had been everything I'd imagined it to be and more. But lying there in a strange bed with the rain beating hard against the window, I couldn't for the life of me work out what the hell I was doing here.

It was time for some tough questions. What was I trying to achieve? What was I trying to prove, and who was I trying to prove it to? Was I taking this journey on the hope that it would heal my wounds, or was I really just trying to be a warrior? To look cool and adventurous to the outside world? Was it about my learning, my growth, my survival, and my joy...or did I still need external validation as the invincible hero?

And the big question—did I really want to be here?

LOOKING THROUGH THE TOOLBOX

When I'd left Whistler a few days earlier, I'd congratulated myself on everything I'd learnt about myself and about life. How smug I'd felt about having nailed some pretty serious life lessons in just three short weeks.

But beware: following smugness comes a fall, or so I was learning. That morning, all my shiny new learnings went out the window as I sat huddled in bed, the covers drawn tightly around me, white-hot tears streaming down my face. The warrior had become a small, fearful girl.

Realistically, I knew what I needed to do to help ease the depth of this emotion—this despair. I knew the process to work my way through it, to get to another place. I had all the tools in my toolbox to ease the pain—and still, I just couldn't shake it.

Step one: acknowledge the emotion. There's no point pretending it isn't there or trying to cover it up. Notice it, acknowledge it, lean into it, and breathe through it. And so I did. But it was still there—raw and stark and gathering momentum.

Step two: move to gratitude. Even a bad day is better when you move to gratitude, right? Well, not this day. I fought it hard. I didn't want to be grateful for anything. I started to write, "I'm grateful for...I'm grateful for..." But it was just words on a page. It meant nothing. My heart was slammed shut. I wanted to hold onto this sadness—it was like putting on a warm coat and I didn't want to take it off.

Step three: meditate. Calm the mind and breathe. Except I couldn't. My mind was like a thousand monkeys chattering incessantly, each one reminding me how much I missed the people I loved. How much I wanted to see them, to be with them. I hadn't felt lonely since I started this trip. *Alone,* yes. Lonely, no. But today, loneliness bit deep.

OK, the toolbox was empty. I had nothing left to throw at this, so I had two choices: hide under the duvet for another hour then call quits on this journey and head for home, or hike Mt. Baker so at least I'd achieved something that day. And then go home. Choice three: continuing on? Not an option. I was done.

Mt. Baker it was, if only to relieve my guilt at giving in. Holding my sadness very carefully so as not to bruise or damage it, I readied Voodoo, and together we rode.

The ride was amazing—at least something was working for me today. As I neared the top of Mt. Baker, I was treated to hair-raising switchbacks—single lane, tight corners that relentlessly curled back on themselves. I'm guessing all the budget must have been spent building this technological marvel of a road and there was nothing left over for guardrails. As I perilously clung to the side of the mountain, I did have a laugh: if I went over the edge, at least I wouldn't need to explain to people why I'd come home!

But even the ride hadn't helped. Time for step four: get back into nature. I power hiked up Mt. Baker—head down, confusion reigning, with a burning in my chest. The pain was so acute, it felt as if someone were treading on my heart. All the while, questions shouted at me.

"Do you really want to be here? Shouldn't you be doing something positive with your life? What happens if nothing changes? What happens if you're still the same person when you go home? What idiot thought this would be a good idea?"

A thousand questions—probably questions I should have answered before I left, but today, they surfaced and were relentless...and I had no answers.

Despite being surrounded by incredible beauty, I'd seen nothing. I'd missed the harshness of the moon-like terrain, the sharpness of the rocks, the rawness of the landscape. After two hours, I still felt an incredible heaviness in my heart. I was overwhelmed, disoriented, and just plain sad. I decided to head back. This wasn't solving anything.

But suddenly, a small, quiet voice—unlike the loud, shouting, questioning voice—told me to keep going. *Just go over the next hill.* Sure. I'd listened to every other voice this morning. Why not a quiet one?

Dropping down the slope, I stopped dead in my tracks. Hidden by the hill, right in front of me, stood the most magnificent glacier. White, shining, gleaming in the sunlight. It was so close, I could almost touch it. I sat on the ground in front of it, completely mesmerised by its beauty. Surrounded by tiny alpine flowers, with a small stream gurgling alongside me, I pulled out the perfect peach—rich, ripe, and juicy. With peach juice running down my arm, I was grateful. Finally.

UNFINISHED BUSINESS

My mind started to quieten, and those biting, snapping questions didn't seem to matter anymore. With the sun streaming through the clouds, bit-by-bit, I took off that heavy, warm coat of sadness and laid it on the ground. I'd carried it a long way.

Step five: be present. Present to appreciate the awesome beauty around me, to set my senses on fire. To smell the dampness of the earth and feel the cool breeze rippling over my skin. That moment—that *present* moment—was pure joy.

And I remembered—for the fiftieth time already on this trip—that while the journey is more important than the destination, being present is just as vital. If we don't have the ability to celebrate what we have right here, right now, then nothing we get materially or experientially will make us happy—right, WuDe? Damn, I'm such a slow learner—when am I going to remember this?

I also realised I wasn't ready to go home. Although I'd come a long way and that hole in my heart had started to heal, it was still gaping. For sure, the skin grafts were taking hold, but I wasn't done yet. To leave now would be to leave unfinished business.

I'm still not sure who I am, but today, I made headway. I expected there would be tough days either physically and emotionally, and that on the really bad days I'd get both. But I hadn't expected the depth of emotion I'd experienced today or the struggle it took to work through it.

But work through it I did, and yet again, once I stopped fighting myself and remembered to let go, I eventually came out on the other side. Trust the process. I'd been shown that so many times already on this journey, but it was another lesson I still had to learn. Do the work, for sure, but trust the process. It'll work out in the end.

DAY 25: EVERSON TO LEAVENWORTH

I love B&Bs. The morning connections were magical. Occasionally, the owners were distant and left you to your own devices, but generally—within minutes of that first coffee being poured—it felt like you were long-lost friends. I loved being part of someone's life, even for just a few minutes.

Those amazing moments of connection set me on fire every single day. A chance encounter, a shared laugh, a snappy rapport in a sliver of time—that's what truly gave me joy. Impacts were being created everywhere I went, both by me and for me. Impacts that could have escaped completely unnoticed or not have happened at all had I not been looking out for them.

That morning, a fiery mother and daughter team joined me for breakfast. They laughed about the amount of coffee I needed to kick-start my day (I was still fragile!), and they also laughed at my brain snap the day before. They explained that Mt. Baker, along with Mt. Shasta, were two of the most spiritually vibrational areas in the Pacific Northwest. It was common for people visiting to have emotional meltdowns.

Really? So, two important pieces of information: number one, I wish I'd know that before, and number two, I'll be in Mt. Shasta in about a week. Look out! Can't wait to see what happens there.

It's amazing the impact the weather has on your emotions. In stark contrast to the bleakness of yesterday, today the Universe had given me perfection. Crystal blue skies with just the tiniest smudge of cotton cloud, gentle sunshine with just a hint of a breeze. The perfect riding day—a perfect, soul-soothing day.

We were rolling, Voodoo and I—still bruised and a little raw from the emotions of yesterday, but we were moving forward. As the sun fought its way through my jacket, slowly warming my bones, I knew I was through the other side. For now. I was a little concerned at the prospect of going to Mt. Shasta given yesterday's meltdown, but that would be a challenge for another day.

OUT OF THE RABBIT HOLE

The beauty of being on a bike for hours is that it gives you time to reflect. To work things through. But when there's just you inside your helmet, it's easy to play the same tape over and over in your head—a conversation that you've had or you wished you'd had, a cutting remark that keeps biting you, a smack you wish you'd given. That thought or emotion keeps looping back again and again and again.

The trouble with looping is that it keeps pulling you backwards, and that's where I was—continually kicking myself for dropping my emotional bundle so spectacularly yesterday. The only thing that stopped it were corners. It was relentless. *Loop, loop, loop—oh, tight right-hander—loop, loop—hold on, sharp left. Man, how did you let yourself spiral so completely out of control? What the hell is wrong with you?*

But it served no purpose.

I remembered an untested technique Ross had taught me to

short-circuit looping: stop, disengage, remove the emotional commitment. *Brilliant!* I gave it a shot. Every time I found myself looping, I physically put my hand up to say "stop" (I had to be careful it wasn't in the middle of a corner at the time), and then I mentally saw myself pulling a plug out of the wall so that I was physically disengaging myself from the thought and emotion.

I made a conscious decision to let go of the story. It took a while— OK, nearly three hours—but every time it resurfaced, I went back to stop, disengage, remove the emotional commitment. Slowly, slowly, I emerged out of the rabbit hole. And I remembered, in stopping the story, to be kind to myself. I'd gotten myself into a black place, and sure I was still a little battered and bruised, but continually beating myself up wasn't going to help.

So I chose to let it go. And somewhere between Snohomish and Skykomish (yep, they're real places!), I felt the weight of judgement fall off my shoulders and bounce onto the road behind me.

WISDOM FROM YODA

Despite the chaos in my head, Voodoo was having the time of her life. The ride was completely a gift, in more ways than one. The first 200 km were pedestrian—if you can have pedestrian kilometres. Big highway riding, single-lane roads where we couldn't pass. But it's amazing how much more you see when you go slow. I really got to appreciate rural America this morning—my favourite sight was two tractors parked outside a diner.

I wondered whether they were husband and wife? (The drivers, not the tractors.)

The beauty of being on a bike is that no minute is ever the same. One minute I was on boring flats racing trains for excitement. (Yep, I embarrassed myself by getting them to pull the horn. Come on—it's cool!) The next minute, I was flying through ravines and clambering up the side of impossibly tall peaks. We were on fire. Beautiful, big sweeping corners, tight hairpins, good visibility, bad visibility—it had it all, and it was perfect.

That's when I knew I was back. The voice in my head finally fell silent, the smile in my helmet exploded, and it felt good—really good—to be exactly where I was meant to be.

However, I'm not so sure the funky town of Leavenworth was exactly where a plant-based chick was meant to be. How can I describe it? It was like stepping into a perfectly picturesque German town—the Bavaria of Washington—complete with cart horses, oompah bands, hanging flower baskets, and lederhosen. Cute and quirky to experience, but a nightmare for anyone trying to eat clean.

Every second store sold meat—from sausages to schnitzels, bratwurst to pigs' trotters—and in between every meat store there was nothing but fudge, ice cream, and pastry stores. The best thing I spotted today? A doughnut wrapped in bacon. *Are you kidding me? Now I've seen it all!*

As I sat on my veranda that night—my dusty boots kicked off and my feet up on the railings—I tried to absorb the enormity of everything I'd learnt and experienced over the last two days. Had it only been two days? How was I still breathing? So many new lessons learnt; so many old lessons reinforced. As I reminded myself that I was trying to put the warrior down, Yoda's famous line crept into my head: "There is no try, only do."

OK, no more trying. Time for doing.

DAY 26: LEAVENWORTH TO ASHFORD

Doing the next morning meant getting clarity on what my living masterpiece for the day would look like. As I sat on my balcony overlooking vineyards and ripe fruit trees—cherries, peaches, and apples—I asked myself, what did I truly want to create today?

I wanted to shine my light brightly. To make incredible connections with people, roll through awesome scenery, be of service (that one was important—people had taken such good care of me that I wanted to give something back). To ride fast and take risks (worry not: calculated risks). Oh, and to remember to be grateful for this blistering adventure.

As Voodoo and I prepared to depart, Maryanne, the beautiful owner of the B&B—a plump, butterball grandma with big arms and an even bigger smile—came out to say goodbye. With a hug, she handed me a paper bag.

"I know you only eat that plant stuff, but I'm worried you won't find anything to eat on the road. So I've made you some blueberry scones. Got up and made them for you this morning. You can eat those, right? They've got real fruit in them!"

There are moments when your heart just stops. *Seriously?* How did I deserve such kindness? I would never have been thoughtful enough to have done that for someone I knew, let alone a stranger! Completely enveloped in her arms, I hugged her back, then carefully stowed my precious scones in my bags. With gratitude pouring out of me, Voodoo and I headed out.

CAREFUL WHAT YOU ASK FOR

Instantly out of Leavenworth, the fun began. First up were forests so dense and heavy that the light struggled to squeak between the trees. The smell was heady. An intoxicating blend of pine and earth that put my lavender to shame. Within minutes, we'd started to climb aggressively through fierce mountain passes, making our way to an impossibly high summit.

The challenge with impossibly high summits is that, as well as being unbelievably beautiful, they're unbelievably cold. Within minutes, I went from happily snug to "Mmm...this is getting a bit chilly," which quickly careered into "Bloody hell—I'm getting frostbite." I could have pulled over and got my heated gear out, but nah. Too lazy, and besides, I looked like a butterball myself with all that gear on. Vanity over warmth, as always.

Just south of Ellensburg, I picked up the 821-S and followed the Yakima River through one of the most striking canyons I'd ever seen. It looked like the Universe had taken a huge bunch of brown-yellow wrapping paper, scrunched it up so it had folds and creases, wound a spectacular river at the bottom, then twisted a ribbon of road all through it.

It was too perfect for words. The contrast with what I'd travelled through just an hour before was insane. It was like I was in two completely different countries. It was warm now. People rafted down the shimmering river alongside of me as I rode through flats, cut through caverns, and traversed passes. The intensity of the ride was staggering.

As well as being stunning, it was also very technical, needing every ounce of concentration I could find. It twisted and turned so sharply, time after time, that it almost made me seasick. (Who'd have thought you could get seasick in a canyon?) But hadn't I asked for an amazing ride this morning? Be careful what you wish for!

At the edge of the canyon, Voodoo and I pulled in for fluids. Alongside was a family in an enormous black RV, towing both a car and a boat and all the comforts of home. They'd been filling up for about two hours before I got there (never wait behind an RV at a gas station), and by the time they were finally ready, we'd become fast enough friends for them to invite me in for coffee. Oh, such a simple way to a girl's heart!

On with the kettle and out with my blueberry scones. OK—maybe it technically didn't count as being of service, but it was close.

HERBAL TEA AND GRATITUDE

Some days on this journey were pure sensory overload—days where I truly believed my body and my soul just couldn't squeeze in another ounce of exhilaration. But somehow, there was always room for just the tiniest bit more. Mt. Rainier was just that tiniest bit more.

Through ever-changing vistas, we flew. Hot, dry glaciers gave way to cool, crisp glades; moonscaped terrain morphed into tropical rainforests. Just when I thought it couldn't get any more impressive, we rounded a corner and there, in all her spectacular glory, stood Mt. Rainier, covered in snow with her head in the clouds.

My home for the evening was a tiny brown wooden cabin with a bright red front door. Ten miniature cabins stood circled together in a dark wooded glade. Perfect for Red Riding Hood. I had Harley riders either side of me, and I figured they'd either be the big bad wolves or protect me from them. Only time would tell.

As I'd checked in, Kenny—the cheeky, Korean owner—interrogated me. He'd lived in the US for over thirty years, but it sounded like he'd just arrived. In a thick accent, he probed inquisitively, "Dat's a werry big bike for a little girl. Does your dad know you've run away? You look tired. Sit, sit—I make you tea."

So I sat.

While Kenny tried to convince me (unsuccessfully) to try yak for dinner at the local Himalayan restaurant, I quietly sipped my herbal tea and smiled. Did I go for it today? I think I did. And the clincher? At yet another gas station during the day, after hearing about my adventure, a farmer in a bright red pickup truck loaded with hay said, "You must really love your life."

I took a moment to let that settle.

Two months ago, the answer would have been very different. Today, with all the gratitude in my heart and soul, I could honestly reply, "Without a doubt."

DAY 27: ASHFORD TO LONGVIEW

Under the heavy canopy of twisted trees and vines the next morning, it was dark as I ran. The sun struggled to make its way through the denseness of the foliage as I listened to the cacophony of birds and the sound of water trickling over rocks. I felt the coolness of the air and smelt the damp mustiness of the earth. The spectacular mountains above the canopy were immense, but it was the small things today that really gave me joy.

And that included my morning with Kenny. I was hoping for a quick getaway—it was going to be a big day—but Kenny had other ideas.

"You like coffee, Missy Sue? I make Americano for you—best coffee inna world. Better than Starbucks!" As a serious coffee drinker, I knew that wasn't saying that much, but how could I refuse? Graciously accepting black hot water from a machine, Kenny and I sat and chatted in pidgin English. I couldn't understand much of what he said, and he couldn't understand my accent, but somehow, we solved the problems of the world.

As Voodoo and I readied to leave, he came out to say goodbye. Twenty minutes after pulling out, I was still laughing in my helmet, his parting words ringing in my ears. "You a nice girl, Missy Sue. Why you out here by yourself? Does no one love you? Why they let you go? You shouldn't be out here alone. Go home!"

Go home? I think we've put that one to bed already. But thanks for the concern!

THE NOTICE OF DEATH

I did have one concern of my own that day: keeping Voodoo fuelled. Gas stations were few and far between in this part of the world. I'd heard there was fuel in the tiny timber town of Cougar, but as always, opinions were divided as to whether or not it would be open. If Cougar wasn't open, it'd mean trying to stretch my fuel for about 220 km. Voodoo had a 200 km tank on a good day—so the last 20 km would be entertaining, to say the least.

But hey, there was absolutely nothing I could do about it. Worrying about it wouldn't make gas magically appear. I could either stress for 200 km and miss this amazing ride, or I could panic if and when it actually became an issue.

It was a good call, because this was a scream-in-your-helmet ride, and I wouldn't have wanted to miss a minute. Under the trusty tires of Voodoo, the second, fourth, and fifty-fourth best bike roads in Washington exploded underneath us as we travelled through the Gifford Pinchot National Forest and alongside the spectacular and still-smouldering Mt. St. Helens.

Most of the route through Gifford was a tree-covered canopy—a magical fairy grotto of filtered sunlight, bright green leaves, and ancient trees twisted and gnarled by the weather. And the weather had tortured the road, making riding conditions more than just a little interesting. The road was completely buckled, bulging, and bent. A nightmare of unpredictability. There were huge dips, crevices large enough to lose a small child in, massive drops-offs without guardrails—one wrong bounce could send you over the side. And for extra adrenaline? The occasional rockslide. *Oh yeah. Love it!*

And I did! The only way I could control Voodoo through the carnage was to ride her standing up. Every bounce flung me off my seat. I needed to stand so that my legs could work as springs to counter the huge bounces and dips. My heart was in my mouth most of the way, but in my helmet I was laughing. Actually, it was probably hysteria. What the hell was I doing riding a superbike as if she were a dirt bike? Was I nuts? (I've got to stop asking that question!)

Because of the dense tree canopy, I had no idea of the elevation I'd gained when, all of a sudden, I popped out from the trees to see majestic Mt. St. Helens right in front of me. She was overwhelming. Powerful, intense—an active, volatile, fire-breathing dragon.

In all the excitement of the day, I'd forgotten to take into account something relatively important: altitude sucks gas. And by now I was running pretty damn low. There was nothing I could do but hold on till Cougar.

As I finally pulled into the gas station, I immediately saw the "Notice of Death"—the paper they tape to the pump telling you there's no gas. OK, now it's time to panic. Instantly, I fell apart.

Shit, shit, shit. You're kidding me! Noooo! So now what do I do? Voodoo's never going to make it. I'm going to run out of gas on the side of the road. Nooo!

Then I looked at it closer: "No Premium."

Breathe. Meltdown averted. Thank you, thank you, thank you. She won't like it—Voodoo was a high-maintenance premium gal—but she'd survive on 87! The definition of gratitude? Being thankful for whatever we can get!

UPGRADED

Knowing it was going to be a busy weekend, I'd booked a cheap and cheerful room (OK, very cheap and not so cheerful) in the bustling town of Longview for a couple of nights. The front part of the hotel looked amazing. It had been built in the 1870s and had hosted everyone from film stars to presidents in its hey-day—but not in the ugly motel cell block unromantically tacked onto the back that I'd discovered myself in. But it was clean. Kind of.

However, the Wi-Fi in my room kept dropping out. I'd had a pretty deep conversation with the guy at reception when I'd checked in. He mentioned that he'd previously been a Crystal Engineer. As I nodded sagely—not having a clue what that was—he laughed. He'd actually been a dishwasher!

Unable to resolve my Wi-Fi problem, he called me back ten minutes later saying they'd like to upgrade me to the—wait for it—Diva Suite. (I'm sure he made that name up specially!) Are you serious? Was there ever a better name for a suite for me, and would I like to move?

Oh, OK. If I have to.

Graciously and effortlessly, I was moved into a palatial two-bedroom suite where I needed to lay breadcrumbs to find my way back to the bathroom, complete with a massive hot tub overlooking a beautiful park. How the hell did I get here? But hey, that's how life rolls on the road—one night a teeny tiny cottage with plastic flowers and a hole in the middle of the bed (sorry, Kenny), and the next, a palace. I just needed to go out and find some new friends to fill up the hot tub with me!

DAY 28: LONGVIEW TO MT. ST. HELENS

I'd planned on staying at Longview for two nights because I wanted to ride right up the guts of Mt. St. Helens—to ride right up to her spectacular peak—hoping that today wouldn't be the day she decided to erupt. Just a day of fun riding—on a naked Voodoo, for once being her superbike self instead of a carthorse weighed down by the Leaning Tower of Pisa.

But first it was maintenance time for my Big Girl. She was carrying enough dirt to support a carrot patch and was in desperate need of a chain lube and some general TLC. I also needed to sort out her 10,000 km service.

It's always tricky getting a service when you're on the road. You never know where you're going to be when that service is due, and most dealers are booked weeks in advance. Oregon was my next port of call, so I tried four dealers throughout the state—all of them happy to help, if I could come back in two weeks. I think not.

Without a service, we weren't going anywhere.

I was desperate. I begged and pleaded (it wasn't pretty) with the last remaining dealer in Oregon. I even promised to have his children (OK, maybe I wasn't quite that desperate). Bless him—after initially saying no, he called me back about twenty minutes later, having shuffled a few clients around so that he could fit me in. He'd need to do it over two days, but he'd get it done. *Cool! Unscheduled play time in Portland!*

I had to laugh, though—he asked me how many Ks I'd done in the past few weeks, and when I told him *8,000*, he repeated back *800*. When I corrected him, there was silence on the end of the phone. His answer?

"You've gotta be kidding me? You've done 8,000 km on an S1000RR by yourself? Are you nuts?" *There's that question again!*

GATE

Finally lubed, cleaned, and booked in, Voodoo and I cantered off to Mt. St. Helens. Instantly, life became interesting for us. Flying in the fast lane on I-5, just ahead of us in the middle lane was a large flatbed truck carrying a full load of garbage cans. They were black bins, about four-foot in height, made of hard plastic.

I know this level of detail, because one flew off the back of the truck, hit the middle lane, ricocheted right in front of me in the fast lane, then bounced onto the other side of the road.

So close! Imagine trying to explain that to your insurance company—you'd been knocked off your bike by a flying garbage can. I was also thankful at that moment that it hadn't been a port-a-potty.

Now, there are bike roads and there are *bike roads*. There are roads that are interesting, roads that are exciting, roads that are thrilling—and then there are roads that are just insane! Roads that make your hair stand on end and then burst into fire! And that was the road to Mt. St. Helens—totally insane!

I was hyperventilating with adrenaline. Huge, flowing sweepers—nothing tight or pokey to tense you up, just big bend after big bend and a road surface smoother than my face. Just pick your line, get your lean, hold your nerve, hold your nerve, hold your nerve—then *wham*! You'd be spat out the other side just in time to set up for the next corner. I felt like a silver ball ricocheting out of a pinball machine, bouncing from side to side. And it was fast—so, so fast. I could barely suck in enough oxygen as we flew up the side of the mountain.

There was, however, an adrenaline rush that I wasn't expecting. As we thundered towards the top, out of the corner of my eye I saw a small, innocuous sign that simply said "Gate."

Gate? What it should have said was, "OMG, slow down! Hit the brakes! The road is closed and you're about to plough through all the barricades and catapult yourself over the top of them!"

Now, I'm not saying that at 150 kph I would have read all that, but it would have made a lot more sense than just "Gate." Nothing like a touch of understatement when the road you're screaming along has been completely blocked off.

HOLD THE DRESSING

After coming to a screeching halt centimetres from the barricades, I surveyed my options, and discovered a well-marked detour route to the top of Mt. St. Helens. (OK, it was well-marked at 40 kph—certainly not at 150!)

Significantly subdued, I rode with a degree of restraint to the top of the volcano. But not for long! Upon meeting a volcanologist at the visitor's centre who told me it wasn't a question of *if* Mt. St. Helens would blow again but *when*, I flew down the side even faster than I'd gone up. Just in case.

Pulling into the sleepy little town of Toledo, I grabbed gas and headed for the diner. I couldn't miss this diner. It was an original, right out of the sixties, with probably the same wait staff still working there. And yes, they had a sixties attitude about customer service! Everything on the menu was serious heart-attack-on-a-plate material. Burgers, fries, steak sandwiches, hot dogs—certainly not the best choice for a plant-based chick.

Foolishly, I asked for a salad.

With a raised eyebrow and the slightest curled lip, my waitress—resplendent in a big white dress, checked apron at the waist, notebook and pencil in hand—informed me, "Nope. We don't do salads."

"OK, you put lettuce and tomato on burgers, right? Then hold the burger. Just give me lettuce and tomato."

"Nope. We can't sell tomatoes and lettuce without the burgers because then we won't have any lettuce and tomato left to put on burgers."

Fair point. Eventually, we made our way through this impasse, but the final straw for my rotund waitress with a tight grey perm and jet-red lipstick was my "...and hold the salad dressing, please."

"No Thousand Island or blue cheese? What's wrong with you?"

How long have you got?

OK, I've had better salads, but I'm not sure I've had better attitudes. Replaying the conversation, I laughed all the way back to my hotel. It was such a victory to have sat with my bowl of soggy iceberg lettuce and overripe tomatoes—hold the dressing.

Later that evening, I wandered over to the park across from

the hotel, fresh avocado and vegetables in hand, and lay on my back under a huge oak tree. Is there anything more magical than lying under an ancient tree as warm, filtered light finds its way through the leaves to dance on your skin?

Trying to absorb the enormity of my day—the exhilaration, the adventure, missing the flying bin—I heard children playing close by. Four mums sat chatting, watching their wild ones swerve around them on bikes and scooters. I'd oversupplied myself on avocado (can you ever do such a thing?), and rather than waste it, I wandered over and offered it to them. Within minutes, I was sitting on the ground with them. Part of their world.

It was a world I hadn't encountered so far on this trip—the world of being a mum without a bike, without a journey, without a story. We were from very different backgrounds, but no surprises: we all wanted the same things for our kids. We wanted them to be happy, to create an environment where they could grow, to make a world where they were safe and not surrounded by fear. Above all, we all wanted to connect and to be connected.

Life was pretty simple, really.

DAY 29: LONGVIEW TO MITCHELL

I felt that connection so powerfully the next morning. I was headed to Oregon, and the anticipation of completely unknown territory made my throttle hand itch. I was antsy for adventure.

As I pulled in to gas up, I saw a slight, unkempt kid sitting on the ground next to the pumps. He held a sign that simply said, "Food Please." He wasn't begging for money—he was just asking for food. One look at him told me he hadn't had any for a while. He was gaunt and hollow, with a blank vacancy in his young eyes. He was in serious need of nourishment and a bath. I couldn't help him with one, but I could help him with the other.

There was a Starbucks alongside the gas station, and though I wasn't sure it necessarily qualified as "food," I invited him to join me. Together, we had coffee and breakfast—well, I had the coffee, and he had the breakfast sandwich.

His story broke my heart. He was just a kid—a sixteen-year-old baby who'd been living on the road for over twelve months. He'd run away from a horrific situation at home and was now homeless. Living from one garbage can to another, sleeping on cardboard, just trying to survive.

My boys were not much older than this beautiful boy. It took my breath away to envisage them living his life—a life of emptiness and hopelessness. He had no one to care for him, no one to love him, no one to make sure he was warm and fed. What sixteen-year-old kid deserved that? I'd been talking to mothers just the night before about the life we wanted for our children. Where was this boy's mum who wanted that life for him?

I rode. Angry and helpless.

The power of connection struck me. We are all one. We are all connected, and we all have a responsibility for each other. I'd staved off his challenges for today, but who was going to help him tomorrow? Who would step up and look out for this precious boy? Who would give him what (I think) he needed most: a warm, loving hug? I sent a prayer of thanks for my own beautiful boys—grateful they would never have to live that pain.

BEER FROM A GLASS

My heart was heavy as I rolled into Oregon, but eventually the wonder of nature started to soothe the physical ache I was holding onto. When I'd talked to Jakey about my meltdown at Mt. Baker, he'd given me sage advice:

"When I'm hurting, Mum, I just get back into nature."

The lessons we learn from our children. He was right. Leaving Washington, I headed south towards Mt. Hood and rode through gentle vineyards and flats before starting to climb. Surrounded by lush forests of impossibly tall trees almost touching the clouds, and with the smell of fresh pine almost overpowering the lavender *still* in my helmet (yep—it was still there), I started to breathe. To let it go.

It was hard not to be completely absorbed by the beauty around me. As we climbed higher and higher, the pine forests were abruptly replaced by charred, blackened sticks—sticks that only days before had been a living, breathing forest. Alongside me, scorched trees still smouldered—the smell of smoke hanging heavy in the air with a haze circling around me and making it difficult to see. The bleakness was eerie—there was a spooky desolation in the remains of what had once been a spectacular green blanket of life.

I rode through the haze, desperate to see Mt. Hood. The smoke was thick, and in some places, I could barely see 100 metres in front of me. I knew she was out there somewhere, but at that point it was hard enough to see the front of Voodoo, let alone a spectacular mountain range. But perseverance paid off. With a quick change in direction, I popped out of the smoke, and there she was right in front of me, in all her awesomeness. Surrounded by haze, she almost looked like a hologram—divine and ethereal in her splendour.

She was truly magnificent.

Working my way through the mountain passes of Mt. Hood had been cold, cold, cold. Funny how the chill of a mountain pass still surprised me, but literally within minutes of passing a sign saying, "Warm Springs Indian Reserve," the temperature went up twenty degrees. How does that happen? Can the weather read signs?

Harsh, desert terrain appeared—yellow, brown, and parched. I felt like I'd stepped into a bad western, complete with cactus and the obligatory tumbleweeds blowing wildly across the road. The landscape was covered in huge crevices so wide and deep that it looked as if someone had taken a giant wedge and split the earth apart. To complete the western, scorching heat almost melted my boots and a wild wind completely encased Voodoo and me in a three-inch layer of dust.

How do you ever prepare for life on the road? Only twenty minutes earlier, I'd been close to frozen. Now I could barely breathe with the heat! Scratching the dust out of my eyes, I pulled in for gas—it was already forty degrees Celsius, and I was on fire. In the shade, I poured a bottle of water over myself and watched it almost instantly evaporate. Not quite the steaming-hot look I was hoping for, sadly.

I'd struck up a conversation with a young guy, and as we chatted, he opened the door of his truck. Out barrelled three enormous German shepherd dogs. The first one smacked me right in the middle of my chest and sent me flying through the air and onto my butt in the dust.

Dust plus water equals mud. *Who would have thought?* And I was covered in it. You know that need I'd had to always look perfect? Well, by now I was completely cured. I'd predicted many scenarios on this trip, but certainly not this one.

Nor had I predicted the sage advice from an elderly, toothless gentleman as I pulled out:

"Ya know, girlies should always drink beer from a glass, and they should ride horses not motorbikes."

OK, I'm not sure what I'm supposed to do with that gem of insight, but I'll tuck it away for future reference. I'm sure one day it'll come in handy!

ROOKIE MISTAKE

Back on the bike—more desert, more dust, more sweat, and a new entrant: sand! The heat had been so intense that I'd opened my jacket up completely, and it was flapping very unglamorously all around me. Under normal circumstances, that wouldn't have been an issue, but behind sand trucks? Not such a good idea.

Sand, as I discovered, flies off the back of trucks and completely blasts any area of skin brave enough not to be protected. Within minutes, my neck and my chest were completely savaged. But how lucky was I? That dermabrasion treatment would have cost me a fortune back home. If only I hadn't had a full-faced helmet on—I could have gotten my face done as well!

In the heat, I'd made a serious rookie mistake. I'd done the unforgivable: I'd passed a gas station. Hot, tired, and more than a little emotional, I pulled into the town of Mitchell—more a slip road off the highway than a town, with a hotel, gas station, diner, and not a lot more. I knew there was gas at Mitchell, so I'd let Voodoo get dangerously low, not wanting to go through the whole circus of refuelling while I sweated profusely in all my gear.

But the gas station in town was closed.

You're kidding me? OK, no drama. I'll fill up in the morning. What? What do you mean the owner is going on holidays and it'll be shut for four days?

I bolted across the road and banged on the door until a slightly reluctant owner, roused from her packing, agreed to fill me up. Mitchell was a cute sliver of a town, but the thought of being there for four days was akin to cleaning the oven with a toothbrush.

Still, as I headed to the diner for dinner, I thought all my Christmases had come at once. There, over the counter, hung the most amazing sign: "All you can eat salad bar." *Seriously?* In this crazy diner straight out of the fifties, where all I was expecting for dinner was atmosphere, I actually have a salad bar? Oh, life is good.

Paper plate in hand, off I went, and yep, no wonder it was an all you can eat. You couldn't eat much. Iceberg lettuce, tomato, cottage cheese, pickles, and olives.

But hey—there was no discussion about the absence of a burger and no incredulousness at the lack of dressing. And, I got to eat as much as I wanted, no questions asked.

Life *is* good.

DAY 30: MITCHELL TO PORTLAND

The ride into Mitchell had been exhausting. It had been hot, hard, and harrowing—not to mention long (close to 500 km), but there'd been a purpose behind the pain. I was determined to see the famous Painted Hills—the John Day Fossil Beds located in the middle of nowhere, hence Mitchell, my less-than-one-horse town.

The ride back out was magical. The air was biting and crisp as the sun tried desperately to climb above the mountains. Slowly, slowly its rays came over the top of the peaks, and the whole desert became bathed in an orange glow. It's such a gift when you're cold on the bike and the sun starts to come out. It feels like you've been touched by a warm hand wherever the sun brushes your body.

Strangely, the sun doesn't hit you all over. It chooses one spot at a time. The top of your thigh, your shin above your boot, a shoulder. But no matter where it touches, you feel it. And you celebrate it.

FACE THE CHAOS

I'd ridden off the beaten track for quite some time, and just when I thought I'd missed a turn, I crested a hill and there they were—these exquisite painted hills. Ochre, orange, taupe, rust, all glistening quietly as the sun came up behind them. My heart literally missed a beat, I was so overcome with wonder.

And they were all mine—without a soul around, I had them all to myself.

I parked Voodoo and just sat, surrounded by silence and in complete awe. These timeless hills with their bands of rich, vibrant colours and gentle pastels of green, purple, and pink were breathtaking in the morning light. For an hour and a half, I sat in the dirt and watched them, their colours changing constantly as the light became more intense.

I knew I had a long ride to Portland, but I couldn't leave. I wanted to hold onto that feeling of complete serenity. And gratefulness! I'd been given an incredible gift, and I wanted to hold onto this place that had truly opened my heart and made me feel exhilarated to be alive.

But time—or, the BMW dealer—waits for no man. Easing back onto the main road, I pointed Voodoo towards the big city. I'd avoided cities at all cost up until this point, but Voodoo needed some TLC, so it was time for me to man up and face the chaos. After weeks wandering solo in the wilderness, I was a little apprehensive about how I'd find civilization. At least I'd get the dirt out from under my fingernails and maybe even get the heels out. *Woohoo!*

ALONE BUT NOT LONELY

I hadn't slept much the night before thanks to some interesting "visitors" in my bed (OK, I'm going to give it the benefit of the doubt—maybe it was just a heat rash. Either way, I'd woken up with some interesting welts). By the time I got to the—way too funky for its own good—town of Sisters, I could barely hold my helmet up.

Grabbing an espresso at a rustic coffee house, I drifted aimlessly to a table under the shade of an enormous tree, where I promptly put my head on the wooden slats and closed my eyes. They were still scratchy and itchy from the dust and sand the day before, and no matter what I did, they just wouldn't stay open. That is, until I was joined by two very cool riding dudes (yep, they were dudes) who wanted to share my table. It's amazing how you can pull yourself together when you have to!

After multiple coffees, I pulled out with my two new best friends who rode the 200 km to Salem with me.

The boys had asked me whether I'd ever been lonely. The honest answer was, "No—with the exception of the Mt. Baker Blowout—never." There's a big difference between being alone and being lonely. You can be alone but surrounded by connections; alternatively, you can be surrounded by hundreds of people and still be lonely.

Even though I was alone, I wasn't lonely because of the incredible connections I was making every day—connections with people that I would never have had the opportunity to meet in the real world.

There was an amazing camaraderie on the road. In the blink of an eye and over the shortest of conversations, it could feel like you'd known someone all your life. Within a few sentences, you could create an instant bond—a trust. A friendship. It was sometimes hard to believe, but there was an affinity that came from nowhere—powerful and strong. Surrounded by that, how could I be lonely?

Funnily though, in Banff, sitting in a restaurant by myself, a couple close by watched me. In her not-so-quietest of voices, the wife leaned over to her husband and said, "Poor thing. She's all by herself. I feel sorry for her. She looks so lonely. Sitting there all alone."

To which her husband replied, "Don't feel sorry for her. Did you see the bike she pulled up on?"

I guess you're never lonely when you're on a great bike!

VOODOO AND THE BEEMER BOYS

And that great bike fearlessly made her way to the Beemer dealer in Portland—the odd rattle and shake from the wild terrain we'd covered making me just a little nervous. It's easy when you're in a car. If something starts to rattle, you just turn the radio up so that you can't hear it. (Is that just me? Ignorance is bliss—if you can't hear the noise, it must have stopped, right?)

Things are not quite that easy on a bike. When she's your home for about eight hours a day, you hear it all, and you instantly know when something's not right. The slightest change in pitch, a tiny rattle, a minuscule hesitation when you surge, an imperceptible whine that wasn't there yesterday.

Since I don't know what any of those mean or what to do about them, they make me nervous. So I do the next best thing to the radio: I sing really loudly in my helmet to drown out the noise. And there'd been a lot of singing over the past few days.

But she was in very safe hands with the Beemer boys in Portland. What a crew. They came from everywhere in the building to marvel at my butt—well, my butt's ability to have ridden a superbike that far and to still be smiling. They showered me with help, maps, boot oil (even my boots had developed a squeak), and the important promise that in two days, Voodoo would be her magnificent best.

Helping me into my cab, a young service tech whispered, "We said two days, but we'll bust a boiler to finish her tomorrow. We know you want to be back on your baby and back on the road."

Gotta love the power of connection!

CHAPTER EIGHT

Portland to Eureka, CA

DAY 31: PORTLAND

Portland was vibrant, alive, and buzzing—such a contrast after tiny country towns and the vast space of nature. For the first time in weeks, I had clean hair, clean nails, and a clean face. For once, I wasn't covered in grunge, grease, or sweat. For once I got to be a girl, heels and all (would you have expected anything less?). I got to be a city-slicker.

I also got to eat. Man, did I eat. After weeks of lettuce and tomato, lettuce and tomato, and well, more lettuce and tomato—I found the very best vegan restaurant in the world just five short minutes from my hotel. I decided to set up permanent camp outside their front door so I could load up with zucchini pad thai in minutes. I almost wish I had a fridge on Voodoo so I could have taken some with me. Almost.

I wanted to really feel the city, so I decided to walk and explore. To step into its colour and cool, funky personality, and to completely immerse myself in its energy. As I tried to burrow into every nook and cranny, I fell in love with its beautiful, wide, tree-lined streets, its quirky little houses, and its embracing character.

I was struck by its vitality, but I was also struck by the size of its homeless population.

I know it's no different to most major cities, but large shanty towns lined the river—communities of homeless people, living in cardboard boxes, lighting fires to keep warm. Again, as in most cities, there were large numbers of people begging in the street. People with mental illnesses wandering aimlessly, not being taken care of. Such a feeling of helplessness.

As I walked, I came across a young girl of about seventeen,

standing in the street, sobbing. I couldn't walk past and leave her, but I had no idea how to help. She had no money, nowhere to go, no one to be there for her. Fortunately, a young guy stopped and offered to take her to a shelter. I was completely out of my depth, unable to do anything other than give her a hug and help her with money. But she needed a lot more than that. Her pain was so raw.

And yet again, I wanted to call my boys and hug them over the phone. It's not just about being grateful for the small things. It's also about being grateful for the big things—for being safe and loved.

THE NOT-KNOWING

There's nothing like walking for hours to give you the opportunity to dig deep. I know it sounds crazy—you'd think there'd be plenty of time for introspection on the bike. Funnily enough, not often. When I'm on Voodoo, I'm busy. I'm planning, plotting, watching, listening, preempting. It's hectic in that helmet.

Walking gave me time for some clarity. One of the expectations I'd had about this journey was that it would give me direction for the next stage in my life. I figured by the time I shut Voodoo down I'd be clear on what my next step would be. But the message wasn't coming. Four weeks into the journey, I still didn't have the tiniest inkling as to what the future would hold for me, and it was starting to scare me.

I knew I needed to let go of the need to know, but damn, I was struggling. I was so used to having clarity—goals and objectives I could head towards with complete certainty, tick off, and then move onto the next one. But not knowing what the future held? That was a cavernous black hole.

I had to make peace with the not-knowing. I had to let go—to not have any expectations of this journey other than the journey itself. Why was that so hard? Why couldn't I just accept that? I let go of that particular rope at least twice a day, but it still ended up strangling me. It's the challenge of being a slow learner, I guess. I was going to be given that lesson time and time again until I finally learnt to make peace with it.

As I walked, I explored my values. The values that I'd held onto so rigorously all my life were starting to slide off me. The need for control, pushing boundaries, being competitive, seeking challenge and adrenaline—they were starting to blur around the edges, and weren't driving me as they had in the past.

In their place, fresh green shoots of new values were emerging—tiny buds were hesitantly starting to poke through my consciousness. Connectivity, being open and engaged, being vulnerable, growth...Two months ago, if I'd seen these values coming up, I probably would have plucked them out of the ground and crushed them. For the first time, I decided to let them grow and see where they took me.

My lesson was to embrace the journey and be open to everything it was bringing me. To be present. To do the work, for sure, but to trust the process and surrender.

It's just so damn hard for a control freak to surrender.

DAY 32: PORTLAND TO CANNON BEACH

After two days off Voodoo, I was back on my partner in crime and putting her through her paces. She was on fire—tight, aggressive, and ready to pounce after being up the hoist. A little slippery at first with her new rubber, she was fast, furious, and feisty. Just waiting to bite. *My kinda girl!* And she looked incredible—clean and shiny as she glistened menacingly in the sunlight. Personally, I could probably have done with two days up that hoist.

Pulling out of the dealership, I met another Beemer customer, also on an S1000RR. A quick chat in the car park, and five minutes later we were riding to the coast—duelling superbikes tearing up the road together.

I thought I was relatively gutsy, but I'd forgotten how wild a twenty-five-year-old without kids, a mortgage, or a concern about life insurance could be! He was smoking, and it took everything I had to keep his brake lights in sight. My excuse was that Voodoo was channeling a carthorse—loaded down with all my gear—instead of the thoroughbred she really was.

But I needed every ounce of that excuse as we tore through the corners together. *Maybe I should be riding a scooter instead.*

It was almost a relief when we pulled into a gas station. He was so relaxed that his heart rate was on comatose, while mine was at cardiac-arrest level. A quick laugh, a big hug and he was gone—back to Portland. Instant friends in a shared moment of time and an impact on a stranger that was never forgotten. I sent a silent prayer of thanks to the Universe—and a promise that I'd "do my job" and ride like an old lady for the rest of the journey.

Well, for the rest of the day at least.

MUMS ALWAYS KNOW

Needing to regroup (OK, to let the adrenaline work its way out of my body), I pulled Voodoo into the shade and sat watching the world go by. Life at a gas station is such an incredible microcosm. It's fascinating to be an observer, to watch all walks of life passing in front of you, and to wonder about the lives people led.

But as it turned out, I was the one being watched. A tiny girl, barely tall enough to see over the steering wheel of her car, pulled in alongside Voodoo. She was beautiful—a petite wraith that didn't look old enough to be driving. She wanted to talk bikes. It had always been her dream to ride, but she couldn't get over her fear.

She thought it was inspirational that Voodoo and I were out

there riding the world together. *Mmm...inspirational?* I don't think so. Curing cancer is inspirational. Taking care of homeless kids is inspirational. Sitting on your butt all day, controlling a feisty machine (and the jury is still out on who controls who), staying in hotels (OK, interesting cabins), and cruising through the US could hardly be called inspirational. I mean how hard is that?

Besides, virtually my whole life had been on a bike. My brother had needed cheap transport to get to work, so under sufferance he'd been allowed to get a bike. But me? No. My very smart and sensible mum told me that under no circumstances would I be allowed to learn to ride, and that if I brought a bike into the house, the bike could stay but I would have to leave. *OK, them's fightin' words!*

So every Sunday morning while everyone slept, I rolled my brother's bike out of the garage so that no one would hear it, kicked it into action, and taught myself to ride. Step one achieved. Then, with a fresh new license in my hand, all I needed was to buy a bike. But that was going to prove a little trickier.

If you want something desperately enough, you'll find a way through. And I did. My brand new, tiny, 250 cc Yamaha spent her first year living secretly in a friend's garage, with my mum none the wiser. Or so I thought. It was only about twelve months ago that she mentioned my first bike. I feigned ignorance. *My first what?*

"Really? Did you think I didn't know?"

Damn. I wish she'd have told me earlier. It would have saved a lot of covert operations in the middle of the night. This did, however, serve as a warning to my boys: mums always know what's going on!

INSPIRATION IN ACTION

From the moment I first rolled that throttle on, I'd been in love. The drama, the energy, the speed—the pure rush of adrenaline was unlike anything I'd ever experienced. Controlling something so wild and willful was exhilarating, and I was instantly and irretrievably hooked.

From 250 ccs to superbikes, from road to track, from teenager to old chook—being on a bike had been my whole life. It was like breathing, in and out without awareness. Putting a superbike through her paces was where I was in my flow, where I was home. Sure, Valentino Rossi was never going to have to worry about the competition, but in my own sphere I was fast, capable, and very much in control. Well, in my own mind at least.

Riding was a natural extension of who I was, not something that I was frightened of. But I could understand this young girl's apprehension. Sitting in the dirt together, we had a deep and powerful conversation about fear and how, even when you identify it, it can hold you back.

The only way to beat fear at its own game was to have the courage to keep taking steps forward. Baby steps if you need them, but to be brave enough to keep moving ahead.

We also talked about how inspiration is only of value if you do something with it. There's no point being "inspired" and then going back to the way things were. Inspiration needs action to be of worth.

I asked her not to terrorise herself about the whole process of riding a bike, but just to think about the first step she could take to own her dream. After giving it some thought, the decision was made: she'd book herself into a course to see whether she actually liked riding. Brilliant! Inspiration in action. She was absolutely going to crush this fear.

Many people considered me reckless for embarking on this journey. Reckless? I'd spent my life on a bike. I was infinitely capable, and usually sensible. Usually. (OK, maybe I shouldn't have mentioned my ride this morning!) But apart from that, how was I being reckless?

With recklessness—as with inspiration and fear—people have very different thresholds. Stepping out of your comfort zone means different things for everyone. I tried to explain to this beautiful girl that she didn't need to be worried about riding a superbike tomorrow, but to start with something that was just a little out of her comfort zone and slowly move up. But no matter what, she needed to step into her fear.

As I sat in the sand on Cannon Beach later that day, I couldn't help but think about the gift that that conversation had been. How many opportunities do you have in life to have a conversation like that? So deep, profound, and life-changing for both of us—all over a bottle of water in a gas station.

Sometimes, lessons are hard fought. You battle ferociously to grasp them and to hold onto the learning. Yet sometimes, lessons are a gift. They appear right in front of you, and all you need to do is cherish them. Today offered a lesson to be cherished.

DAY 33: CANNON BEACH TO MANZANITA

Before embarking on this journey, I'd had two big health problems: ulcers that wouldn't heal, and insomnia. According to Louise Hay, stomach problems were caused by never being enough—continually feeling the need to prove yourself and to achieve. So every day on my bike, I rolled affirmations around in my head to remind myself that I was more than enough and that I was perfect just as I was. (Even though I do have very ugly feet.)

Flushing my pills away back in Ainsworth Hot Springs was a conscious choice to trust something bigger than myself. I knew that somehow this journey would heal my soul. And if it was going to heal my soul, it might as well sort my body out too. A double-header—two for the price of one.

So far, so good. The ulcers were pretty much under control. Now for the insomnia. It really wasn't a surprise that, when I read further in Louise Hay's book, insomnia was caused by fear. By not trusting the process of life. In other words, needing to be in control, being driven by goals, demanding clear direction, and being fully in charge.

Had she read my bio? So, I'm supposed to just surrender? To say "yes" to whatever life throws at me? To trust whatever happens and just go with the experience? I don't think so. That's not gonna happen!

I'd sat with that information for about three weeks and—being a serial controller—had refused to give in. But, as always, pain is the greatest motivator for change, and after about a week of slivers of sleep, I decided I needed to face my fears.

Physical fears didn't faze me, but spiritual ones? They were the big, scary monsters. My chat with the newest female addition to the bike-riding fraternity the day before had pushed me over the edge. How could I encourage her to face her fears when I wasn't brave enough to face my own? Without knowing it, she'd made me see that I too had to step up.

EXACTLY WHAT I NEED

Now in the middle of peak season, accommodation had been getting harder and harder to get. A couple of nights, it almost looked as if I'd be sleeping under a picnic table in the local park because all the hotels were full. So for the past few days, I'd been booking hotels ahead, just to be safe.

After yesterday, I figured it was time to walk the tight rope without the net. As I meditated that morning, I asked myself what I needed to do to really trust the process of life—to surrender to my quiet inner voice and not my loud, shouting mind. What did I need to do to let go of control and stop forcing everything?

I figured I needed to go with the flow and leave accommodation up to the Universe. But there was still a controller lurking in me, so I decided to visualise exactly where I wanted to stop for the night. I wanted a sleepy little town, maybe cute shops and houses. A surfing village with a pristine beach. A little off the beaten track—not too touristy. Somewhere serene.

OK, Universe. You've got the order. I'll leave it with you now, shall I?

The past few days had been easy, and I really felt like a long, hard ride along the coast. About 30 km after leaving Cannon Beach, I saw a sign pointing to a little village called Manzanita. I was still warming up, and there was no way I was ready to go off-road yet. But Voodoo seemed to have other ideas, and yep, you guessed it: somehow, we found ourselves in a sleepy little surf village—exactly like the one I'd asked for.

It was perfect. A couple of small hotels, a smattering of restaurants and the most pristine white beach I'd ever seen. It went on for miles—shiny white sand, crystal clear water—even more beautiful than what I'd asked for.

Well, thanks, Universe. Yep, it's perfect, but I'm not ready to stop yet. I need exactly this in about 300 km, OK? See what you can do.

But the message came through loud and clear: *this is what you asked for!*

I decided to test fate. I'd try the three motels, and if I got a room, I'd stop for the night. The first motel: full. The second motel: full. *OK, so it's not meant to be.* The third motel: one room left. *OK, so it's meant to be.* Maybe there is something to this "trusting the process" after all.

My room wasn't going to be ready till the afternoon, so that gave me time to head out to Oceanside, a spectacular little village perched on a high clifftop about 80 km away. It was famous for a walk-through cave on the beach, so it looked like I was going to have the best of all worlds today: a reasonable ride, some sightseeing, and a stunning place to shut down.

RETRACE YOUR STEPS

On the bluff overlooking the beach, I pulled over to take photos. Now, I have a very strict protocol with my gear. When I'm changing location, if I don't have a thorough checking process, the potential for disaster is huge. If I lose something, it's gonna hurt.

On and off my bike, I always do a check: *wallet, keys, phone, sunnies—and yep—lip gloss.* It serves me brilliantly—except for today, when I forgot to do it.

As I got off Voodoo, an uber-dreadlocked surfer cruised over to talk. He asked questions, we chatted, he took photos of me, I took photos of him, phones were exchanged to take photos of each other, more chatting, we said goodbye, and I headed off down the road to the cave.

Traipsing through the sand in my bike boots and jacket, I headed to the cave. The beach was so beautiful that I stopped to take a photo. *Phone? Holy shit, not again! My phone was AWOL. Missing in action. Noooo! Damn, damn, damn. It's gone!*

The good thing about wearing my boots was that I could see exactly where I'd walked, so I retraced my steps along the beach. But nah, not there. Back on the bike, I crawled the 500 metres back to where I'd been taking photos, desperately scouring the side of the road. Not there.

I can't begin to tell you what it feels like to know that the only way you communicate to your outside world in a strange, distant land has vanished—for the second time, no less. (OK—maybe not such a strange land, but a distant one at least!). For sure, a first world problem. But a big one.

Trying to breathe and figure out the next step, I decided to throw it out to the Universe. What did I have to lose? It probably wasn't the best of ideas to use the Universe as an insurance policy, but at that stage, I had nowhere else to go. So I asked: "My whole life is in that phone. People won't be able to find me without it. I have to have it. Please help me find it."

As I sat on Voodoo, I felt a huge need to go back to the beach. *You're kidding me, right? I've already checked the beach—I've retraced step by step. It's not there.* Again, I heard, "Go back to the beach!" I've always been a little deaf!

In the absence of any other solution, I went back. As I walked along the beach, still following my original boot steps, a young girl ran towards me. As she reached me, she looked up and smiled, my philandering phone safe in her tiny hands.

"Is this your phone?"

Is this my phone?! Yeessss! Thankyouthankyouthankyou!

When I stopped hugging her, I asked how she knew it was mine.

She replied, "I didn't. I found it earlier, but the minute I saw you I knew it was yours." Maybe the wild look in my eyes was a giveaway.

SHIFTING

Sitting on the pristine white beach at Manzanita a couple of hours later—the sand curling between my toes, the sky a brilliant purple-orange—I struggled to make sense of the day.

Sometimes it felt as if I were learning too much too fast. Things were moving and changing around me faster than I could comprehend, faster than I could absorb. I needed less growth or a bigger brain. *Did I have to keep learning? Couldn't I sit on Voodoo and ride just for the hell of it?*

But I'd made a shift. For just a brief moment, I'd let go of my fear of not being in control. I'd surrendered. I'd trusted the process, and I'd been OK. In fact, I'd been more than OK. I'd been taken care of.

The trick would be being brave enough to do it again tomorrow.

DAY 34: MANZANITA TO YACHATS

All the way along this journey, I'd been voraciously reading. I knew that if I wanted to heal the gaping hole in my heart, I needed to learn everything I could on the way. I'd made the commitment not to watch TV (not a hard choice when you're faced with fifty-seven channels of crap and reruns of *Gilligan's Island*) and not to read newspapers or magazines but to completely immerse myself in my world—the world of healing.

At the end of every day—after the boots were off, the dust had been washed from my shirt, socks, and undies in the bathroom sink (it was generally more a case of swirling the dirt around, but it was an improvement!)—I'd bunker in and read. I'd be lucky to get two pages out before my eyes would droop shut and I'd wake myself up with an embarrassing snort, but I persisted. I was desperate to learn.

One of the books that fascinated me was *The Untethered Soul* by Michael A. Singer, where he'd made a bold statement. *If we wanted to tap into the energy of our bodies, all we had to do was completely open our hearts.* Simple, right?

That morning, as I ran along the pristine white beach that I'd so cheekily asked for and then ungraciously almost rejected, I knew exactly what Mr. Singer meant.

With the sun gently coming up over my shoulder, I ran and played like a kid. Skipping in and out of the waves, jumping over tiny rivulets, dancing on the beach, singing at the top of my voice. I even tried out some old gymnastic moves (probably not such a good idea—some things should be left well alone!). The beach stretched for miles, and with not a soul around, I careered in and out of the bright aqua water. The golden glow of the morning on my face, the bracing spray of the surf on my body. My heart hadn't just opened—it had exploded.

As I sat on the sand shaking the sand out of my shorts after a back flip had gone horribly wrong, I figured that no matter what came my way, I could handle it.

IT HAPPENED SO FAST

It was an easy cruise down the coast—not necessarily by choice, but RV mania had hit Oregon. The road had become a slow-crawling caravan of bikes, 4WDs, and camper vans meandering from beautiful beach to beautiful beach. The coastline was often hidden by a fortress of pine trees, so it was a blessing to be going slow (I can't believe I just said that!). It gave me a chance to peak through the branches to get a glimpse of the elusive coast.

Trying to spot the water sometimes was a little like trying to find the Yeti, which apparently came from around here. (Yeah, yeah. That Yeti sure gets around. This was already the sixth place I'd found claiming him!)

Early in the afternoon, a blanket of dense fog descended, so any chance I had of spotting the coast disappeared. As it circled around me—eerie and pervasive—I was lucky to be able to see the road 100 metres in front of me.

With fog comes damp, and very quickly damp turns into cold. Not only was I riding blind, I was riding frozen. *What gives? It's the middle of summer, and I'm a block of ice. Think warm thoughts, think warm thoughts.* Surprisingly, seeing myself on a beach in Barbados sipping piña coladas just didn't cut it.

About 15 km from our home for the night—the seaside town of Yachats—I checked my gas and decided against fuelling up. We were in gas heaven on the coast, and I knew I wouldn't have a problem. But on the outskirts of town, I changed my mind and turned into a gas station for a high-speed gas and go. As I pulled in, a shiny new Corvette—black and fierce—pulled out.

I filled up quickly, desperate for a hot shower and a warm bed, and headed back out, virtually at my destination. A few minutes out of town, I eased Voodoo out of a tight corner and onto a long, flat straight...

Just in time to see the black Corvette flip over and slam onto its roof in the distance.

I was there within minutes, but people were already working hard, trying to release the unconscious driver. As the emergency teams worked, there was nothing I could do but wait helplessly by the side of the road.

The road was closed for about an hour as police measured and interviewed, the fire brigade cleaned up glass and mangled metal, and the tow truck cleared away the evidence. After gingerly picking my way through the debris, I found a hotel, and within minutes I was sitting on the bed in my soulless room, shaking uncontrollably.

It had been so close, and it had happened so fast.

It had all unfolded right in front of me and I'd been powerless to help. If I hadn't stopped for gas, I would have been very close to the accident. Although that didn't bear thinking about, it reminded me how vulnerable I was out there. For the first time, it scared me. In an instant, everything can change. I'd done nearly 9,000 km on Voodoo in just over a month with another two months to go. The reality of spending that amount of time on the road suddenly hit me:

Maybe people were right. Maybe I was reckless.

I'd been OK on the side of the road waiting for the ambulance. I'd been OK talking to the police. But by the time I'd gotten to my hotel, unpacked Voodoo, and dumped my gear on the floor, I was not OK. I shook and cried inconsolably.

I needed a hot shower, a cup of tea, and a hug. I was in desperate need of a hug.

Short of heading to the bar to find a hug, I settled for a hot shower and tried to let the warm water wash the shock and fear out of my system. Eventually—curled up in my bed in a tight a ball of vulnerability—I finally stopped shaking.

DAY 35: YACHATS TO ROSEBURG

I pulled out the next morning, still feeling exposed and unsettled. I hadn't slept. It seemed like every time I closed my eyes, the accident unfolded in front of me. At 4:30 in the morning, I gave up trying to sleep and headed out for a run. Normally, that's my go-to fix for everything, but this morning I carried a big black cloud of fear all the way out and all the way back.

I'd had a conversation with Connor the night before, and he'd reminded me that I couldn't keep thinking about near misses because there were probably about a hundred near misses every day that I didn't even know about.

When did he become the grown-up? He was right and I knew it, but I couldn't let it go.

I was seriously spooked. For the first twenty minutes, I rode Voodoo with trepidation. I was hesitant, tentative, fearful…and I needed to pull in for coffee to give myself a shake down. You can't afford to be defensive or apprehensive on a bike. With 1000 cc of power demanding your attention, you have to be confident or mistakes will happen. It's that simple.

Warming up over coffee, I made the call to let my fears go. I was feeling rattled, and I knew I had to consciously change that emotion. I thought about how I wanted to feel instead, and instantly the words "on fire" came into my head. *Really? That's how I wanted to feel?* OK, it *was* about ten degrees and I was already frozen, so if nothing else that seemed like a positive alternative. It felt like a big shift from "rattled" but it was going to be a long day. I had plenty of time.

Here's an admission: every morning, I load up, kiss Voodoo's tank, and say, "Let's knock it out of the park today, Big Girl," and every evening I unpack, kiss Voodoo's tank, and say, "Thanks, Big Girl. We nailed it."

Her tank is embarrassingly covered in lip gloss (how come it leaves your lips in seconds but it's impossible to get off a tank?), but what the hell. She's my Big Girl and I'll kiss her if I want to!

Leaving the coffee shop, I stepped back onto Voodoo, leaned on her tank, and kissed her. "We've got this, Big Girl. We're in this together, and together we'll be fine."

And we were back.

Well, I was, anyway. Voodoo hadn't gone anywhere!

TIME TO BREAK OUT

With the fog of yesterday a distant memory, the coastline

opened up and showed itself in all its glory. Long white beaches, quirky little fishing villages full of colour and character, breathtaking headlands. Spectacular.

It was also spectacularly cold. I had so many layers on, I was trussed up like an overweight turkey ready for Thanksgiving. Seriously—if I'd fallen off the bike, I would have bounced I had so much gear on. It's not a good look when you're trying to be cool, but for once I didn't care. I was happy to trade looking like a bloated sausage for the tiniest fragment of warmth.

Earlier in the morning, I'd considered heading inland. The coast was glorious, but after a couple of days, the wild interior was calling me. I missed doing the big miles in wide open spaces filled with huge sweeping curves. I missed dipping and dropping, and the feeling of rolling on the gas perfectly as I pulled Voodoo through fast, spine-tingling corners. Two days picking RVs off one-by-one on single-lane roads had me feeling like a caged animal.

It was time to break out.

I turned Voodoo east, heading towards Crater Lake, and instantly the whole world changed. With not an RV in sight, we were free. Threading our way through deep purple mountains, we tore through the countryside. Voodoo flowed effortlessly through rolling turns and expansive corners. Oh yeah—the girls were back, and we were on fire.

EXPERIENCING THE MOMENT

That turned out to be literal as well as figurative. As frozen as I'd been, within fifteen minutes of heading inland, it started to get warmer...and warmer...and warmer...and then damn hot! Bit-by-bit, the layers came off. Slowly, I went from looking like a stuffed turkey to a giant watermelon with my red jacket completely undone and flapping wildly as I tried desperately to grab even the slightest hint of a breeze.

But we were loving the freedom. We were low flying, Voodoo and I—riding hard and fast. There wasn't a car in sight, and we were flowing—back together as one. As we flew over the crest of a hill—a huge empty straight in front of us—out of the corner of my eye, I spotted a side road with a tractor sitting at the junction.

Instantly, I knew we were in trouble.

I was braking before he even pulled out, and pull out he did, at the massive speed of about 10 kph. It's hard to wash off huge speed in a very short space. Fortunately, I saw it all happening and went for Plan B—yet again—the other side of the road. Disaster averted.

As we pulled into Roseburg for the night, sweat poured down every square inch of my body. My hair was stuck like glue inside my helmet, and I could barely breathe for the dust inside my visor. It wasn't a pretty sight—I stank and was desperate for a shower.

I'd picked out a cute little B&B on the internet the night before. I hadn't booked it, but it looked gorgeous. And it might have been, fifty years ago. But today, paint was peeling off the walls, garbage was piled high in the yard, the shingles on the roof were falling off, and I was sitting in front of it—sweating like a piglet in forty-degree heat.

There were times—and this was almost one of them—that I came close to losing it.

But hey—a deep breath, an air-conditioned room, and a cold shower twenty minutes later had me reminding myself that an experience is only good or bad depending on the meaning you give it.

Being frozen could have been a "bad" experience—being barbecued could have been a "bad" experience. But if I let go of the meaning, I could just go with the flow and accept the experience for what it was: *amazing.*

(OK, maybe all but the tractor bit. To give him his dues, he probably wasn't expecting to find an S1000RR barrelling down the highway at flank speed!)

DAY 36: ROSEBURG TO CRATER LAKE

In a past lifetime, Crater Lake had been Mt. Mazama, an active volcano sitting at an elevation of 3,600 metres. About 7,700 years ago, a massive volcanic eruption triggered its collapse, sending ash and debris over 500,000 square miles, covering most of Oregon and even into Canada. A huge caldera—an upside-down mountain—was left, now known as Crater Lake. At 580 metres, it's the deepest lake in America and one of the deepest in the world—fed only by snow and rain.

It would be the fourth of the Seven Wonders of Oregon that I'd seen—I'd already nailed Mt. Hood, the Oregon Coast, and Painted Hills. The only challenge? I wasn't sure how I was going to get there.

BACK TO THE DRAWING BOARD

I'd done the math the night before. Roseburg to Crater Lake was about 190 km. I could make it there on one tank—only just—but unless I could get gas at the park, I wouldn't have enough to get me out again the next day. As usual, there was nothing definitive about gas being available, so I was in a pickle. Do I take the safe option and not risk it—but miss this incredible spectacle that I'd been busting to see? Or do I risk it, and maybe still miss the spectacle because I'm stuck on the side of the road without gas? These were the questions that kept me up at night!

I had a brain wave the next morning (they are few and far between, that's for sure). I'd buy a five-litre container of fuel, strap her to the back of Voodoo, and have a back-up plan for once. *Look at me being safe!* Boring for sure, but hey—I've been called worse.

The only challenge with the plan was that, five gas stations later, I was still without my fuel can. It turns out, Oregon is considered a fire state—a tinder box ready to explode into flames. It's even illegal for you to pump gas yourself. An attendant has to start the pump for you. Carrying a potential fire bomb of gas on the back of a bike? That was never going to happen. So much for the brain wave!

OK, back to the drawing board.

At the last gas station in town, I decided to check one more time to see if someone could give me a definitive: could I get gas in the park? The two guys behind the counter—a father and son—had no idea, but they called out for reinforcements. Bob. Bob would know for sure.

Now, beautiful Bob, the grandfather, was about ninety in the shade—a venerable gentleman clad in denim overalls that were about four sizes too big for him, a straw hat and cowboy boots completing the picture. He had the most heartwarming smile, and even though I'm sure he drank most of his meals through a straw—I could only see three teeth—his smile lit up his whole face. He was divine!

The three generations of Bob and I pored over my maps, which by now—after countless attempts at folding—were full of holes, usually right in the middle of my next destination. Bob sent a snail-paced Steve off to get a new map for me.

"You've gotta excuse Steve," said Bob. "He's getting old. He's a lot slower than he used to be."

I guess everything is relative when you're ninety.

With bated breath, I waited for Bob's verdict, as with craggy fingers he pointed to key destinations on the map, mumbling quietly himself. Checking and rechecking.

He took a deep breath. "Now girlie," (you could tell he was old if I was a girlie) "Ya see here? Now that's Glide. You'd b'gettin' gas at Glide—that's about twenty miles from here—and then you see here? That's Diamond Lake. Sure as eggs, you'll get gas at Diamond Lake, and that'll getcha in safe and sound. Mark my words."

Really? You sure? There's gas at Diamond Lake? Sweet—I'm in!

"Mind you, girlie, it's been nearly twenty years since I've been there. Things mighta changed somewhat since then."

Oh.

But by this stage I was committed. I was going for it. Glide would give me a 30 km buffer that I wasn't expecting. If worse came to worst, I had a plastic tube with me and could siphon gas from someone—preferably after asking!

OUTRUNNING THE FIRE

There are two entrances to Crater Lake—the north entrance that I was headed to, and the south entrance at the opposite end of the park. Life got just a little more complicated when I pulled into Glide and saw a huge flashing sign: "Crater Lake North Entrance closed due to fires."

Are you serious? How many more challenges was this upside-down mountain going to throw at me today?

A few more, it seemed. Using my universal knowledge bank (the guys at the gas station), we pulled out my shiny, new maps and found another route to the south entrance, but my survival still depended on there being gas at Diamond Lake—and now, because of the extensive detour, gas at the park.

The guys were 100 percent sure there'd be gas at Diamond Lake. Most days. (!)

Throwing caution to the wind, I decided to just enjoy the ride and to go for it. There was no point worrying about it until I got to Diamond Lake, so I might as well let Voodoo fly.

I loved riding in the early mornings. It was cold, but I loved the crispness of the air, the smell of the trees, the sound of the wind, the zing and energy of nature around me. I loved the solitude. I loved having the road to myself—the quiet of just me and the road, the silence in my helmet.

I realised that I'd been constantly surrounded by so much beauty over the past few weeks that it was easy to take it for granted. Another breathtaking forest, another stunning stream, another terrifying mountain pass, another awesome valley. As I rode, I made a pact with myself: every day, I would look at the world with fresh eyes and in wonderment—in appreciation of my amazing surroundings.

One thing was for sure: I would never take gas stations for granted. Despite a 20 km diversion because fire had closed the main road, gas was eventually secured at Diamond Lake (one down, one to go). Now all that remained between me and Crater Lake was a 160 km, smoke-shrouded detour down the side of the park to sneak in through the south entrance. *Easy!*

Not so easy. All around me, roads were being closed. The fire was gaining momentum, and alone on the road, I felt just the tiniest bit exposed. What happens if I get cornered here? There ain't a lot of exits on this road if the fire were to change direction.

The smoke was thick and heavy—even with my visor shut, it permeated my helmet, singeing my eyes and turning them into red, watery road maps. With visibility obliterated on either side of the road, I gently picked my way along the side of the park, coughing heavily as smoke made its way into my lungs.

As I finally made it to the south entrance of Crater Lake, any breath I had left was completely taken away. Nothing prepared me for how exquisite it was—the intensity of the water colour, the harshness of the crater rim, the size and sheer magnitude of the crater itself—the enormity of nature at her astounding best.

I'm sure Mazama herself would have been pretty spectacular, but you've gotta love a good explosion. Even through bleary, red-rimmed eyes, the hole she'd left was one of the most mesmerising sights I'd ever seen, and certainly worth all the excitement of getting there.

DAY 37: CRATER LAKE TO MT. SHASTA

Sometimes, being in the clutch of such overwhelming nature made it impossible for me to sleep. I was often so overwhelmed by what I'd seen and experienced that I was totally wired. Sleep was often wishful thinking. The good news about not being able to sleep was that my eyes were always ready—wide open in excited anticipation of a sunrise.

At 5 a.m., as I glanced out my window, I saw the sun starting its warm-up routine above the crater rim. Grabbing my shoes, I headed out into the purple light and ran to the opposite side of the crater to catch the sun rising up over the verge.

You know how sometimes you just have to hold your breath, because what you're seeing seems almost too perfect to be real? If you breathe, the real world might just creep in?

That was my sunrise. Dusky pinks and deep purples surrendered to reds and oranges as the sky then became a brilliant golden fire all around me. I held my breath at the moment of aurora—that sliver of a second when the sun hangs in suspended animation just before it rises. And then it was up!

For about forty minutes I sat there, captivated by the luminescent sky and the sun's shining reflection on the other side of the crater. I was struck by yet another comment from WuDe: "Every day, there's a sunrise and a sunset."

Every day starts and finishes with something truly magnificent. Every day, we get to make a new start—we just need to be up in time!

AT THE CROSSROADS

And it was time for me to be on the road. I was heading to Mt. Shasta, and after my "experience" in Mt. Baker (OK—let's call it what it was: my meltdown!), I was more than a little apprehensive. I'd heard a lot about Mt. Shasta. It's an active volcano known for being a place of high spiritual vibration and the location of a number of vortices, or transformational energy flows. No wonder I was nervous!

It had also never been featured on any of my plans. As "interesting" as it sounded, it had always felt a little "woo woo" for me—especially the old me! But for some reason, it was pulling me. Having learnt to let go of control and surrender to the unknown (well, for today anyway), I found myself heading there.

But first, a decision needed to be made: take the easy, direct route to Shasta—breathe it in early, get settled, and have a relaxing night—or take the much longer route via Ashland, which was a renowned blistering bike road. Tough choice. At the crossroads, I weighed my options. I was tired, emotional, and deserved an easy afternoon. I deserved to turn left and head straight into Shasta for some TLC.

Instead, I turned right.

You're surprised? I plunged onto Highway 66, a completely psychotic road between Keno and Ashland which had me screaming in my helmet within minutes. (Maybe I was the psychotic one!) What a road. It started through flats and dairy farms where, for once, the enemy wasn't deer, elk, or caribou, but wandering cows. The good thing about cows is that, although they'll stop you as dead as a deer, they're not prone to bouncing all over the road. Thank God. Can you imagine?

Leaving the flats, this biting, snappy road wound its way up and down an incredible mountain ridgeline. There were massive straights where Voodoo and I absolutely floored it—full throttle down. And then instantly we were thrown sideways—tight corner after tight corner. At one point, nausea nearly kicked in. It was like being on a giant roller-coaster shunted from side to side, then we'd come out of a corner and get to floor it all over again. Rinse and repeat for 90 km.

Just when I thought I'd had enough—and yes, I'd like to stop for lunch now, please—I popped out of the woodlands and into the desert. Why wouldn't I have expected that? Within minutes, I was clinging to the side of a mountain, pulling my way through 25 km of the tightest switchbacks imaginable. If I hadn't felt seasick earlier, I did now.

Equilibrium was finally restored about 10 km south of Ashford. But by then we had a new challenge: the fires had returned and the air was again heavy with smoke. When I finally pulled into a B&B, the owner—who probably needed just a little more finesse in his approach to customer service, took one look at my eyes as I pulled my helmet off and said, "Shit, you look like you've been on the booze all night. Actually, you look like you've been on the booze all week!"

Charming! Nothing a hot tub and half a bottle of Visine wouldn't fix.

DAY 38: MT. SHASTA

It was going to take more than Visine to be able to see Shasta. The plan had been to spend the day hiking. I'd pictured the perfect day. A gentle stroll up this awe-inspiring mountain—wildflowers at my feet, jumping over tiny streams, the sun warming my bones, with maybe the odd mountain goat or two for company. It was going to be gentle, serene, and soothing, and as I breathed the crisp, cool mountain air, I would smile and be at peace.

So much for planning!

From the minute I scrunched my tired, red, reluctant eyes open, I knew I was in trouble. A mood blacker than my boots had not just descended on me, it had engulfed me. I could tell by the way it had made itself comfortable in my head that it wasn't going anywhere fast.

How does that happen? You go to bed calm, at ease, peaceful, yet wake up in such darkness. Where does that come from? What happens in between while you sleep? I'd love to stay awake and see that process of transformation.

I knew that how my day went was up to me. I could choose to stay belligerent—agitated, anxious, overwhelmed—or I could choose to let it go. To be positive, upbeat, and enthusiastic.

I pulled the curtains back.

The supposedly spectacular Mt. Shasta was completely shrouded in smoke. The plan had already gone to shit. *Fine. Decision made.* I chose to stay belligerent. The Shasta energy had struck, and I wasn't even out of bed.

One of my strengths is determination (regularly referred to as "stubbornness" by those around me). When I commit, I commit 100 percent. And so I did. I threw everything at it. I chose to be at my belligerent best.

BURIED ALIVE

A gentle, peaceful stroll was now out of the question. I wanted pain, and I wanted lots of it. Nothing fuels being miserable more than punishing yourself physically. Leaving behind the planned wildflower walk, I chose the most rigorous nine-hour route on the map and headed out—head down, feet focused, and angry.

Completely encased in smoke, I relentlessly pushed my way up the mountain. The steeper, the more challenging the terrain, the better. I wanted my body to hurt. I figured if my body hurt badly enough, it would stop me having to deal with the hurt my soul was feeling.

They say an emotion buried is an emotion buried alive. As I pumped, pushed, and pulled my way up the mountain, six weeks of buried emotions came out of the grave kicking and screaming—and yes—they were very much alive. My head felt like its own volcano, spitting out questions like molten lava. Every fear I'd been carrying came pouring out of my head. It wasn't pretty.

Sometimes, being on a bike can be a safety net. Although there can be "free helmet space" to think, usually I'm pretty focused on staying present—a prerequisite for staying alive! That means I can carefully partition what I focus on. I trot out the stuff that's easy to resolve and carefully smother the tough stuff.

But walking is very different. When you walk, it's just you, space, and time—it can get raw and it can get ugly. One of the challenges of spending so much time on your own is that you don't have anyone to sense-check you—to tell you you're crazy or you'll be OK. When it's just you, peace and belief have to come from deep inside you. Today, peace and belief stayed buried. Instead, I had only questions. There was no rhyme or reason to them. They were random, and they were relentless.

Who are you if you're not a CEO anymore...what are you trying to prove...what if you never find your purpose...why do you have to always be in control...why can't you let go...what are you going to do next...you need to know what you're doing next... for God's sake, you need to know...how come you don't know?

I don't know, I don't know, I don't know! Stop asking questions I don't have answers to!

Man—where had this stuff been hiding? Obviously, my smug I'm-working-through-all-this-shit-I'm-doing-great persona had plastered over the cracks, but there's nothing like an uphill battle to reveal the real holes in the wall. The fears were still there—exposed, raw, and painful—and for the first time in six weeks, I felt scared. Was I actually making progress, or was I still a fraud? Was I still pretending that everything was perfect when really nothing was changing?

Overwhelmed and confused, I ceased the relentless forward motion and stopped in the middle of the track, my body shaking with emotion. And dammit! When was I ever going to see this mountain?

THERE ALL ALONG

I turned around, and there in all her majestic glory stood Mt. Shasta—just as perfect as I'd imagined. She'd been hidden behind smoke and clouds, but as I'd walked—head down and furious, the smoke had cleared and the clouds had vanished. She'd been there behind me all along. Peaceful, serene, and breathtaking. And I'd nearly missed her.

On this journey, I was discovering that nature heals. The wonderment of nature seeps into your cells and slowly, slowly, it permeates the cracks and closes the wounds. If you let it.

I sat down exactly where I'd stood. Right in the middle of the trail, in true awe, watching this glorious mountain as tears streamed down my face.

As I watched, I felt Mt. Shasta start to heal me. Just as the smoke had vanished, leaving her crystal clear, so my mind began to clear when I stopped fighting and faced my fears. Sitting in the dirt, the things that mattered were solved. Even if I didn't have the answers, I would trust the process.

For today anyway, I could let go of the things that didn't matter. I knew they'd be back to bite me—it would never be that easy— but every time they came back, they'd be weaker.

No matter how imperfect my progress, I had to keep making the effort to change. Then one day, I'd wake up and it wouldn't be an effort. That was the plan, anyway.

DAY 39: MT. SHASTA TO EUREKA

The great Shasta Shake Out had taken its toll. I woke up bruised and shaken from the day before. Maybe I needed to give these high-energy places a miss. They were certainly sending me into spiral dives. But when I looked closely, they were dives I needed. Every time I managed to find my way to the other side, another layer had been peeled back (OK, ripped off) leaving a raw wound, but a wound that, like a muscle after training, would grow back stronger and healthier. But damn—did it have to be so painful?

I'd planned an easy riding day. I was heading towards Happy Camp (yep, really—*Happy Camp*) on the Klamath River, about 200 km from Mt. Shasta. It was a one-horse town in the middle of a Native American title area, but a great stepping off point for some amazing bike roads through the interior of California. And I was in need of a serious ride to shake out the cobwebs.

We cruised out just before lunch, taking our time, playing in the sun, and exploring quirky little towns all along the route—towns like Weed and Yreka. At a health food shop in Yreka, I struck up a great conversation with the young owner who joined me for a green smoothie. (Gotta love California—even in the middle of nowhere you can find kale!)

She asked me where I was headed for the night, and on hearing Happy Camp, she reached over to a piece of paper and wrote a number on it.

"Here. This is my cell number—call me if you need anything at all. Any time, OK?"

Mmm...OK...not sure why I'd need it, but thanks. People are so friendly here, aren't they?

WRONG PLACE, WRONG TIME

The minute I turned off the highway at Yreka, my world became a giant canyon, alight with dramatic desert colours—orange, red, and ochre. Steep, twisting roads wound themselves carelessly through the desert mountains, traversing huge and impressive peaks and valleys. The climbs were so steep it felt as if Voodoo was actually going to fall backwards. And the descents? Hair-raising but exhilarating.

The deep, impressive canyons came right to the bottom of the road. I could almost touch the sides as I skirted through narrow, tight gaps. Together—the canyons and I—we hugged the Klamath River, where it was deep enough for people to raft and shallow enough for me to see brightly coloured fish. All the way through the canyons I had just one word in my helmet: "Wooowwww."

About 15 km from Happy Camp, I pulled into a small store to get water. The heat was blistering—California desert at its burning best. An eclectic group gathered outside trying to find shade. Gaunt, unshaven guys who'd just finished the Pacific Crest Trail mixed it with a gaggle of wild boys—dusty, dirty, and very drunk—who were trying unsuccessfully to hitch into Happy Camp. They were funny and harmless as I swatted them away from Voodoo, but I was a little concerned as I pulled out, wondering what I was headed towards.

I found out soon enough. As I pulled into town, the first thing I noticed was just about everything was boarded up. There were only a few shops and houses, but all the windows and doors were covered with wood and corrugated iron. *OK, interesting look.*

The one motel in town looked as if it had seen better days, but haven't we all? I was a little apprehensive as I watched three guys sitting out front surrounded by beer cans and smoking something very herbal. (You can smell everything on a bike.) But I figured it was only for one night. I needed to toughen up, princess. I could handle anything for a night, especially if it meant I got to ride the second-best bike road in California the next day.

But my instincts began to kick in, and for the first time on this trip I felt I was in the wrong place at the wrong time.

HAPPY CAMP

It constantly amazed people that I hadn't had an issue feeling threatened on this journey. I'd never felt uncomfortable. I'd never been harassed. Maybe it was the size of my boots or the thick layer of dust constantly covering me that stopped guys hitting on me.

My whole experience with guys on the road had been one of consideration, kindness, and generosity. Admittedly, naively perhaps, I always expected to receive the best from people. And so far, that trust had never let me down. Maybe that's what I would have received in Happy Camp, but for the first time ever it didn't feel like it.

As I pulled into the local store for water, the five guys sitting out front in the tail of a pickup truck stopped talking, put their beers down, and looked.

Now, there are looks and there are *looks*, and these looks weren't good. These were the looks I'm sure the Wolf gave when he spotted Little Red Riding Hood in the woods. The hair on the back of my neck stood up.

Being brave, cool and completely unfazed (well, on the outside) I wandered into the store, grateful that the owner was a woman—a big, bouncy woman at that, sassy and tough on the outside but a sweetheart on the inside. She asked me where I was headed, and when I told her I wanted to cross the Salmon Mountains and ride to Callahan, she just shook her head.

"Honey, fires closed that road this morning. It ain't gonna open for days."

Damn. I had another couple of options, but they too had been hit badly by fires. Those roads just weren't going to happen.

It was late in the afternoon now. I was hot and tired, and despite the potential challenges of my exotic hotel, I wanted a shower and to shut down. But when I told her I was staying in town for the night, she leant across the counter. Putting her face really close to mine, she quietly but forcefully said:

"No, you're not. You're not staying here. This is not a safe place for you. Now drink your water, make sure you've got gas, and get out of town. Tuck your hair inside your jacket, put your helmet on, and just go. Don't stop for anything or anyone. Go, and go now. Ya hear me?"

Now the cell phone number made sense.

I didn't need to be told twice. I pulled out my maps and had one option: Eureka, which was about another 200 km away. On a good day, that would have been a breeze. But it was already past four in the afternoon. I had at least another three hours of riding through a fire-shrouded desert to get there. I was hot, tired, emotional, and now, very spooked.

But staying wasn't an option, so into the desert we went.

A TREAT FOR VOODOO

Coming out of the desert and into tight, aggressive mountain passes required tough, technical riding that needed more control and energy than I had to give. Voodoo and I bludgeoned our way through the corners—the smoke so thick I could barely see 50 metres in front of me. My eyes were stinging—it felt like I'd been peeling onions in my helmet.

The road was foreboding. There was no traffic—just me and Voodoo alone in eerie desolation. Eagles circled above us, fires smouldered around us. There was a strange, negative energy that I needed to get out of—fast.

Feeling vulnerable and scared, I reminded myself that an experience was only good or bad depending on the meaning I gave it, but it was a hard sell. Nothing was going to shift this experience from "challenging" to "amazing." Just one long word rattled unconvincingly in my helmet:

"You'reOKyou'reOKyou'reOK." *Focus. Just ride. Don't think.*

Finally, after pulling into a hotel at Eureka, I lay my head on Voodoo's tank and kissed her. Yet again, my Big Girl had gotten us through. And tonight, she would be rewarded. As I checked in, Doris—the elderly receptionist—asked if I'd like to bring my bike inside.

"Of course, that'd be great. Thank you. Do you have a garage?"

"No, dear. We have a ballroom. We like to make sure we take as much care of bikes as we do guests."

Seriously? Five minutes later, I gunned Voodoo up the curb, through the hotel lobby, and left her sleeping in a giant ballroom surrounded by fairy lights. It was just what she deserved!

CHAPTER NINE

Eureka to Death Valley, CA

DAY 40: EUREKA TO CHICO

The ride to Eureka had knocked me around physically and emotionally, and I struggled to get my head and my body together. It
was drizzling—not enough to warrant a full-on wet-weather panic
attack, but enough to encourage me to hide under the duvet all day.

It was a close call, but I decided to toughen up and go for a run. Maybe it was the leftover energy from yesterday, but as I ran along the seaside wall and through the fish markets, I felt vulnerable. Then again, maybe fish co-ops aren't the best places for a woman to be running first thing in the morning. After getting strange looks and even stranger comments, I called it quits and headed back. I needed to get on Voodoo and get moving.

It was hard waking a sleeping Voodoo from the luxury of her ballroom suite. My room had been good, but it sure as hell hadn't come with fairy lights. Feeling as grey as the sky, we packed up and cruised past a few coffee places. I needed somewhere with energy and pizzazz to pull me out of my gloom, but nothing felt right.

Eventually, I found exactly what I needed: a quirky Mexican bagel house full of character, buzz, and surprisingly good coffee. It was hard to stay miserable in such a funky place, though I gave it my best shot. But slowly, the tension and the apprehension slid from my shoulders as I settled down for some serious people watching.

A cool dad and his gorgeous young son immediately caught my attention. There was such a spark between them that was captivating to watch. I guess there's a fine line between observing people and stalking, but I couldn't take my eyes off them. Is there anything more special than a father and his son, laughing together and sharing a visibly powerful bond?

As I headed out to brave the rain, the dad stopped me at the door. He'd watched me pull up on Voodoo earlier and was fascinated about our adventure. Did I have a couple of minutes to tell them about it?

Have I got a couple of minutes? Hey, I've got all day! It's miserable out there and I'm trying to stall anyway, so you bet. Pull up a chair!

Sometimes, the Universe gives you exactly what you need, exactly when you need it. We talked about life, adventures, taking every opportunity to be in the moment, and what it really means to make life count. Brian and his beautiful son were the perfect gift on a cold, wet Eureka morning. With their joy and enthusiasm for life, they reminded me why I was on this journey, and it was impossible not to be reinvigorated.

DEVASTATION WITH PURPOSE

Full of energy, inspiration, and a lot of coffee, I headed out—finally excited to face the day. And what a day. Out through the flats, through gentle meadows ablaze with wildflowers, a blanket of rioting pinks, purples, and yellows everywhere I looked. The vision was complete with captivating towns, cows, the odd tractor, and hay bales rolled tight. The meadows gradually transformed into a magical forest of giant redwoods filtering golden beams of light between the branches of behemoths. I felt like Voodoo, sleeping beneath her ballroom fairy lights.

And the road? Just heart-stopping. It was a ribbon twisted at both ends until it turned back on itself, then placed gently amongst the trees. It turned, it curled, we went backwards, we went forwards—all the while laughing with pure joy.

But this amazing road wasn't done with us yet. Leaving the forest, we started to climb...and climb...until suddenly, out we popped onto an amazing ridgeline—a beautiful mountain range behind us and the scorched remains of a once-stunning forest around us.

I'd been desperate to ride this road—Highway 36—but fire had closed it for days, with many side tracks still smouldering. The devastation was staggering, but somehow there was beauty in this process of nature—of regeneration and an opportunity for new life to emerge.

NOPE, NOT A DOCTOR

After traversing the once lush ridgeline, we began a descent—into the harsh, yellow dryness of the desert. Seriously, how many scenery changes can a girl and a bike handle in one day? I never knew what to wear! I'd started the day in the rain at a chilly nine degrees, and now I was battling dirt and dust at a steaming thirty-nine degrees. Was there ever going to be an in between?

I pulled into the tiny town of Platina for gas, though the word "town" is probably an overstatement. It was more a diner with a gas pump—but a very welcome gas pump at that.

The diner was straight out of the sixties, complete with wood paneling and nothing but big red bar stools. It had everything you could possibly want to eat (as long as that was a hamburger or a hot dog) and everything you possibly wanted to drink (as long as that was a Coke or a beer). Luckily, I just needed gas.

As I fuelled up, a group of Harley riders sitting in the sun threw me a question: "Say, Missy—could you settle an argument for us? We're trying to work out what you do, and we think you're a doctor. Are we right?"

A doctor? They obviously haven't heard of my bedside manner!

I shut Voodoo down and played "yes or no" while they guessed my occupation. Eventually I had to tell them the truth so I could move on—that I was a fighter pilot—and they seemed happy with that. It was a better answer than what the Harley guys the week before had guessed—that I was a pole dancer. *Seriously?*

GOOD LUCK

The real craziness started after I left Platina. They obviously ran out of money building this road which meant two things: number one, they decided not to level it, so for fifty wild kilometres, it felt like we were on a giant, scary roller-coaster with rollers so fierce that I nearly lost Voodoo a couple of times when she completely dropped out from underneath me.

And number two: because there are so many hairy curves, they must have decided not to bother with any speed guiding signs. They'd taken a "Well good luck with that—I hope it works out for you" approach to corners, which meant our only option was to feel our way through them. Halfway into a corner, I'd often think to myself, "Mmm...might have been better if I'd taken this at 20 kph instead of 50..." But hey, it all added to the excitement.

Later that afternoon, I sat in the sun in Chico—an eclectic little university town, complete with colourful Victorian mansions set on wide, shade-tree-lined streets on the one hand, with a campus buzz on the other. The world wandered past me. Guys throwing Frisbees, professors bustling with papers, lovers arguing, an old dog trying to get the energy to chase a stray cat but deciding that dismissal was probably the better part of valour... the cacophony of life flowed in front of my eyes.

Four hours after I'd switched off, when I closed my eyes I could still feel myself flying over the rollers and leaving both my stomach and, on a couple of occasions, Voodoo behind.

And I laughed.

DAYS 41–42: CHICO TO TAHOE

The roads from Chico to Nevada City to Tahoe were unlike anything I'd ever ridden—roads destined to soothe the soul and excite the spirit. My objective was to always take the most amazing bike roads possible, which meant I often zigzagged all over a state, eking out wild and crazy backroads, to connect one "scream in your helmet" road to another.

The squigglier a road looked on the map, the more adrenaline I knew it would pump. Very rarely did I go direct.

The randomness of my selection criteria meant that I never knew what to expect. I just started Voodoo up every morning and stepped into the adventure. Whatever we experienced would be what we were meant to experience, even if I didn't understand it at the time. What better way to learn to surrender to the unknown?

What I didn't expect, as Voodoo and I traversed through the staggeringly beautiful Sierra Nevada Mountains was how over-whelming our experience would be when we just surrendered to the roads—when we ignored the destination and focused purely on the journey. When we just focused on being present to everything and everyone around us. The Sierra Nevadas were mind-blowing. The Universe must have contemplated long and hard about what it needed in order to create the most awe-inspiring mountain range, then carefully, piece-by-piece, combined each exquisite element, so that no matter where you travelled or where you looked, you would be in a constant state of awe.

And I was in awe.

There were deserts—striking, yellow, and harsh. Dry dust bowls of scorched earth with orange rocks glistening under a heat so intense it created a shadowy haze that hovered on the horizon. In contrast, the majestic pine forests were lush and cool, bathed in beams of golden brilliance. Impossibly deep gorges peppered the route, spanned by bridges—engineering masterpieces—that completely defied logic and gravity. I held my breath as we crossed, with just the slightest degree of trepidation, marvelling at both the awesomeness of nature below me and the awesomeness of the construction (hopefully) holding us up.

Serene canyons carefully wound their way along the bottom of the range, while alongside, slow flowing rivers meandered gently—the occasional fish jumping high out of the water. The colours were soothing—ochre, deep orange, taupe, the subtle darkness of the canyon rocks, the intensity of the blue-green water. Could it be any more impressive?

It could. Purple-blue peaks still speckled with snow wrapped in impossible mountain passes, fierce and treacherous, surrendered to beautiful lakes—water of azure, with rustic cabins dotted between the pine trees.

Yep, I think the Universe checked just about everything off.

In gratitude, all I could do was kick back and say *thankyouthankyouthankyou*. I couldn't have asked for anything more.

ONE OF THE BOYS

But the Universe wasn't finished with me quite yet. In its infinite wisdom, it had decided to give me the ride of my life. Schizophrenic roads—where one minute the elevation and descent were so steep they would give me vertigo—then gently sweeping corners so rhythmic they'd almost rock me to sleep. Insanely tight hairpin bends and drops-offs so acute that Voodoo was almost vertical gave way to slow, wide bends where we dropped and flowed.

I was as schizophrenic as the roads. I was tense, relaxed, apprehensive, calm, terrified, chilled, and wired—usually all at once. I just had no idea what was going to happen next or what this incredible road would throw at me. Intensity, exhilaration, and adrenaline burst their way into my DNA, and hour after hour after hour, I was on fire.

But—as hard as it was to believe—I hadn't just stepped into this amazing adventure purely for the awesome scenery and breathtaking riding, although the Sierra Nevadas had certainly given me that. I also wanted to learn—about myself, about life, and about what it truly meant to feel content and at peace.

Over those few days, while winging my way through the beautiful backcountry of California, I received a valuable lesson—one that the Universe had given me at least six times—either because it was important for me or because I was a very slow learner. Probably both. Either way, it came to me through connecting with amazing, beautiful people that briefly but powerfully touched my life in a few short days.

First up were "The Boys" in Chico—five wisecracking, cheeky gentlemen in their late seventies. They'd been friends for fifty years and still met most mornings for coffee. After asking me to join them (I probably looked about seventy, so I guess they figured I fit right in) I sat back and watched in awe. They were full of energy—debating, arguing, agreeing to disagree. They figured they had all the answers to the problems in the world, but they were so old now that no one bothered to ask them the questions! After they departed, I caught up with a young barista—a college kid with three degrees and no idea what he should do with his life. I'm still not sure how we got to that depth of conversation between "A large Americano, please," and "Do you want room for cream?" But by the time I'd drained the last dregs of my coffee, we had a plan for him—or at least a good first step.

Later, in another powerful connection, there was the beautiful Stop-Go lady who was skillfully controlling construction traffic over a tight, narrow gorge. She was dressed to kill—even in construction gear—with immaculately polished boots and bright red lipstick. We talked bikes and love and being true to yourself.

It's amazing what can be divulged in a fifteen-minute conversation at the head of a construction queue.

She'd always wanted to ride, and as I pulled out, she told me she was inspired to get a bike now. After seeing her stand in thirty-nine-degree heat for hours and still look gorgeous, I was inspired to get my act together and stop looking like I'd been pulled through a hay stack backwards. (Mind you, I think it'll take more than lipstick.)

JUST BEING MYSELF

It'd been a pretty wild weather day—one minute I was riding through cool, crisp forests, the next I'd be riding through deserts with harsh, searing heat. It was like standing in front of an open fridge door one minute, then sticking your head in the oven the next. Fortunately, by lunchtime only one option remained: heat, and lots of it.

Sweltering, I pulled into a gas station. I couldn't bear contemplating fueling up until I'd ripped all my riding gear off. As I tried not to make a complete spectacle of myself struggling out of my jacket, a young guy wandered up to me, put his cool hand on my sweaty shoulder, and handed me a bottle of water.

"I think you need this. Make sure you stay hydrated out there." *Sweet.*

Late in the afternoon, I pulled into yet another gas station, where an old guy in a beat up pickup truck alongside me decided to ask fifty questions. Where was I from...was I on my own...was I scared...where was I headed...why was I travelling...Here's the kicker: every time I answered him, he'd high-five me! It made filling up a pretty slow process, but where else did I need to be? He obviously needed to be somewhere else, though, because eventually his friend in the passenger seat got out and told me to stop answering his questions or they'd never get home for dinner.

After finally making it into Lake Tahoe, with its pristine azure waters encased by mountains and forests, I thought about everything the past few days had given me. Magnificent scenery and blistering roads, sure—all important elements of the journey—but my encounters with people had given me far more.

None of the people I'd met on the road had known my history. None of them were aware of what I'd achieved or accumulated. None of them cared about my business card, my title, my role.

On the road, that meant nothing. The only thing that mattered was who I was—right then and there, in that moment of time.

What mattered was how I engaged with the world—how I connected with these inspiring, captivating people. How I chose to show up. People who didn't know the warrior or the superhero in me liked me anyway. How's that for a surprise? They liked me for just being me. Or for being a feisty Aussie woman on a pretty cool superbike.

Either way, it felt good. Maybe—just maybe—I didn't need to be anything but myself. I still wasn't really sure who that person was, but time would tell, I guessed.

DAY 43: TAHOE AND MONITOR PASS

Lake Tahoe is fascinating. The natural beauty is staggering—a striking, vivid blue freshwater lake surrounded by the majestic Sierra Nevada ranges. The lake crosses two state boundaries— the northern part in Nevada and the southern in California. Obviously, the lake was so stunning that both states wanted a part of it. Completely understandable!

But the township that surrounds Lake Tahoe? Well, it has kind of a "Heidi meets Vegas" feel, where kitsch A-frame motels and houses are overshadowed by big casinos and flashy billboards. It's where nature meets the concrete jungle, and it's pure sensory overload.

Breathtaking scenery notwithstanding, I came to Tahoe specifically to ride the infamous Monitor Pass—voted the very best riding road in all of California. Monitor Pass is on Route 89, about 50 km southeast of Lake Tahoe, between the tiny towns of Markleeville and Topaz Lake. At an elevation of 2,500 metres, it's 30 km of pure riding wonderment, exhilaration, insanity, and zing. Get the picture?

I'm sure they wanted to make the Pass longer, but they figured a human body could only cope with 30 km of such intense emotion. I'd ridden it a couple of years before, and the adrenaline from that experience was still running through my veins. I knew what to expect, what the road would demand of me, and exactly how I wanted to ride it: fast, furious, and fearless. I was ready.

We left Tahoe at first light. Voodoo was naked—the Leaning Tower of Pisa stacked neatly on my hotel room floor—which meant she was ready for action. My Big Girl was ready to fly, and without the extra weight of the bags to hold her down, I knew I'd be flying too. (Probably off her as I struggled to keep her on the ground.) But hey, that just added to the excitement.

IN PERFECT SYNC

Cutting through the Sierra Nevadas to the Pass was sublime—pink, purple, blue mountain ranges stacked one behind the other stretching far into the distance, a pastel blue sky dotted with wisps of white cotton clouds, and the gentle warmth of the sun as it slowly made its way upwards. The perfect day for the perfect ride.

I could barely sit still waiting to get to the Pass. But I had to calm myself down—to remind myself to be present and to really sink into the incredible sights around me. I was getting closer, and I could feel the excitement starting to percolate at the bottom of my stomach.

Bring it on, baby—this was going to be epic!

The instant I turned left onto the Pass, my heart leapt. For the briefest of seconds, I looked down at Voodoo—almost trying to hold her back—but it was too late. She'd seen the road and she was off—it was on for young and old. For thirty wild kilometres, it was a blur of wildflower meadows, fertile green valleys, canyons of reds and yellows, huge cliffs, scorched forests, deserts, mountains, caverns. The scenery—rich and intense—changed as quickly as my heart was beating. Each corner took me to yet another world, and no three minutes were the same. (Maybe if I'd gone slower it wouldn't have changed so fast!)

But going slow was not an option on this road, except through the nail-biting switchbacks that unfolded, one after another, like a giant yellow ribbon twisting down the mountainside. They spiralled and zigzagged—they sucked me in and spat me out. Not to be trifled with, they demanded my utmost attention.

But Voodoo was all over them.

It was pure magic to be riding my naked Big Girl without bags or equipment to slow us down—nothing but pure, raw energy and fire. Together, we flowed. The feeling you get when you're in perfect sync with your bike is unlike any other. It's about energy and bliss, control and confidence. It's about excitement and anticipation. We were one.

The first time down, I rode to remember—to get the feel of the road, to know what twisted where, to understand how far I could push it, to get my head into the right space before turning around and riding back to the top again. The second time down, I rode to forget—to forget everything but the thrill of flying and the joy of riding hard, fast, and just a little over my level of capability. I wanted to sign my name on the Pass today. To know that I'd ridden like the wind and I'd nailed it. There was only one sound in my helmet as we hurtled back down the Pass, screaming it for a fast 30 km:

Fuuucckkkkthisssisssaaaawsoommmme!

ALIVE AND ZINGING

After I'd ridden back to the top the second time, I was seriously tempted to give it a third go, but sometimes you just have to know when to stop. Quitting while I was ahead, I turned for home.

Needing water and to breathe, I pulled back into the tiny town of Markleeville. But before I even had time to step off Voodoo, tears starting to roll down my face. Small ones at first, then huge, fat tears, creating wide rivers of dirt on my cheeks.

I cried uncontrollably. Not the beautiful, gentle crying you see in the movies, but the snot-covered crying that makes your eyes red and your face blotchy—true crying that comes from the heart.

In that moment, as I stood in the dirt alongside Voodoo, I was crying for everything. Everything that had been, and everything that was.

I was crying for my adventure—for the sheer, raw beauty of nature I experienced every day. I was crying for the incredible opportunities I'd been given. For the pure joy of each and every moment. For the learning. I cried for the extraordinary gifts, the growth, the wildness of my world. For the love and support, the connectivity that surrounded me wherever I went.

And although my heart was overwhelmed, I was on fire. Every fibre of my body—every cell, every tiny bit of DNA—was alive and zinging with gratitude.

Two months ago, this ride would have been all about the ride—breathtaking in its intensity, full of adrenaline and excitement. Pure bike, pure exhilaration. But today? It had become much more. It was the full experience—soul, spirit, emotions, and body. The total package.

Two months ago, I couldn't have imagined my heart ever being cracked as wide open as it was today. But it needed to be. It had been shielded for way too long. As I cried and snuffled in my helmet all the way back to Tahoe (by the way, don't cry or sneeze in your helmet—it never ends well!), I was grateful.

Grateful for the day. Grateful just to be.

DAY 44: LAKE TAHOE TO SONORA

Starting each day with an intention was initially a hangover from my goal-driven, need-to-achieve days. But it had slowly morphed into being about how I wanted to show up in the world. My intention set the energy for the day and gave me clarity on the person I wanted to be. It also gave me the chance to reflect at night. *Had I really gone for it? Did I nail my intention?*

Sometimes, my intention would come from meditation. Sometimes it would come over coffee; sometimes it'd come from something I'd learnt. But what really shocked me was that, no matter what sparked it, it was starting to come from my heart.

For the first time, I was beginning to respond to how I felt in my heart rather than in my head. My head often told me one thing, but when I was brave enough to step into my heart, I often felt something very different. My head was about achievement; my heart was about being. The two were very different.

I'd read a great quote:

"You cannot get through a single day without having an impact on the world around you. What you do makes a difference, and you have to decide what kind of difference you want to make."

My intention for the day—or the difference I'd decided to make as I headed to Sonora—was to be of service. Every day, I'd been blessed with people taking care of me, going out of their way to help me, and giving purely of themselves. I'd had coffee in RVs, carried sage, been given water and fresh berries. People had shared their worlds with me. They'd been vulnerable and had chosen to connect with me at such deep levels.

Being of service would be my thank you.

NO MATTER WHAT

The best way to be of service today would be to put a spark into the lives of every person I came in contact with—to help them feel valued and positive about themselves. Seemed easy enough—but the Universe decided to put me to the test straight away.

Checking out of my hotel, there was a problem with the bill. The receptionist was surly, and no amount of my high-energy charm cracked her scowl. *OK, tough audience. It'll get easier.* On the way out, I held the door open for a couple and gave them my 1000-watt smile—you know, the one you save for first dates. But they just walked through. No acknowledgement, no smile, nothing other than being smacked by their bags as they passed.

OK...don't lose faith...keep being of service no matter what comes back.

But it wasn't easy. Cruising into a coffee shop, where I normally connect, the barista was snappy and sullen. *OK, you're not going to beat me—I'm going to be of service to you whether you want it or not!* I threw everything I had at him, but he wasn't having any of it...until suddenly, between taking my money and handing me my coffee, he snapped. Positively.

Over Americanos, we became friends as we dug into fears for the future—his and mine—and what we were both going to do when we grew up. *Finally.* Being of service had kicked in.

REMEMBERING INTENT

A few days earlier, a magazine had asked me to write an article about Jakey—to tell his story about the tough times, the helpless times of desperation, and about coming out on the other side. As I wrote in the coffee shop, the tears began to flow.

It was an amazing story for sure, but the pain of telling it was acute. The feelings of hopelessness and despair—of watching my son drowning and not being able to throw him a lifeline—were still so raw. Even though I knew the story had a happy ending, it was still heartbreaking to write.

My new bestie barista loaded me with coffee for bravery and serviettes for the tears. I'm not sure whether he was being kind or if he was worried I was going to scare away business, but either way, it gave me space to write. After hitting *send*, I wiped my tears one last time, pulled back my shoulders, and hit the road.

Pulling into a tiny diner in Cooktown for water later that morning, I chatted briefly to a craggy guy with a lived-in face as he ate his breakfast. As we chewed the fat about bikes, he suddenly shouted to the waitress, "Hey Michelle—bring a plate of French toast for the chickadee here. She looks like she needs a good feed. Now," turning back to me, "what's your name? Siddown and have a chat. You can afford to be ten minutes late."

Indeed. I ended up being over an hour late. But what a treat! After circumventing the non-plant-based French toast and settling for coffee, I discovered he'd been at school with Kenny Roberts—the first American to win the Grand Prix Motorcycle World Championship. And he was best friends with Keith Code—my legendary coach at the California Superbike School. *You're kidding, right? In the middle of nowhere I'm discussing bike legends with a guy eating hash browns? Only on the road!*

Paying for gas later that afternoon, an amiable lady behind the counter noticed my accent (how could you not?) and asked if I had any Aussie coins on me. Her granddaughter was doing a project and needed foreign coins. Now—here's the thing. At the bottom of my roll bag, I knew I had Aussie coins that I'd tossed there when I'd emptied my wallet. But unpacking and repacking that baby was an engineering feat I just didn't want to initiate.

Then I remembered. *Damn!* My intention today was to be of service.

Pulling Voodoo into the shade, I dismantled the Leaning Tower of Pisa. Ta-da! A bunch of Aussie coins were found. She was so excited that she wanted to buy them from me. With our exchange rate, I'd probably have ended up owing her money. But when I gently refused, she insisted on giving me a bag of doughnuts to say thanks. *Doughnuts? What's a vegan to do with doughnuts?* But into the roll bag they went. I knew I'd find someone along the road to re-gift them to. Beats re-gifting socks, I guess!

En route to Sonora, we passed through the old gold-mining town of Angels Camp. It was scorchingly hot by the afternoon. As I sat stopped at traffic lights, I had to continually rock from one foot to another in the forty-one-degree heat to stop my boots from melting on the boiling tar. As I rocked, I read the town goal, posted on the side of the road—and I smiled:

"To be in a state of being. To be committed to kindness and service. We're dedicated to creating a kinder and gentler place—a place of service."

Seriously? Just in case I'd missed the message with my intention this morning, it was being sent to me again. There are no such things as coincidences.

IT'S WHAT YOU MAKE OF THEM

I finally made it into Sonora—melted boots and all—and shut

a tired and overheated Voodoo down at a beautiful Victorian manor at the top of the hill. It had once been the home of Mark Twain, and I could imagine him sitting on the shaded veranda, drinking lemonade by the pitcher.

As I was checking in, the owner—a vivacious woman in her early forties—told me her story. She had two beautiful boys, aged thirteen and fifteen, who had both become severely handicapped following a routine vaccination. They were now unable to speak or communicate, and she had four therapists caring for her boys on a rotational basis, twenty-four hours a day.

Together, we watched her precious boys playing on the slip-and-slide on the lawn, and my heart broke. Her dreams for their future had been dashed, and life was never going to end up the way she'd planned when she'd married her childhood sweetheart twenty years ago.

But she was strong, determined, realistic, and inspirational in her spirit and positivity. If I hadn't already felt blessed at how Jakey's story had turned out, I did then.

Life has many unexpected turns. Nothing prepared me for the challenges I'd faced with Jakey. Nothing prepared me for the adventures I'd had on this journey. And nothing had prepared this inspiring mum for the heartache she'd experienced with her boys. She said to me:

"There's a purpose for everything. Life gives you experiences for a reason, and what you make of those experiences is how you choose to live your life. As difficult as this experience is, it is the right one for us to have." Could I have had a more powerful lesson?

DAY 45: SONORA TO MAMMOTH

Leaving Sonora early in the morning, it was already thirty-five degrees by the time we'd reached the end of the driveway. Within minutes, I felt like a fried egg on a griddle. But gradually, we started to climb into the sharp coolness of the Stanislaus National Forest.

We passed by petite villages with evocative names like Strawberry, Sugar Pine, Confidence, and Mi-Wuk. I kept rolling their names around in my head—they sounded too precious to be true, and they certainly looked the part. Log cabins, smoke fires burning, the smell of pine heavy in the air. It was like riding through the enchanted forest.

The road that threaded itself through this lushness was a complete surprise. It was one of the top ten bike roads in California, so I knew it'd be good—but I wasn't expecting heaven. It was different to Monitor Pass. Monitor was sharp, ferocious, and aggressive. This was gentle and laid back, but undeniably powerful.

Its corners did 270-degree turns back on themselves. I'd find my sweet spot—give it enough throttle to get my weight on the back tire, hold my nerve, hold my nerve (there was a lot of holding my nerve), spot the way through, and then power out. Again and again and again. Everything was big. Sweeping turns, big drops, wide bends—nothing tight or scary, just the perfect soothing ride for the soul.

A CLOSE CONTEST

As I reached Dardanelle, I pulled over for air—and to give my cheeks a rest. I'd been smiling so much in my helmet they were hurting and I looked like a chipmunk. Gazing out at the brilliant Sierra Nevadas, I decided I was done. I was complete—busting with joy and smiling from ear to ear. The ride up had been such a rush that I figured nothing could beat it.

But I hadn't figured on Sonora Pass.

The second highest pass in the Sierra Nevadas, Sonora Pass climbs to a staggering height of over 3,000 metres—which is very high, considering the road for most of the climb is nothing more than a goat track clinging by a tenuous thread along the side of the mountain. For extra excitement, there are no guardrails. At any moment, you could plummet to your death over the side. It was treacherous, hazardous, and spine-tinglingly terrifying.

It was astoundingly beautiful, and I loved it. Completely.

OK—I'm going out on a limb here—until today, my favourite road in the whole wide world had been Monitor Pass, hands down. It was a close contest, but today, by the slimmest of margins, Sonora emerged victorious and claimed the title.

This pass was feisty. It bucked and kicked, bit and spat—some of the corners were so tight, I had to have two goes to get Voodoo through them. (Thank goodness there was nothing coming the other way!) For what felt like hours, my heart was in my mouth (better than my usual foot, I guess) as we gingerly navigated impossibly narrow hairpin bends and zigzags, barely suspended off the side of the mountain.

The first rule of riding a bike is the bike will always go where you look. I was too scared to even peek over the edge of some of these cliffs, because I knew that's where we'd end up. I couldn't pull over for a breather because there was no edge of the road— only a very sharp drop-off.

This bucking bronco of a road twisted and turned like a cork-screw, and just when I thought I was completely spiralled out, we hit a sign: "Dangerous Corners Next 15 Miles."

You've gotta be kidding me! What the hell do you think I've been doing for the last thirty miles? You've gotta love a road that throws everything it's got at you the last fifteen miles!

Unexpectedly, in the middle of this chaos, we suddenly found ourselves in a magnificent glade of redwoods. A forest of overpowering red giants aligned majestically in the sun. I desperately needed grounding after flying through the air all morning. Yanking my helmet and my boots off, I sat with my back against an enormous red colossus, sank my toes into the dirt, and just breathed.

For half an hour, I sat—the sun streaming through the branches, the smell intoxicating me—and I breathed. I breathed appreciation. I breathed exhilaration. I breathed wonderment. (OK, I did actually hug a tree—and kissed it as well—but if you kiss a tree in the forest and no one sees, is it still kissed?)

IN THE END

Sonora Pass had it all, and it had taken everything I had to give. If I hadn't looked like a complete goose, I would have gotten off Voodoo and laid on the ground at the end of the pass—first to give thanks that I'd made it through alive, and second to sleep. I was completely toasted. Combine serious concentration, technical riding, a little tension, and a touch of fear (OK, a lot of both) for eighty long, torturous kilometres at nearly 3,000 metres, no wonder I was wiped. But oh, so happy.

Exhausted—we finally rolled into beautiful Mammoth Lakes— where, despite it being thirty degrees late in the afternoon, my thoughtful hotel owner upgraded me to the suite, "Because it has a fire." I wasn't sure I'd use it, but the sentiment was lovely. As was my dancing partner later that night.

At an open-air concert, green juice in hand, I shuffled badly and slowly to the music, taking in the vibe and reliving the day. Suddenly, I found myself dancing with a beautiful young Rasta with dreadlocks past his waist and a smile that just about singed my eyes. This gorgeous boy was either high or blind, but somehow, he didn't notice that my moves looked more like a water buffalo on roller blades. As the sun slowly slipped out of the sky—while he grooved, and I hoofed—I thought of Ernest Hemingway:

"It's good to have an end to journey towards, but it's the journey that matters in the end."

This was shaping up to be one hell of a journey.

DAY 46: MAMMOTH TO DEATH VALLEY

In the dark, I headed out into the mountain trails of Mammoth. I needed to stretch my legs and run, but the steepness of the terrain gave me more than I'd bargained for. Nearly eight weeks on the bike with my knees up around my ears for hours every day hadn't done my thighs any favours. My trainer was gonna have his work cut out for him by the time I got home. Breathing heavily (OK, wheezing), I wound my way through the trees, pushing hard to reach the top before sunrise.

It was cold. Really cold. Even in my frenetic scrambling up the side of the mountain, I was frozen. Looking back, I should have appreciated that brief moment of frostbite—a few hours later, I would have given anything to be shaking with cold. But that moment was yet to come.

Still, as a reward for my valour, I was treated to the most exquisite sunrise. The fires were getting closer, and a constant haze had hung in the sky for days, often making it difficult to see and even more difficult to breathe. But this morning, the smoke was a gift.

Acting as a filter, it reflected divine rays of pink and purple across the sky as the sun—a fiery scarlet orb—pushed its way up from the horizon. The intensity of the colours took whatever breath I had left. I stood, frozen but mesmerised. The most perfect start to the day.

ARE YOU INSANE?

Riding to Death Valley was going to be a challenge. As well as being a torturous ride, it was also going to be hot—damn hot. Despite everyone over the past few days warning me about heading into the desert in the hottest part of summer, I'd chosen—as always—to ignore sane advice. In my stubbornness, I was going anyway. I mean, how hot could it get? Besides, Australians are built to handle heat!

The plan was to get away early—cover as much of the 370 km as

I could before lunch, before it got too hot. But as I was learning on this journey, plans were only made to be foiled, and the foils were worth it.

As I loaded Voodoo, a young guy in his late thirties packed his Harley beside us. Not your typical Harley rider for once—a cool, sharply dressed guy with a buzz cut and not an ounce of leather, tattoos, or bandannas in sight. It's funny (or it's sad) how we (OK, I) jump to quick judgements. Out of the corner of my eye, I saw him and instantly thought, "Yep, accountant pretending to be a wild boy, riding his Harley to escape actuarial boredom."

When am I ever going to learn?

We shared stories as we loaded, and within ten minutes, we'd stopped talking and had moved to hugging as he cried. Six months ago, his best friend had contracted cancer, and my new friend had nursed him until he'd died in his arms. Just a few weeks ago. He was out riding his Harley, trying to clear his head and to pull himself together.

I wept with him. There was nothing I could say or do to take the pain away. All I could do was hold space for him in his anguish.

I was honoured he'd shared his story with me and that, for even a few short minutes, I'd been able to give him a shoulder. He did have some interesting advice for me, though, as I pulled out: "You're seriously heading to Death Valley? Are you insane?"

Not the first time someone's told me that, and it certainly won't be the last. But on reflection, it was probably a very accurate comment.

TOUGHEN UP, PRINCESS

Dressed for arctic exploration, Voodoo and I headed out—and damn, it was cold. As we powered south on Highway 395, I huddled in behind the screen to get out of the wind, gripping Voodoo's tank like a long-lost lover, desperate for even the slightest degree of warmth.

Highway 395 was a serious four-lane highway that powered through the countryside. It was a "blast-and-drone" road—one that gave me distance and let me cover as much countryside as I could in the shortest time possible. Hopefully without attracting too much attention from the infamous California Highway Patrol, of course.

The scenery would have been amazing, but the fires had worsened overnight, and the horizon held nothing but layer after layer of hazy, purple-hued mountains silhouetted in the background.

But slowly, the smoke started to clear—and with that clearing came scorching heat. Within seconds, I went from frozen turkey to barbecued chicken. I realised I was in trouble. It was already thirty-five degrees at 9:00 a.m., and I wasn't even close to Death Valley.

The minute I turned east towards Death Valley, the pain hit me. I was coping at thirty-five Celsius, but within ten minutes the temperature skyrocketed. It was like being in a fan-forced oven at 200 degrees—not that I've ever been in a fan-forced oven. By the time I'd reached my first gas station, the temperature had hit forty-one, and within twenty minutes, it had spiked to forty-seven.

A group of Harley riders pulled in behind me, and one guy had just enough time to put his side stand down before he fell off his bike and collapsed on the ground with heat stroke. We're talking sizzling.

For another 165 km, I powered through one of the toughest rides I've ever done. At one point, I ripped off every piece of metal on my body—my sunglasses, watch, and necklaces—because they were burning holes into me. I had to constantly pour water over my hand grips because they were too hot for me to hold, and even my iPhone had packed it in, saying it was too hot before switching itself off. I wish I could have done the same thing. Instead, I had one choice: *toughen up, princess!*

I was incredibly close to the end of my tether by the time I'd arrived at my destination—the aptly named Furnace Creek. The last half hour had been really tough—the temperature had risen to forty-nine, and as well as coping with the heat, I had a very real fear about Voodoo's capabilities.

I was the only one on the road (funnily enough), and the feeling of desolation was a little unsettling. I had to stop the conversations rolling around in my head. *When the Germans built this bike I know they built it for snow, but did they build it for deserts?* The last thing I needed was for Voodoo to overheat or blow a tire on the scorching griddles they called roads. I was pretty sure there wouldn't be a cavalry around to save me if she did.

But no—my Big Girl was amazing. She did her job effortlessly. I, on the other hand, took a hammering. On a bike in the sun, you conservatively add another five degrees to the outside temperature due to the additional heat coming off the bike, and my body count certainly reflected that.

My eyeballs already looked like beetroots after riding through smoke, but now they felt blistered and ready to peel. My legs were completely scorched by the sun—even in riding pants. They were burning so badly that I'd tried to protect them with my hands—an impossible feat when you can only use one hand at a time. My legs have never been my greatest feature, but they looked even more interesting with second degree burns.

I had to shut the cooling vents off in my boots because the hot air flowing through them started to cook my toes. This made my feet swell up an extra two sizes, and I needed a passing bellman to help me pull them off. My head looked like a melon—and not a cute, small one—I had scorch marks all over my body where metal objects had left huge burns, and my lips? Well, move over Mick Jagger. They looked as if they'd been flapping out a car window at 100 kph.

Back to my friend in the car park: was I insane? Oh, you bet!

But despite the battle scars, as I watched a brilliant orange sun drop slowly behind dusky purple mountains (from the air-conditioned luxury of my hotel room)—as I watched the desert in all its dark and moody splendour come alight in front of me—I knew it had been worth it.

But maybe not if my eyes peeled!

CHAPTER TEN

Death Valley to Moab, UT

DAYS 47–49: DEATH VALLEY TO VEGAS

My body took a couple of days in Death Valley to recover from the onslaught. Burnt bits, scorched bits, and dehydrated bits all competed for attention—demanding to be soothed, creamed, or watered, and usually all at the same time.

But my soul? My soul was healing beautifully.

I ran out into the darkness each morning to breathe into the desert. To feel the ferocious, dry heat right through my bones, reviving and restoring as it seeped deep into my body.

I ran to be in awe of the exquisiteness of the sunrise. To watch breathtaking colours light the sky as the desert awoke—a rising orange sun gently piercing the blueness of the night, turning the clouds a dusky pink, setting purple mountaintops aflame as the golden light hit their peaks.

I ran to have my senses ignited by the unforgiving beauty of the desert. To absorb the harsh starkness of the terrain—black, lunar, and cruel. To smell the brine as it rose from dry, unrelenting salt flats. To listen to the comforting silence of being alone, and to wonder at the contrasts: fragility and strength, bleakness and bounty, intensity and serenity.

I ran to feel insignificant. To feel lost in the timeless majesty of the Valley, where for millions of years, the world had stood still and nothing but the present mattered. To remind myself that the things that concerned me, frightened me, worried me today wouldn't mean a thing in the years to come.

In this vastness—in this extreme edge of nature—I knew I was healing. Nature didn't ask questions. It didn't have expectations or make demands. It just was. In nature, I got to just *be*—the real me, open-hearted and joyous. Free of the personas, the armour, and the paranoia. The desert didn't care if I hit targets or performed well. On this journey, nature was teaching me how to breathe. It was teaching me how to celebrate the simple—to find real joy in the smell of the earth or the fragility of a flower. It was teaching me to crack my heart wide open in gratefulness for the sheer beauty around me.

Six weeks ago, if anyone had told me I would find pure and complete happiness in the smell of pine needles, the colour of the redwoods, or the warmth of the sun, I would have laughed— and probably been a little concerned.

But slowly, slowly, the beauty of nature was healing me. I could feel it in my heart. I could feel it in my soul. I was letting go. I was accepting. I was moving forward.

THE WIDE VIEW

It was just as well, because I needed every ounce of serenity and sanity nature had to offer in order to survive Vegas. As much as

I wanted to avoid it, Vegas stood between me and the Grand Canyon. It was a necessary evil. (Isn't it always?)

I have an interesting perspective on Vegas. On a racetrack, we're taught to take a wide view—lift your head up, use your peripheral vision, and get a very broad view of the track. If you focus too acutely, everything happens fast—very fast—and that degree of speed can be dangerous and frightening.

In Vegas, I take a wide view. I see it from a distance and don't look closely at anything or it gets too intense. After the peace and tranquillity of the wide-open spaces, I braced for an assault on my senses, and it didn't disappoint! After a couple of days, I was ready for the ashram—ready to spend months in solitude and silence. But the craziness can be infectious.

After parking Voodoo outside my hotel the first night, it took me about thirty minutes to unload. Everyone from the valets to taxi drivers and hotel guests wanted to take pictures of Voodoo and talk about her. She was quite the celebrity. It's like when you're pregnant—for some reason, people think they have a proprietary right to rub your belly. Or they did with mine! In Vegas, it's as if everyone has the right to say whatever they want, as loudly as they want, and to take the high ground on any conversation.

My favourite was a very cool limo driver who pulled up alongside Voodoo and, in a strangled New York accent, threw at me:

"Damn, girl. Issat your bike? Now that's a might' fiiiine bike—you look like you stole it. You really ridin' that thing? Nah, what's a chicken like you doing ridin' a man's bike? You gotta get yourself a scooter y'hear? Wass your man saying about you ridin' dat thing? You allowed?"

In a three-minute conversation, he admired my bike, told me I didn't look like I could handle it, suggested I'd be better off on a girly bike, and decided I shouldn't be allowed out at all without my "man's" permission. Only in Vegas! (I hope?)

THE SISTERHOOD

And only in Vegas would your riding boots catapult you into people's lives. My riding boots are Sidis, and they're amazing. They're comfortable, they're cool looking (well, as cool as riding boots can be), they do the job day in and day out, and I love them to death...

But they squeak. The more dust I get in them, the worse they get.

As I stood in the queue at Whole Foods (plant-based heaven), a tall, elegantly dressed woman in front of me turned and said, "I heard you coming—you must be wearing Sidis. Mine are just as noisy!"

Yay! A sisterhood rider!

Between avocado and quinoa, we traded beliefs about what it

was like to ride as a woman and how easy it would have been to stay in our comfort zone—safe and secure and never knowing what we were capable of. We talked about negativity and that very early on—particularly as women—we learn to limit ourselves, our dreams, our beliefs, and our expectations. But somehow, on a bike, those limitations could be shattered.

Where did that come from? Who would have thought that standing in a queue at Whole Foods could have engendered such insightfulness, all in the space of about five minutes? As I wandered back to Voodoo, I was struck by the truth of our conversation. The only thing that limits us is ourselves. And yes, it's a hard pattern to break, but the possibilities are endless once we cut through our limiting negativity.

To seal the deal, she'd left a small piece of raw carrot cake in a brightly coloured box on Voodoo's seat with a beautiful card inviting me to be interviewed on the power of women for her magazine.

Now who would have thought—me, the masculine warrior, being comfortable talking about the power of women? Go figure!

WHAT HAPPENS IN VEGAS

But for all its fun and insanity, there's a darkness about Vegas—a heavy energy that I struggled with. I found it hard to walk through a hotel lobby at 6:30 in the morning to see the room packed with people desperately playing slot machines. At one point, I watched an elderly man, his eyes dull and listless, mechanically pump coin after coin into a machine. In his other hand, he held a cigarette and beer, which he alternately consumed by lifting his oxygen mask—the tank sitting alongside him.

And yet, there is incredible beauty. At the crack of dawn one morning, I headed out to Red Rock Canyon—a towering sandstone formation about fifteen miles west of Vegas, famous for the vivid, rich red of the rocks and its powerful peaks and canyons.

The plan was to run the breathtaking trail that went through, over, and around the canyon. That was the plan. Unfortunately, despite hating the stereotypical "Women can't navigate" profile, I had to accept that this woman actually can't.

I lost the trail within minutes and found myself high, dry, and stranded in a cactus bed, miles from anywhere.

I knew without a doubt that being so completely lost in the middle of the desert and without cell coverage, I'd certainly die of either heat exhaustion or dehydration within hours. Fortunately, once I'd stopped snivelling, I looked around and discovered I could actually see the road. (OK, so that was embarrassing!)

It was a perfect contrast of everything Vegas is—flashy but fabulous, brash but beautiful, wild but wonderful. *Only in Vegas, baby!*

DAY 50: LAS VEGAS TO THE GRAND CANYON

Riding out of Vegas was just as wild as staying in it: eight-lane highways, traffic jams, heat, and fumes. After the luxury of riding through gentle country towns and having the roads to myself over the past few weeks, I'd forgotten about the confrontation of big city living and the impact of peak-hour traffic. Within five minutes of leaving my hotel, I was on a freeway parking lot, surrounded by huge interstate trucks either side of me, and completely choked of movement.

Nothing like a spot of lane-splitting to get some forward motion. Lane-splitting is the art of making yourself as narrow as possible in order to suck it all in and ride between stopped or slow-moving traffic.

It's a fine art and one that requires fearlessness. You need to be able to ride a straight line at reasonable speed without wobbling or you'll collect the side mirrors or the doors of the vehicles alongside you. (Getting the death-wobbles between traffic never ends well!) It also requires a touch of foolhardiness, as you pray no one's going to decide to change lanes as you're coming through or open their car door to empty their ashtray while they're stationary.

Both have happened to me in the past, and it does make you a little gun shy. But the alternative is sitting in the heat, surrounded by fumes. So even though it's illegal in most states, the temptation to just get the hell out of Dodge and power through bumper-to-bumper traffic outweighs the risks every time.

ON THE FREEWAY

It was always going to be a long, hard haul heading east from Vegas to the Grand Canyon, so I'd braced myself for 500 tough kilometres of mainly highway riding.

Sometimes, if you need to crunch distance, there's no other choice but to slog it out on the freeway. But freeways take their toll. Being at speed on a highway for long periods of time is a physically demanding experience. It's the equivalent to being in the heavy-duty spin cycle of a washing machine.

There's very little protection on the freeway. No trees or mountain ranges to shield you from crosswinds, downdrafts, or the air foils that slide off the back of fast-moving trucks. You have a choice: you can go slow and be thrown around less for a longer period of time, or you can get into a tuck position behind your screen to stop the winds from turning you into a kite, put your head down, and be sucked into a vortex, but for a shorter period of time. A hell of a choice, really.

The wild winds that whipped across the flats made life intense as they threw me all over the road. It was diabolical riding, intensely physical, and more than a little scary. At one stage, it was so out of control that I was tempted to pull over, but what good would that do me? I'd still be in the middle of nowhere, I'd still have another 300 km to do, and there was no point just hoping the wind would drop. *Toughen up, princess. Get on with it!*

As I stopped for gas, a young guy I'd overtaken pulled up to the pump alongside me. He laughed as he got out of his car. Putting a comforting arm around my shoulder, he shook his head.

"Dude, that wind was giving you a kickass slap. I'm a rider. I know what that feels like. I've gotta say, you're a better man than me. I'd have packed up and gone home hours ago!"

I'm not sure I'm a better man, though I may be a dumber one. And "Dude?" How come I'm still such a man—is there nothing feminine about me?

Looking at myself in the bathroom mirror, I figured there probably wasn't. No amount of hair product or red lipstick was going to erase the look of having been through a wind tunnel. But I wore that look with honour. I'd had my ass kicked, and I'd survived.

INNER BEAUTY

With only 80 km to go, the traffic around me suddenly ground to a halt, and I found myself in a freeway parking lot waiting for an accident up ahead to clear. I was only 3 km from the turn off to the Grand Canyon—so close, but not close enough. With no other choice, I sat in the shade of a large truck and waited the ninety minutes it took to clear a fiery collision.

I was tempted to lane split and get ahead of the traffic, but my conscience kicked in and I decided—unusually—to suffer with the rest of my road colleagues.

Being stuck in the jam was like being in a circus as people around me did whatever they could to pass the time in the heat. Guys flew drones (really useful for keeping us updated from the front line), kids threw Frisbees, Harley riders cracked open beer (interesting choice!), and truck drivers sat in the shade playing cards together. They were obviously used to delays.

The enforced break gave me a chance to reflect on a chance encounter I'd had in Vegas the day before. When I'd arrived back from running Red Rock Canyon, I was dirty, sweaty, dusty, and above all, I smelt *really* bad. I was covered in grime from head to foot, and as I pulled my helmet off, it left a huge smear of blackness across my face. Fortunately, I didn't see that at the time.

Stepping off Voodoo, I was approached by a guy who looked like he was just about to play golf—crisp yellow polo shirt, chinos fully creased (who creases chinos?), and deck shoes that looked as if they'd never been to sea. To my embarrassment, he wanted to hear about my journey. *What, right now? I stink—can I at least have a shower first?* But no. In all my sweaty glory and in his pristine immaculateness, we sat on the curb and talked.

As was becoming the norm on this journey, the bond was instantaneous. For an hour, we talked about journeys, life, challenges, the fear of stepping forward. It was an intense conversation, honest and right from the heart. We laughed just like old friends—at ourselves, our lives, how ridiculous we looked—me in my filthy magnificence and him having just stepped out of a Ralph Lauren catalogue.

Eventually, the smell of my feet was too much even for me, and I stood up to excuse myself to take a much-needed shower. As we scrambled from the curb, my new friend gave me one of the most important presents I've ever received. He hugged me tight, saying I had beauty that came from my soul. He told me I radiated a powerful energy and that I needed to shine my bright light constantly for the outside world. (Commenting on my inner beauty was all he could probably say at the time, given the state of my outer beauty!)

Although in my heart, I knew what he said was true, in my head, I still struggled to believe it. Until today. It was interesting that yet again I needed external validation to help me really understand the point. But hey—whatever it takes to get the message through.

His words made a powerful impact on my heart and soul. True beauty has nothing to do with the external body. It simply comes from how you make people feel. If you can help someone feel positive, valued, or energised, you've achieved something amazing.

It's also up to you how you choose to radiate that beauty every day. I'd come to realise that the greatest gift I could give was my attention—to really listen. And the greatest gift I could receive was when someone told me I'd made their day, or they appreciated our conversation, or I'd inspired or challenged them to do something different.

When I'd made that connection with someone, it was the ultimate joy. Nothing felt better.

That connection is a conscious choice I have to make—not just every day, but with every opportunity I have to talk with someone. If I can't be bothered making the effort to connect, I get exactly the same energy back. The conversation becomes a transaction, not a connection. But when I make the conscious choice to connect? Everything changes. Even if the changes are tiny, life is never the same.

DENNIS CHANGED HIS LIFE

As if to reinforce that message, as I travelled the last 70 km, partially along the infamous Route 66, I met Dennis—an older guy from the UK who'd shipped his bike out from England and had been riding for seven months. There I was, all smug from having ridden from British Columbia, while he'd ridden in from Alaska and had camped the whole way.

He had a courageous story. His only son had been killed in Afghanistan five years ago, and he was riding to reconcile with his loss. Despite this, Dennis radiated such excitement and exhilaration, continually looking for the next adventure in life. His bike was painted in camouflage and was completely covered with photos and small mementoes from his son's life. It was a celebration of the beautiful son he'd lost, and of life—a constant reminder that life was precious and he needed to live it.

He was such a powerful example of consciously changing your story. I'm not sure how you could you ever turn the raw loss of a child into something positive and empowering. But Dennis did. After spending years in grief and in blackness, he'd decided to change his story into something meaningful and compelling.

In his inspiration, his dazzling light was shining so brightly I needed sunglasses. Together, we rode into the Grand Canyon—the rain was coming in sideways by the time we hit the village, but I couldn't wipe the smile from my face. Was there anything more beautiful than shining your light?

DAY 51: BRIGHT ANGEL TRAIL

In complete blackness the next morning, I crept out of my tiny hut on the outskirts of the Canyon rim. My pocket-sized cabin was basic—a bed, a chair and not much else—but it was a welcome relief after the excess of Vegas. It was just what my soul needed—to sit in simplicity and absorb the lessons I'd been given over the past few days.

At five in the morning, I headed for the trail. I'd watched the sun set over the rim the night before and had been mesmerised by its intense beauty. But today, I didn't just want to be an observer. I wanted to immerse myself in the canyon—of course, on the Bright Angel Trail. (Could there have been a more appropriately named trail after the past few days?)

It was a challenging trail—no surprises there. It was 19 km there and back, from the Grand Canyon rim to Indian Camp, then onto Plateau Point, which literally dropped into the Colorado River.

The good news was that this beautiful trail was downhill all the way—a 3,000-metre drop in elevation.

The bad news was that it was uphill all the way home.

DEEP IN THE CANYON

It was cold as I headed out, and the sky was still blue-black, but I wanted to be deep in the canyon for the sunrise. In total darkness, I "felt" my way down the trail for the first few miles, leaning onto the rock walls to make sure I didn't lose my balance and topple into the abyss below.

True to form, being geographically and navigationally challenged, I hadn't worked out that the sun would rise on the other side of the canyon (the sun rises in the east and sets in the west, remember?). So I missed the sunrise completely. But the Universe took pity on my blondness. Instead of a sunrise, I got the heart-stopping beauty of the sun bouncing golden rays of light onto the mountains in front of me. (Hah, not so blond after all!)

As the sun slowly rose (behind me), I got to see into the canyon for the first time. It stopped me in my tracks. Firstly, because I suddenly realised how incredibly steep the side drop-off was, and I'd been walking by Braille for about an hour. But secondly, because I'd never been surrounded by such depth of awesomeness.

When you see the Canyon from the top of the rim, the immensity is almost overwhelming. But when you're right in the middle of it, surrounded on all sides by such incredible majesty, you get a different perspective on just how magnificent this wonder of nature truly is.

To be able to touch the canyon as I walked—feel the coolness of the rocks, the sharpness of their edges, inhale their damp scent—it was sheer joy. A couple of times, I was so overwhelmed I actually kissed the rocks—I was so excited to have them at my fingertips. (It's OK, I was the only one on the trail.)

I was so grateful to be there and to be able to catch the morning light as it came up through the canyon. The colours changed constantly as the sun hit the mountains—a full spectrum of rich reds, vibrant oranges, deep purples, and buttercup yellows. And this intense, fiery beauty was all mine. There wasn't another soul on the track as I walked down, down, down in complete solitude. It was just me and the Canyon, the sunlight, and the wind—and together we made a great team as I headed towards the Colorado River.

I hadn't had a good record on being present during my big nature hikes. So far, the score was Mountains: 2, Me: 0. But today was different. Today, I appreciated the grandeur and majesty of the journey and let the canyon and this experience seep deep into my bones.

When I finally reached the Colorado River, I found a ledge that hung right out over the drop-off (I had to remind myself that I was brave—bloody hell it was a long way down). Completely alone, in the warmth of a golden sun, I pulled out breakfast—a rich, ripe peach. Below me, the majestic river in all its brown, muddy glory, carved its way through the canyon, breathing life into the harsh, beautiful terrain. Surrounded by more majesty than I could ever have imagined, I felt like a tiny dot on this vast and imposing landscape. But I also felt peace—real peace.

I sat dangling my feet over the edge for about half an hour, thinking about how much my life—my values—had changed in fifty short days. In the past, my values had been hard-edged—adrenaline, challenge, pushing boundaries—but as I careered through the canyon, I realised that the shoots of new values that I'd recognised in Longview were actually beginning to blossom.

Without needing to be true to anyone but me, I'd been able to give space for new values to emerge. Connection, growth and learning, freedom and inspiration. I was grateful for the lessons this trip had given me every day. In the sunshine, I smiled. But not for long.

BACK UP THE TRAIL

Life was very different coming up the trail. By now it was busy, and the hard slog began—step after step, always onward, always up! The trail was littered with packs of mules carrying smug passengers (they were riding after all) that took up the whole trail. The mules I didn't mind, but their continual "catering off-loads" I did. The smell was strong enough to singe my eyeballs!

On breathlessly reaching the top—my lungs burning and my thighs exploding with pain—I found a quiet rock in the shade, away from the chaos, and just sat. In less than two months, my life had changed dramatically. The speed of change actually scared me. I felt like I couldn't keep up. Some days it felt like I was almost overtaking myself, and I had no idea who I would be at the finishing line.

In some ways, it was daunting to say goodbye to some of my old values. I had no idea where these new values were going to lead me, but I guessed it was going to be another amazing adventure.

The thought of letting my warrior go completely had been

terrifying, but I figured she would never leave me completely. The trick would be to use her by choice, rather than as a default.

But there was no point worrying about the future—what would come would come. And right now? Right now was magic, and I was at peace in my soul.

DAY 52: GRAND CANYON TO ZION

When I awoke the next morning, I felt anxious—concerned yet again about what happens at the end of all this. The future demanded attention. It wanted to agitate me. No matter how hard I tried to ignore that fear, it still came out of nowhere and tried to bite me. Today, it latched on hard.

I needed to focus on the journey—to make amazing connections, to reach out and be a spark in people's lives. To have my eyes open in wonderment, and to inspire and be inspired. *Yep, I knew that.* Expecting this journey to give me all the answers created unnecessary pressure. *Yep, I knew that.* I needed to abandon my commitment to knowing what the future held and just focus being present to allow freedom, expression, and inspiration to come through. *Yep. I knew that, too!*

Yet despite that insight and knowledge, the fear of the unknown future still rose up every now and then. This morning, it erupted like a volcano.

THE CARPENTER IN THE CAR PARK

Holding my fear next to my heart (if I didn't know what to do with it I was going to keep it safe by holding it close), I headed out to the car park to gear up. With the Leaning Tower of Pisa almost assembled, I suddenly felt someone at my shoulder. Alongside me stood a handsome young guy with long blond hair escaping from a ponytail and tattoos covering his arms. He had literally come from nowhere.

His story drew me in. He'd been a carpenter for most of his life, but despite having created a successful business, he'd felt empty. Despite flak from everyone around who believed he was crazy, he'd walked away from his profession and his old world. Overnight, he went travelling—becoming an artist, a jewellery maker, and a musician. He'd found it impossible to ignore the calling of his soul and chose to live the life that was true to him. Not the life others expected of him.

He explained that he had no idea what the future would hold, but that he was OK with not knowing. There were things he wanted to achieve—he'd let the Universe know what he wanted and was now surrendering to the journey. The future would unfold as it was meant to. So he'd let go of the pressure of needing answers. Knowing the destination wasn't important. Immersing himself in the present—being alive and awake to everything around him—that was important. If he gave into fear about the future, he'd miss out on the gift that life was creating for him right now.

Are you serious? In my fear of the unknown future panic, this is the message I get—from an unknown carpenter who just appeared alongside me in a car park?

At the end of our chat, we hugged long and tight, and he literally disappeared back into the woods. Out of nowhere, just when I needed it most, I'd received the most powerful message. Let go of fear. Surrender and just focus on the present. Focus on the life I'm living right now, on this incredible experience. It wasn't that I couldn't think about the future, but I didn't need to worry about not having the answers. Being present would allow space for expression and inspiration to come.

But where had this message come from? And how?

I could no more explain the most perfect message I'd received today than I could explain why my husband Robbie was still alive.

PINS AND NEEDLES

When our boys were small—Jakey was two and Connor was just six months old—my healthy, athletic, non-smoking, non-drinking husband (OK, I'm not counting the occasional glass of red wine) decided to die.

OK, he didn't decide to. His body did.

The night before, he'd been fine. We'd been out to dinner, and he'd been his usual cheeky, irreverent self. There was nothing to indicate how dramatically our lives would implode over the next few hours—except for my dark premonition. Gazing at my sleeping boys as I thought about how blessed we were, I was suddenly overwhelmed with foreboding that something in our perfect lives was about to go desperately wrong.

It did. Early the next morning, Robbie woke, and in barely a whisper, he uttered just one word: "Pins." We were in trouble. His face was a clammy, ashen grey, his body completely bathed in sweat.

Somewhere in the place you store useless information, I remembered that pins and needles in your arm was the sign of a heart attack. But that made no sense. He was thirty-eight—strong, vital, and ridiculously healthy. Robbie would be the last person in the world to have a heart attack. It just wasn't possible. And yet...

In cold, calm fear, I asked, "Have you got pins and needles in your arm?"

With his eyes closed, barely moving, he gave the tiniest of nods—and so began our journey into darkness.

It was 6:00 a.m., and I figured I could get to the hospital faster than the ambulance could get to us. Scooping my sleeping babies out of the warmth of their beds, I threw them into their car seats and half-dragged, half-carried Robbie out to the car. By the time I got into third gear, he was unconscious in the front seat.

With Robbie in my arms, I ran into Emergency screaming for help. Even as I said it—"I think my husband is having a heart attack"—I still didn't believe it could be true. I almost expected they'd give him something for indigestion, slap me for being a panic merchant, and send us back home. But no.

Within seconds, the empty ER burst into life. People came running from everywhere, and Robbie was frantically whisked away from me. Cold, alone, and terrified, I stood in the ER and listened to the desperate attempts to bring him back to life.

My boys were still in the back of my car—fast asleep, completely oblivious to the devastation that had just struck our world. I carried them into the ER, barely able to breathe.

Moments later, as I stood breastfeeding a tiny Connor with Jakey playing with blocks at my feet, a young doctor broke the news. "You'd better come in and say goodbye. He's not going to make it."

There was only one answer to that.

"We're coming in, but we're not saying goodbye. He's not going anywhere, so get your ass back in there and fix him. Now!"

He went back.

Weeks later, when I met up with this unfortunate recipient of my wrath, we hugged tight and laughed hard, reliving my tirade. He figured Robbie didn't have a hope in hell of surviving, but he knew better than to argue with a mother breastfeeding a baby!

Behind the screen, the team working on Robbie had all but given up. As they'd tried to stabilise him for surgery, he'd had heart attack after heart attack. For nearly two hours, he'd been classed as clinically dead. There was an occasional blip on the monitor, but his heart had otherwise stopped beating. Despite many of the team wanting to call it—to pronounce him dead—the head heart surgeon had seen the boys and me and told the team he wasn't prepared to come and tell *that mother and her tiny boys* that they'd lost him. So they kept going.

Thank God.

His heart suddenly kicked back in, and they rushed Robbie to surgery. He was given the almost impossible odds of a 2 percent survival rate. For a couple of weeks, we lived in a chasm of darkness. While Robbie's life hung in the balance, another fear had emerged. Even if his body survived, would his brain be irreversibly damaged after having been "dead" for two hours? There was nothing we could do but hope and wait.

Robbie defied medical history. As they brought him out of his induced coma, I held his hand, desperate for any sign that his brain was still active. They'd tested him while he'd been in a coma, and the results had not been good.

My own heart almost stopped when his eyes fluttered open. He slowly turned his head to me and asked quizzically, "What happened? Where am I?"

"Baby, you had a heart attack."

"No shit. Really? Was it serious?"

Was it serious? Spare me!

We learnt, much later, that Robbie's heart attack had been caused by a rare blood disease. To this day, the doctors couldn't explain how he survived. Or how his brain hadn't been irreparably damaged after having been starved of oxygen for two hours. (I've noticed damage—usually, when I ask him to buy toilet paper, he says he "forgets.") The doctors have no idea. They don't even have a theory other than quietly chalking it up to a miracle. They've tried to replicate what happened with Robbie in other emergency situations, but the patients have never survived. Yet Robbie did, and we'll never know how.

There are some things in this world we're not meant to understand—things like quantum physics and black holes. (OK, maybe we're meant to understand them, but I'm not capable of it.)

I can't explain how Robbie cheated death, and I can't explain how a blond-haired, tattooed angel dropped in this morning to give me the message I desperately needed to hear. Sometimes, all you can do is hold the miracle in your heart, wrap it in love and light, say thank you, then get on your bike and ride.

Late in the afternoon, we pulled into Zion National Park in the southwest of Utah. It was close to dark, but I still couldn't resist a quick delve into the park to breathe in its awesomeness. As the shimmering orange sun slipped behind the majestic cream, red, and pink sandstone cliffs that towered more than 600 metres above me, I held my breath and softly whispered, "Thank you."

Another miracle.

DAY 53: ZION

I had always wanted to experience Zion. For years, its raw beauty had held me in its spell, and I had the perfect vision of how our first encounter would be.

I would run Zion. I saw myself—graceful as an antelope—running like the wind in the early morning light. Golden, yellow light would bounce off the dusky red canyons as this 250-million-year-old world slowly opened its eyes. I would wind my way through tight canyons as I traversed up hills and over streams, running trails of yellow and red dust.

I felt myself soaking up the silence, deeply connected to the beauty of nature around me—in complete awe of its magnificence. My heart would be cracked open. It would be both spiritual and physical at the same time—an experience that would stay with me my whole life. Just me, complete silence, and the awesomeness of Zion.

I'd held that dream in my mind for a long, long time—I just needed to turn it into reality. My trail of choice? Angels Landing—considered to be one of the top three trails for both beauty and challenge. Perfect! Just after 6:00 a.m., I walked to the trailhead shuttle to find the queue already trailing out of the park.

Are you serious? Who are all these tourists and what are they all doing up at this hour? Didn't they know I want peace, tranquillity, and serenity? I've got a dream to manifest!

Two buses later, jammed in like a chicken on a battery farm (another good reason to be plant-based), I was dropped at the start of the trail along with everyone else on the double-trailered shuttle.

WE'RE IN IT TOGETHER

It was chaos. It would have been easier to elbow your way through the Boxing Day sales than to get started on the trail. Runners pushing to the front, hiking hellions randomly waving poles, backpackers carrying enough food for a zombie apocalypse, people playing music at a deafening volume (Where are your headphones, people?), elderly people on walking frames (OK, that was impressive), and one guy lugging a five-litre container of water for a four-hour hike. (Always take your hydration seriously.)

Somewhere in the middle of this zoo, I still held onto that dream of mine—of flying up the canyon, light on my feet. (OK, that *was* a dream and was never going to happen!) Of having the place to myself, being bathed in golden light, and experiencing the heaven, the peace, and the tranquillity of the canyon *all to myself.*

Think again, baby.

After a tiny temper tantrum at the bottom of the climb—it was tiny, but definitely a tantrum—I had to rethink my dream. What do you do when you suddenly realise your dream isn't going to become a reality? You change your dream, of course! Instead of it being about me, I had to work with what was around me: a mass of humanity, all looking for the same experience.

A friend had asked me a few days earlier what gifts I brought to the world. Tough question. It rolled around in my helmet for days as I searched for clarity. Interestingly, it felt that my gifts had changed since the first day Voodoo and I had wobbled out of town. What I gave to the world two months ago was probably very different to what (I hoped) I gave now.

After serious consultation with myself—sometimes it's hard being the only voice in your helmet—I decided my two gifts were connectivity and inspiration. This was the perfect opportunity to test that theory.

Instead of trying to break all land speed records (as per my usual *modus operandi*) and instead of being frustrated with people slowing me down on the trail, I would use the opportunity to chat and encourage people as I ran.

When you put the energy out there, it always comes back double.

I ran with three guys in their early thirties who had nineteen kids between them (good Mormon boys). I ran with a serious ultra-marathon runner who blitzed up the canyon and left me in her dust (maybe she was the one I'd seen in my dreams and it wasn't me at all). There was a guy who'd invented spy-monitoring for the US Air Force (that was all he would tell me!). It was exhilarating. (Maybe I'd gotten the gift thing wrong—maybe *inspiration* was what other people gave me instead of the other way around.)

The running was tough. It was straight up, with twenty-seven tight switchbacks that sorted the men from the boys. Unfortunately, I fell into the "boys" category. I figured if I kept lifting my knees it would still be classified as running. *Yep, still dreaming.* It was more like walking on my toes, but hey—I was moving.

At the bottom of a steep vertical climb, a small group had started to cluster. The climbing wasn't challenging, but we were high and the drop-off was reasonably terrifying. People were stalled, frightened to climb any higher. As a team, we had to get the whole group moving or none of us were going to get to the top.

What a treat it was to watch a group of strangers work together to help each other achieve their goals. That alone was worth letting go of my dream. And the view from the landing was magnificent. It wasn't quite the solo experience I'd envisaged—it was pretty crowded up there. But it was crowded with my inspiring new friends, and that just made it all the more perfect. And so, the dream didn't become a reality. The run I'd pictured in my head for years dissolved in front of me, but in so many ways, it was even better. I'd connected with amazing people while surrounded by majesty and beauty that took my breath away.

I've learnt on this journey (usually the hard way): things don't always go to plan. I can't control the plan, but I can control how I react. My tantrum at the bottom hadn't been pretty, but after a shakedown, I changed the story. I changed how I wanted to react, and voila! A new and improved dream had appeared. Amazing.

DAY 54: ZION TO BRYCE

The Universe must have decided I'd learnt my lesson, and in its infinite wisdom, the next morning gave me the run I'd held in my heart for years. It's amazing—when you detach yourself from how something should be, you end up getting what you're meant to get.

Early the next morning, I decided to forgo the trails and their assorted masses and to run through the park. In complete darkness, I ran a ribbon of road that wove its way through the canyons, slowly climbing dizzying switchbacks until I reached the peak.

It was glorious. As the sun eased over the top of these magical cliffs, I realised I was living my dream. The canyons exploded in golden yellow as sunlight bounced off the red mountaintops. As I watched, the colours changed in front of my eyes—muted purple and taupe became fiery ochre and orange, the mountains ablaze with colour. It was everything I'd imagined it to be.

But there was something about the sheer magnitude of Zion that overwhelmed me. Even after my dream-come-true run, I felt disoriented, disconnected from myself. From the beauty around me, from people. Worse, I felt disconnected from my journey.

It felt like I was just going through the motions. Run, beautiful place, ride, run, beautiful place, ride. *What the hell was I doing here?* Yet again, "Big Nature" had struck. Where did this blackness come from? Did it just sit in the back of my head, waiting for the perfect opportunity to strike? I'd just had the most perfect morning, but not even that was going to save me. I felt completely adrift.

I needed to wrestle back control. That would save me. I needed firm ground underneath me—to know exactly where I was headed—to have a clear direction to aim for. Forget all this surrender and trust crap. Take me back to goals and objectives. I wanted my old world back—the one where I was in charge and called all the shots.

Really? How well has that worked for you?

Oh. Damn.

As much as I wanted the safety of my old life, deep down I knew it hadn't worked for me, that it would never work for me again. As much as I wanted control, I had to let it go. A great teacher had taught me that it was OK to feel like crap—but only for five minutes. After that, it was self-indulgent.

Having stepped well into the "self-indulgent" state, I needed to step back into my journey—to re-engage and reconnect. Breathe.

Does this ever get any easier? Do I have to keep showing up, doing the work? I'm tired of growing. Can't I just go out and ride?

Apparently not!

Being a slow learner, I kept getting the same lessons—again and again. And today? When all else fails, step back into gratitude. I was beginning to learn (not quickly enough, obviously) that gratitude was a practice. You have to work on it every single day. The more you practice it, the easier it gets. It wasn't enough to just think about gratitude. To really feel it in my soul and for it to turn me around, I had to consciously express it.

Large black coffee in hand, I shook myself out, and I wrote.

I'm grateful for the amazing connections I make every day. I'm grateful that I get to create a living masterpiece every day. I'm grateful that I get to ride a beautiful, mind-blowing piece of machinery. I'm grateful for the freedom, the opportunity, and the incredible adventures that this journey brings.

Kinda hard to be disconnected after that. It's amazing what a little alignment will do for you.

For good measure—just in case my gratitude slipped out from underneath me as I rode—I decided to nail the day by setting three kickass intentions: to connect with everyone around me, to feel joy in the beauty of nature, and to be grateful for this incredible journey.

TOOK ME LONG ENOUGH

Before I could leave, I had unfinished business with Zion. I needed to make peace—to find that connection. Pulling Voodoo into the shade of a deep red canyon, I finally worked it out. The trick with Zion was the opposite of Vegas and its wide view.

Trying to comprehend the magnitude of its beauty was just too overwhelming.

Instead, the answer was to narrow my focus. Concentrate on one structure at a time and give it my total attention. Rock face by rock face, I examined the striations, the colours, the sharpness of the cliff face. The vegetation desperately clinging to the rock face trying to eke out life. The weathering. The cracks and the crevices.

Finally, finally I got it. The pure majesty of Zion. The depth of its awesomeness. I got my connection—spiritual and emotional. Took me long enough.

It's amazing—when you set intentions, how opportunities come out of the woodwork. The first was a young guy who had discovered me on Instagram—he messaged later that day saying he'd been so inspired by my journey that he'd packed up and hit the road himself. He wanted to thank me for giving him the courage to step into the unknown. *Intention one: check.*

I almost felt guilty about my second intention. It was impossible *not* to feel joy in the beauty of nature as I rode to Bryce. After travelling peacefully through gentle pastures and grasslands, I took a left on Highway 12 and instantly found myself in the limestone wonderland of Red Canyon, surrounded on either side by brilliant red, orange, vermillion hoodoos catching the afternoon sun. *Heaven: check.*

At dusk, I settled into the comfort of my tiny wooden cabin in Bryce. A podcast I'd listened to that morning had talked about not having the courage to realise our dreams. They said, "People dream about riding a motorbike across the US, but who actually does it?"

Me. That's who.

And I'm so very grateful. *Intention three?* A resounding *check!*

DAY 55: BRYCE TO CAPITOL REEF

Utah is known as the land of the dinosaurs, and it'd take me a million years to be able to absorb and explain the incredible brilliance I experienced. It's a very different kind of beauty to the gentle beauty of BC and Alberta or the harsh desert beauty of Nevada and Arizona. It doesn't have the vibrancy of Oregon and California. It's stark, dynamic, and overpowering. It stops you dead in your tracks, makes your eyes pop in wonderment, and shocks in its intensity.

Travelling from the red-pink hoodoos of Bryce Canyon to the fierce majesty of Capitol Reef had been truly sublime. I tried desperately to capture it, to hold it forever in my memory bank.

No fifteen minutes had been the same. The terrain, hues, and formations changed constantly, creating total sensory overload. Salmon pink rocks turned red with a touch of putty, then putty with a touch of red, then vermillion, then chocolate, and then the whole colour spectrum started again. Rich, red hoodoos gave way to stark vertical walls of muted grey, which then transformed into russet pinnacles and spires—all encased in the distance by giant pink and purple turrets that looked like slowly eroding castles from a fairy story.

It felt as if I'd stepped back in time as I made my way through this prehistoric landscape. I felt insignificant and small—unable to influence anything around me, and yet still integral.

Through the pass, an eagle soared above my head, tracking me as I rode. His wingspan completely blocked the sun, casting a deep shadow over me as he flew. For minutes, we travelled in parallel together—him in majestic ease, and me in complete awe.

SCOTT IN THE BLACK RV

A day of contrasts, of incredible beauty—but what day would be complete without crazy connections? Pulling up for gas just outside Escalante, I was followed in by a huge black RV. As it came to a halt alongside me, the doors burst open and three excited middle-aged ladies jumped out and ran over to me.

"We've found you! We've found you! We've been tailing you for days. We saw you at the Grand Canyon, we saw you in Zion and in Bryce. We've been watching out for you the whole time and here you are!" (Remind me not to take the scenic route next time!)

Not quite sure where this was heading, I introduced myself and Voodoo. It wasn't often I was stalked, but as strange as it was, I figured I was safe with three older ladies! As it turned out, they weren't procuring me for themselves—they told me that Scott was desperate to meet me.

Scott? Who the hell was Scott?

Scott belonged to one of the ladies—an ex-professional bike racer who'd been desperate to talk to me about my journey. Unfortunately, he was currently asleep in the back of the RV. (Who can sleep in the back of an RV?) Not to be deterred, his wife gave him a shove, and within minutes, we were camped around the coffee pot exchanging stories about bikes and life on the road.

Scott and the ladies weren't my only new friends that day. Later, coming into Capitol Reef, I pulled into an overlook, blown away by the glory of everything below me. As I stood, breathless in awe, a scruffy dude on a Harley pulled in alongside me. In companionable silence, we leaned on our bikes looking out at the valley below.

Quietly, he reached into his side bag and pulled out two bananas. Without a word, he passed one to me. Together we ate—the only thing said was, "Thanks." Sometimes, words just aren't necessary.

DAY 56: CAPITOL REEF TO MONTICELLO

The next morning, the great gas game was about to get serious. Voodoo and I were staring down the barrel of a 210 km stretch without a gas station. For once, it wasn't even a question of whether or not the gas station would be open or whether or not a tanker had come through. In between Hanksville and Monticello, there was nothing but tumbleweeds—not a gas station in sight. Could I nurse Voodoo through? She was good for about 200 km depending on how I rode her, but 210? There was only one way to find out.

Some things just don't bear worrying about. I'd be in serious trouble if we ran out of gas in the middle of the desert, but after having decided to go for it, there wasn't much more I could do. I handed it over to the Universe and went for a run.

SO, WHAT DO YOU DO?

The seasons were changing. The days were getting shorter, mornings were staying darker, and it was now cool until lunchtime. There were reports of snow in Wyoming and Montana, and although that filled me with more than a little apprehension, I'd worry about that if or when it became an issue. Nothing like sticking my head in the sand (or in the snow, as it later turned out).

For now, I ran—into the blackness of a purple-blue sky and out through the canyons. I could barely see the road in front of me, the sky was so dark. Slowly, the light began to change. Behind me, pink clouds started to build up as the sun eased over the mountains, sending slivers of yellow light behind the black clouds. Within minutes, the canyons were completely illuminated, set aglow with the golden rays bouncing off the mountains.

Once I could see more than three steps in front of me, I braved the off-road and headed into the rich red dirt of the canyons. I clamoured over big fat boulders and wound my way through sharp spires and beehive hoodoos. It felt as if the world had been created in just three bands of colour—the red of the earth, the purple of the mountains, and the yellow gold of the peaks and sky.

I had no idea where I was going or how long I'd be out. I just ran. The only sound I could hear was the pounding of my heart and my shallow, ragged breath as I pushed up the hills. (Man, I was seriously out of shape!) I eased my tired body down onto a forgiving boulder. Breathless but content, I looked at the desert around me. Sometimes it still surprised me to find myself completely alone in the middle of raw nature with nothing but my running shoes to get me home.

Less than three months ago, my shoes had been eight-inch stilettos, and the only thing I navigated was the way to the dry cleaners. The changes to my life and to me in such a short period of time still shocked me. There are times now when I almost don't recognise the person who first threw her leg over Voodoo and wobbled off down the road in fear. I'm sure, sitting here covered in rich red dirt, not many other people would recognise me either. Maybe that was a good thing!

So if I wasn't that person anymore, who was I now? Sitting on my comfortable rock in the cool of the morning, I pondered the great mysteries of the universe—or at least the answer to that question. I figured they were probably one and the same.

I used to have a place in this world. A title, a flashy business card that told people I was successful. It said, "Get out of my way—I'm someone to be reckoned with." (Well, probably only in my dreams, but sadly, flaunting it gave me much-needed validation.) If I had a kickass business card, then I was a kickass legend. And in my own head, I was.

People continually asked me on the road, "So, what do you do?" It was a qualifier. It let them know where I belonged in this world. For the first few weeks on this journey, I went straight into the story that had always kept me safe—the one that let people know that although I was cruising on a motorbike, I was still a serious player.

"Well, I have a business...it's five companies, blah blah blah..." But eventually, I realised two things. Number one: they didn't care. Number two: neither did I! It stunned me to realise I was telling the old story out of habit, and that finally—after years of clinging to it—external validation just wasn't important to me. Who'd have thought?

In the middle of the Utah desert, caked in red dust and sweat and surrounded by cacti, the only card to my name was a credit card (OK, I had a couple just in case I lost one). My business card was long gone. So now the answer was simply, "Right now, I don't do anything. I'm just adventuring." It doesn't have quite the same clout as my previous titles. It doesn't open doors or let me be smug knowing I'm doing something "grown-up." But it does give me incredible joy, freedom, and complete release from title-tyranny. My business card is just that: a card, a piece of paper. It's not who I am, and it feels amazing!

SOMEONE NEW

Letting go of my title also released me from the fanatical need to achieve—to set goals, to blast objectives, and to smash targets. Both my boys were born on the day they were due. It's pretty unusual for that to happen once, let alone twice. The general consensus from my team was that my boys were both scared of not hitting their "On-Time Arrival Targets." I laughed...kind of. Looking back, I wasn't sure I really liked the old me. She sounded diabolical.

But she was who she needed to be at the time. Being that person had gotten her to where and who she was. Now, however, I had a choice. I could stay with her in all her pain and glory, or I could honour her, be thankful for how she'd gotten me here, and then carefully put her away while I stepped forward in my new skin. New skin trumps a business card any day!

Leaving a big part of my old self in the desert, Voodoo and I rode out into the visual overload of Capitol Reef. Red, ochre, white, vermillion, putty, yellow, green—sometimes colours on their own, sometimes together—combined with spires, hoodoos, massive amphitheatres, castles in the sky, flat tops, flat lands, fertile pastures, harsh desert...It was a day of greatness and grandeur as we criss-crossed the inimitable Colorado River.

THE GREAT GAS GAME

Hanksville was the last gas stop before the 210 km Gas Game, and a group of riders—all squeezing the last bit of gas into their tanks—weighed into the great "Will you/won't you make it?" debate. It didn't exactly fill me with confidence when, after hearing I was heading to Monticello, they all said, "Are you serious? On that bike? Are ya gonna make it?"

Not what I needed to hear!

The general consensus was that I should go for it, despite horror stories about those who'd "gone for it" and run out of gas in the desert. But you can't take the risk out of the risk-taker (or something), and I didn't want to carry fuel. Oregon had made me nervous about crossing very hot deserts with a loaded bomb of gas on board.

Filling Voodoo up within an inch of her life, I switched her into "rain" mode and decided to go for it.

But suddenly, liquid began spewing out of her. My heart was in my mouth. It looked black—like oil. Not a good position to be in as you're about to head into the desert. As always, I had five different opinions about what it was...but it turned out to be gas. I'd overfilled her, and fuel had come out of the release tank. *Goose! Had me worried there for just a minute.*

I should have had more faith in my amazing Voodoo.

She rolled easily and seamlessly through the harsh Utah desert—fuel-fat and in defiance of her very precise German tech specs. She didn't even hit her reserve tank. Sometimes I wonder whether she plays with my head just because she can.

She certainly has a personality and a following all her own, my Big Girl. As I pulled into Needles, a couple in an RV asked if they could take a photo. *Sure! Oh really? Just Voodoo? Not with me?*

You'd think after two months I'd be used to her being the celebrity of our team. But today, she did me proud, and I was only too happy to let her take the glory.

DAY 57: MONTICELLO TO MOAB

Monticello was in the middle of nowhere. It was a truck stop smack bang at the intersection between I-191 and I-491. There was a main street, a bunch of no-name hotels and gas stations, a supermarket, and not much else. It was a characterless little town, but that was OK. It was just a pit stop on the way to Moab, and for one night, I could do with "uneventful." I should have known better than to make that assumption after everything I've learnt on this trip.

I woke up the next morning feeling flat. Sometimes, I forget just how physical this journey is. Managing 210 kgs of high-performance machinery, hour after hour, when your feet don't touch the ground (not that I put them down while we're riding)—putting her through her paces in every kind of weather and terrain imaginable (yesterday we had hail, and man that hurt)... it takes its toll.

If there's even the tiniest incline, she's almost impossible to manoeuvre when I'm parking her (that's the issue with not being able to touch the ground). If there's dirt or gravel, she slides from under me. And the daily process of humping bags, loading bags, unloading bags, re-humping bags is demanding. Not to mention the omnipresent pressure of navigation to make sure I'm in Monticello and not Montana. Not that I was complaining—but as a short, small bundle of contradiction, I sometimes got tired. (I can't even believe I've admitted that. See ya later, Superhero!)

Waking at my truck-stop hotel room, one eye opened cautiously and looked around. Riding boots, helmet, jacket—damn. I was still on the road. And I didn't want to be. I wanted to be somewhere warm and smelling of pine while a Swedish Viking called Sven massaged hot oil onto my aching body. *Yeah, right. What miracle was going to make that happen in the middle of I-191?*

However, when I stopped grizzling, I did find another miracle. Right across the road was an amazing juice and raw food restaurant. *Go figure.* Not quite Sven, but it'd do! Gearing up, I rode all of the twenty-two metres to the other side of the road, parked Voodoo, and headed in for some green magic.

BRAZILIAN BOYS

While lovingly nursing my fresh green juice, I thought about energy. A friend had reminded me pointedly that I needed to consciously put positive energy out into the world every day. *I know, I know, I know. But can I just have one day off? Can I just have one day where I keep all my energy to myself?*

Apparently not. As I struggled with the decision to put it all out there or hold it all back, the doors of the juice bar burst open and in walked six Brazilian dirt-bike riders—scruffy, dirty, and chaotic—with enough energy to power a solar plant.

Their English was worse than my Portuguese, but we sat together as riders for forty-five minutes, trading bike stories through hand gestures, Instagram, and by drawing pictures on serviettes. I couldn't understand a word they said except for "louco," which they called me after they realised I'd been on Voodoo for eight weeks on my own. Their cheekiness and pure joy for life was infectious.

They'd given me an energy injection right into my butt, and it was time to put it to good use.

Heading out towards Canyonlands felt strange. For days, I'd been surrounded by huge monoliths. The rainbow of sandstone formations was somehow comforting when I rode. There was a security in their magnificence, and I loved not knowing what structure or colour I'd see next—a continuous birthday party where the presents never stopped. *My kinda party!*

But today the towering rocks disappeared, and in their place was...nothing. Zip. The road was as flat as a pancake and just about as boring. Then suddenly, after a quick left turn, the road dropped thousands of metres, and we fell into the most awe-inspiring canyons imaginable. We'd been riding on the top of the rim, and all the wonder lay thousands of metres below us. Flat-topped mesas the colour of chocolate, huge monoliths that looked like the Acropolis on steroids sitting atop massive weathered rock, horizontal striations with vertical columns, fins, arches, and towering pinnacles—all carved by the glorious Colorado River that wound its way along the base.

For extra excitement, we got to experience Utah's backroads at their finest. In order to terrorise the local cow population and unsuspecting motorbike riders, unmarked cattle grids littered the road.

Now, being unmarked wasn't a problem for cattle. They can't read the signs anyway. But for bike riders, it was a nightmare.

Hitting a cattle grid at speed usually means losing both your bike and your dignity as you fly through the air—usually separately—before trying to land the bike squarely in order to not spear into the bushes. Not pretty.

To add insult to injury, road cracks in Utah were filled with thick, black tar strips that looked suspiciously like liquorice. That may be fine when you're in a car, but on two wheels, it's like riding on an ice rink. The ultimate adrenaline rush was to come 'round a corner to find a cattle grid right in the middle of it laced with liquorice strips on the other side. I'm sure I provided maximum entertainment for the people behind us.

GIVE ME ALL YOU'VE GOT

Canyonlands gave me a day of almost unspeakable beauty and majesty. But as incredible as it was, the true magic of the day was how I connected when I decided finally to put the energy out there. It's funny—I knew it was a conscious choice to shine bright, but despite knowing how amazing it would make my day, sometimes I fought it.

There were days where I just wanted to sit alone and unbothered in the darkness of a coffee shop. There were days when I wanted to pull into a gas station and not have to engage, to not be peppered by the same questions over and over again. There were days when I just wanted to ride and be left alone. (OK, maybe just minutes, not days. But they were there.)

Ideally, I'd wanted to hide in the shadows today—or at least until Sven had straightened out my back—but no. The Brazilian boys left such an explosion of energy in their wake, I had no choice but to absorb it. As a result, I shared trail mix with Harley riders from Chicago, talked to an old guy who'd driven tour buses for rock groups (I think the drugs were still in his system), and was pulled over by two Dutch guys in a Mustang who'd overtaken me and wanted to have a chat. *Of course!*

I met the owner of the Needles outpost and his corgi, Haggis (Haggis made more sense than the Harley riders), and I flagged down a German driver as a giant panel flew off the back of his RV, almost decapitating me. I even got to practice my German by the side of the road, though he kept answering me in impeccable English. Obviously not the day for my linguistic skills.

Despite my occasional bouts of resistance, moments of connectivity gave me my greatest joy. I loved the complete unpredictability of each connection. I never knew what the day would bring. It was as if I said to the Universe every morning, "Give me everyone and everything you've got. Leave nothing behind. Throw the kitchen sink at me as well."

And usually, it did.

DAY 58: MOAB

I decided to stay a couple of nights in Moab. There was so much extraordinary beauty to explore right outside town—more of Canyonlands, Dead Horse Park, and the impressive Arches National Park—and I just loved this funky little town, full of energy and attitude. There was a real buzz to everything and everyone. It was colourful—mainly from the red desert—quirky, and full of characters. There was everyone from old timers drinking beer in the sun to uber-cool dudes doing wheelies on their mountain bikes down Main Street.

But it was the Bike Brotherhood who made my time in Moab. The night before, I'd heard chaos coming from the car park of my hotel. Sure enough, it was my Brazilian buddies, looking the worse for wear, having ridden off-road through the dirt and dust all day, now noisily unloading.

We went to dinner at a Mexican restaurant, and it's safe to say that alcohol didn't improve their linguistic skills—or mine. I was hopeful that margarita after margarita would make them easier to understand, but no. It just made them even more hyper, if that were humanly possible. They'd had a great day on the road, and I got to relive it with them again and again—or I think that's what we were talking about. Their energy and sense of chaos were infectious, as was their ability to plough through guacamole. Many avocados suffered mercilessly to feed these guys!

There is an incredible camaraderie between riders on the road—particularly between non-Harley riders. I'm not saying Harley riders are pretentious—I'm not brave enough to say that, especially to their faces—but they have their own code. They're seriously into their image, and many tend to be a little aloof and harder to connect with. But the rest of us? Any time there's a chance to shoot the breeze with a brother (or a sister), we're there—exchanging stories, giving tips, asking for advice, comparing bikes. We just can't get enough of it.

Comparing bikes can be a little interesting at first. It's almost like we're dogs sniffing each other's tails. "So, what kinda mileage do you get? How much does that sucker weigh? What'll she do 0–100 in?" It's like we have to get the sniffing over and done with first before the stories will come out. In real life, chances are we'd have nothing in common—but on the road? There's a tough, powerful bond among riders.

THE BROTHERHOOD

While having breakfast at my favourite hideout—The Peace Cafe—two cool dudes—brothers touring together on GS1200s (very grown-up, off-road bikes) cruised past. Our paths had crossed a few times over the past few weeks, but we'd never spoken. Before they'd even made it into the restaurant, we'd spent an hour on the footpath laughing and telling stories.

They gave me some great tips for travelling light—to reduce the weight of their gear, they'd made the unanimous decision (it had to be unanimous) to wear undies for four days in a row: normal, inside-out, front-ways, and back-to-front. (Call me old-fashioned, but I'm happy to carry the extra three grams it takes for my knickers.)

We also compared wildlife horror stories. They'd come 'round a corner in the dark the night before and just missed hitting a cow. Hitting a moose or a caribou, as I've come close to, is street cred. But a cow? That's just plain embarrassing!

As I pulled into Arches later that day, two guys who had been part of the "Will you/won't you make it?" gas debate in Hanksville pulled in behind me. It was like meeting old friends. We jumped off our bikes and hugged each other tight. The guys laughed, "We've been sooo thinking about you and wondering if you made it. Even though we said go for it, we weren't really sure." *Now they tell me. And they'd been so confident at the time!*

Later in the day, I met another two GS riders who were headed to Colorado, as I was. They pulled out their maps and showed me where all the gas stations were (now that's the ultimate in conservatism—these guys could do more than 300 km on one tank before breaking a sweat!), plus some cool sweeper roads along the way. But they were worried about me riding on my own. The fact that I'd just ticked over 15,000 solo kilometres on Voodoo didn't impress them. They wanted me to ride with them in the morning just to be safe.

Now seriously. How often in life do you meet a complete stranger who worries about your safety to that extent? Only with the brotherhood. Only on the road.

IT'S A MAN'S WORLD

Interestingly, I'd had a couple of different responses to the sisterhood. I hadn't seen many solo women riding across the US. There'd been women riding in Harley groups, but few on their own. You can imagine my excitement in Vegas when I'd pulled into a gas station and who should pull in alongside me but another female rider on a touring BMW.

I was so excited! *Yay, sisterhood!* I bounced over to her like an excited puppy and hit her with a barrage of questions—where have you come from, how long have you been travelling, how's the road treating you?—the usual fifty questions I get every day.

I desperately wanted to connect with her. It was fantastic to meet another female rider.

She didn't seem to think it was so fantastic.

She gave me monosyllabic answers to everything. That is, until she heard I'd just come from Death Valley, when she proceeded to lecture me about how "idiotic" I'd been coming through there in the heat of summer. Now, I can take being called "idiotic" by my friends—and they're generally right—but I wasn't taking it from a complete stranger!

Women are sometimes our own worst enemies. In the bike world—which is generally considered to be a man's world— women should be there for each other. It wasn't about competition, it was about connection.

But maybe it wasn't a gender thing. Maybe she just wasn't a nice person. And maybe I needed to curb my puppy excitement. Either way, the rebuff stung just a little. (OK, a lot.) In the middle of nowhere, it would have been magical to have shared stories and connected with a sister. Not this time, I guess.

The good news is that, every day, there is a community of riders who do want to connect. They give me support, consideration, encouragement, and engagement. Our machines and our love of adventure bring us together no matter who we are, what we do, what we ride, how we ride.

That connection opens the door like we've been friends for years. And that's exactly how life should be.

CHAPTER ELEVEN

Moab to Jackson, WY

DAY 59: MOAB TO TELLURIDE

I was eager to run the trail to the iconic Delicate Arch—the most spectacular formation in Arches National Park. I wanted to be there by myself to watch the sun ease over the top of its soaring pinnacle and to soak up the intensity of this natural beauty without anyone else around.

I was desperate to *run* Delicate Arch—the problem was, I didn't want to *get* there.

It'd taken me 15,000 km, but I'd finally found a flaw on my Big Girl. Because she's more a track/race bike, she's not really built to be out after dark. Something like her owner, really. Her headlights and high beam are virtually useless. They really give you more of an indication of where the road is rather than show you the way. In a well-lit city area at night, they're bad enough, but in the total blackness of a national park, they're almost deadly.

As much as I wanted to run, I was seriously spooked about riding 25 km of total darkness to get to the start of the trail. I'd be lucky to see more than twenty metres in front of me, and there was no way I wanted to find that "deer in the headlights" or some other unidentified animal in the dark.

Bed seemed a very warm, safe, and attractive proposition.

THE DELICATE ARCH

But eventually, Chicken Girl decided to brave it, and out we went. Purely by Braille, we felt rather than saw our way to the trail. I could barely see my hand in front of my face (not sure why I'd want to do that anyway!), and there were a couple of hair-raising moments when I thought the road went one way and it completely went the other. The good news? No animals were hurt in the making of this ride.

As with most things that frighten us, the rewards are there when we have the courage to step up to the plate, and I was truly rewarded. It was a beautiful time to be in the park—to be in total darkness and then see the light slowly changing—the sky turning yellow and pink—a complete 360-degree, breathtaking light show!

I'd had an unsettling day in the park the day before. It had been beautiful but heaving with spectators—tour buses, RVs, and four-wheel drives clogging roads and vistas. With big sites naturally come crowds. That's the trade-off, I guess. (I'd still like to ban them, though!)

But this morning, I had it all to myself, and it was as magical as I'd imagined it to be.

It was just becoming light when I started to run—which was lucky because I was in grave danger of getting lost. It's always a challenge being the first on a hidden trail when you suffer from

Navigation Numptiness! I scampered over rocks, jumped over rivulets, climbed up stone staircases...and suddenly, there she was. The exquisite Delicate Arch silhouetted against the dark blue morning sky.

I clamoured over the final cliff face, dropped into the natural amphitheatre surrounding her, and sat in total solitude. The Arch blazed with vibrant oranges, yellows, and reds. I was completely mesmerised by the displays of light and colour, by the sheer magnificence of the Arch as she came alight in the sunrise. It was just too perfect for words.

Reluctantly, I had to let my beautiful Arch go. I'd had my moment in the sun and the solitude I'd been craving, but I was headed to Telluride and had a big day to create. Besides, coming up behind me were six buses filled with tourists, and they scared me more than deer.

A QUICK DETOUR

Telluride had been a last-minute addition to the journey. A few days earlier, I'd heard about the Telluride Wellness Conference featuring the inimitable Deepak Chopra, the legendary whole-food nutrition expert T. Colin Campbell, and my all-time hero—ultra-athlete Rich Roll. Yep, the same Rich Roll whose journey had given me the confidence to embrace my own plant-based power.

Telluride was close, if you call a quick 800 km detour close, and I'd learnt to say yes to the universe when it sent me an opportunity.

Before heading out, I juiced up at the Peace Cafe and gave some serious thought to what it would take to nail my living masterpiece today. It took me all of about three minutes to decide. I wanted adventure, challenge, inspiration, and connection. Easy—should have that knocked off by lunchtime. I'd already run Arches, so Challenge was ticked off. Time to fire up Voodoo and bring on Adventure!

I'd loved the incredible red majestic beauty of Utah—but it was a sharp, ferocious beauty, and in truth, I'd missed green. I'd missed lush green pine forests reaching to the skies, being surrounded by purple-blue mountains. Turning east out of Moab across the border, I finally got them. How does that happen? Does nature know where state boundaries are and shift the scenery accordingly? Another great mystery of the road.

In the blink of an eye, all the *bigs* disappeared—big sandstone, big pinnacles, big spheres, and big canyons gone. In their place were glorious meadows teeming with wildflowers, mountains covered in pine trees, sparkling flowing rivers, and sunflowers everywhere. How do you not smile when you see a sunflower lifting its precious head up to you? (OK, it's lifting its head to the sun, but it *feels* personal!)

And the road? Corkscrews and sharp, tight turns over impossibly narrow mountain passes, huge sweepers at the base of the mountains, and perilous twists where I needed to remind myself to keep breathing. Occasionally, the Universe gave us a break and the road would open up onto a glorious straight where we tucked and rode like the wind, only to come to another mountain and repeat the tight, twisting torture. Be careful what you ask for: Adventure, well and truly nailed.

HOW COULD I NOT BE HAPPY?

Telluride was an old Wild West mining town (aren't they always old Wild West mining towns?) that had done a great job of keeping its heritage beautifully intact. There were three flavours—old mining rustic; colourful, wooden Victorian; and condos of wood, steel, and rock. It was an eclectic mix, but it worked. It was gorgeous.

Sitting in the sun outside a juice bar, I held the beauty of the day and everything I'd experienced in my heart. My body still flowed from the rhythm of the ride. It's a crazy phenomenon: often when you stop the bike, your body keeps going. It's still flying through the bends and leaning into the corners, trying to hold onto every last little bit of adrenaline. Green kale juice in hand, I closed my eyes and went with the flow, smiling as I relived corner after corner.

I must have looked in need of medical attention as I sat there smiling to myself. But that didn't deter the owner of the juice bar who wandered out to talk, and we conducted the usual journey banter, before he surprised me with a whammy. He asked something I hadn't been asked before: *what made me so happy?*

I was glad I looked happy and not a little deranged sitting there, but seriously? I'm travelling 'round the US on an amazing piece of machinery, where every day is nothing short of mind-blowing. How could I not be happy? But he kept digging. He wanted to know more. What nourished me? What nurtured me? What gave me the courage to grow?

Woah. Can't I just sit in the sun and drink my juice? No? OK, let me think.

So many things came to mind, but one thought that stuck was how blessed I was to be surrounded by people who loved and supported me. Even though they didn't like what I did and didn't understand why I needed to do it, they were still right there behind me. They say you're the sum total of the five people in the world you're closest to. Being surrounded by people brimming with love, support, and belief, it was no wonder I was happy.

Later that night, that purposeful pushing of a stranger helped me make a decision. It was time to let go of relationships that didn't serve me or nurture me. I made the commitment to only surround myself with people who fed, stretched, and watered me—who helped me grow to be the best me possible. Final ticks of the day: Inspiration and Connectivity achieved. Gotta love strangers!

DAYS 60-62: TELLURIDE TO RICHFIELD

It had been an amazing few days in Telluride. Its mellow, relaxed charm had soothed my soul. Nestled in the San Miguel Mountains, it was peaceful, gentle, and quietly magical. Just what I needed to rejuvenate after nearly nine weeks on the bike.

The conference itself had been incredible. Nearly three days of inspiration, insight, and growth as world-renowned speakers powerfully challenged concepts and beliefs. Some views were controversial and a little difficult to come to grips with, but I aligned with most. How could I not, as a plant-based aficionado? It was easy at first to be smug as I listened to the presenters. *Yeah, yeah, I do all that. That's how I eat, I know all that.* But from experience, smugness comes just before a fall.

I loved Rich Roll's simple philosophy: change your plate, change your life, change the world. I'd changed my plate by becoming plant-based, I'd changed my life by optimising my health, and yes, I'd changed the world in my own sphere by not contributing to the impact of animal agriculture. But I'd done that unconsciously, and now I wasn't sure that was enough.

I'd stepped into being plant-based because of taste initially, as well as the old anorexic attraction of not being able to put on weight eating carrots. (Though I have gone orange in my time.) The benefits were all about me, and in my own bubble, I'd figured I was doing well. But listening to the shocking evidence of the impact of animal agriculture on health, the environment, and of course animals, I knew it was time to personally step up and develop a deeper advocacy about my choices.

Leather was my biggest downfall. I was embarrassed to say it, but my life was leather. I guess there were only so many times I could use the defence that on a track, a hemp race suit wouldn't give me much protection. But that didn't excuse the rest of my leather-loaded wardrobe! I guess it's progress not perfection, so although I made the decision to keep what I've got, I committed to never buying any more.

MANIFESTATION

Before this weekend, I'd read a lot about manifestation, and although I was skeptical, I was fascinated about the principle of thoughts informing energy, then energy creating an experience. Trust the Universe to give me a brilliant opportunity to address my skepticism!

The main reason I'd come to the conference was to listen to Rich Roll. His book *Finding Ultra* had given me the confidence to go plant-based, but it had been his weekly podcasts on health, nutrition, sport, and wellness that had had the most significant impact on my life and growth. I wanted to thank him for the inspiration he'd provided in my life. And so—as you do when you're going to be one of hundreds of attendees—I threw down the challenge to the Universe and asked if I could meet him personally.

The first morning of the conference, I wandered past three coffee shops before eventually settling on Starbucks. The person in the queue in front of me? Rich Roll.

He very graciously spared me some time, despite me being in his quiet coffee space, and I got the chance to thank him for the impact he's made in my world. Don't you love it when a plan comes together? Although I'm not quite sure it's ever a good idea to put the Universe to the test!

Through the whole weekend, it was fantastic to be surrounded by kindred spirits and to not feel like a strange science experiment ("You're what? Plant-what? Does that mean you eat grass?") It had been a thought-provoking, controversial, and dynamic two days, and I'd been honoured to be part of it—even if I was the only raw food advocate with chain lube under her fingernails!

SIXTH SENSE

Two days off the road, and I was itchy. Fortunately, I had a long six-hour ride to get that twitch out of my system. I was headed to Richfield, Utah—three hours south of Salt Lake—where I'd been an exchange student over thirty years ago. I was hoping my exchange family would recognise me. After all, I hadn't changed much in thirty years—I still looked the same, it was just that everything was lower. Sadly.

I'd had a tough decision leaving Telluride in the morning. I could leave very early in the dark and cold but stay dry, or I could leave later to get the light and be warmer but get rained on. Mmmm...always a tough call. In the end, cold and dry won out. But just after we pulled out, it started pouring with rain—so I ended up being both cold and wet in the dark! My favourite combination! Funnily enough, no amount of telling myself it was "just an experience" made a difference.

For 200 km, I grumbled—loud, cranky, and miserable in my helmet—mainly about the fact that I was still trusting the weather forecast on an iPhone!

Except for the weather, my sixth senses were working overtime that morning. As I flew through pasturelands just as dawn broke, a thought crept in: "Be careful—farmers aren't going to expect to see an S1000RR in full flight at this time of the morning. Chances are, they'll pull out without looking." Sure enough, 'round the next corner, that's exactly what happened. Out of a driveway came a farmer in a very big truck who probably got a bigger shock than I did as I swerved past him.

Ten minutes later, my next piece of inspiration came through.

"Watch yourself. This is exactly the time deer will run out of nowhere." Yep, you guessed it. About thirty seconds later, a deer and her fawn jumped right out in front of me. Thinking they'd run forward, I tried to cut behind them. The doe did exactly that, but not the fawn. She stopped then bolted back towards me. I came very close to wearing the spots on the fawn's back, and she came very close to wearing the decorative headlights of an S1000RR.

I wasn't sure whether I'd had a sixth sense, or if I'd just wished the excitement on myself. Either way, I decided not to do any more thinking.

GOING HOME TO RICHFIELD

Leaving the lushness of Colorado behind at the border sign, I stepped back into the world of harsh, stark monoliths that turned from red to white—salmon pink, green, and yellow in-between. Every change in colour meant a change in rock formation, with each almost more spectacular than the next. Utah was very different from the gentle beauty of Colorado, but stunning nonetheless.

The road was perfect, fast, and furious, and on the highway, I could easily power through the nearly 600 km I had to travel. But the wind terrified the life out of me. Wherever I could, I rode in the centre of both lanes so I'd have space to manage where the wind threw me. I wasn't heavy enough for Voodoo in the deadly combination of speed and wind velocity. She desperately needed another twenty kilograms to stop her from blowing either off the side of the road or into oncoming traffic. It was a ferocious battle all the way in, but hey—I loved a good fight.

It had been close to thirty years since I'd been to Richfield, and being the girl I am, I wanted to arrive in some kind of reasonable shape after all this time. I knew I was never going to look my best after six hours of wind and rain, but I was hoping to at least pull off a "cool but dishevelled" look so that the first impression would be, "Woooowww. You haven't changed a bit!" (Like that was ever going to happen.)

After having saved my skin twice this morning, the Universe decided I'd had enough good luck. Thirty minutes before I arrived, the heavens opened again, and I was completely soaked to the skin. But there was more excitement to come. Just as I pulled into town, the biggest dust storm I've ever seen descended.

Do you have any idea what happens when you're completely soaked and then ride through a very red dust storm? I looked like something out of Mad Max.

So much for the smooth entrance. I looked and smelt like a Labrador that had just rolled in a mud bath—and not as cute. But my family didn't care what I looked like or even what I smelt like. Luckily for me, they loved me just the way I was. Miracles do happen!

DAYS 63-64: RICHFIELD

I hadn't been back to Richfield for over thirty years because I'd been frightened. Being a seventeen-year-old exchange student in Utah had been one of the most amazing twelve months of my life. I'd instantly fallen in love with the beautiful family who'd bravely volunteered to take this wild Aussie teenager into their home, despite not being able to understand my accent, my strange food, or my fear of hunting. They treated me like a daughter from the minute they met me—which also meant they grounded me from time to time. (It was usually well-deserved!)

Richfield was a close-knit farming community completely surrounded by mountains. I think that's where I got my love of mountains. I loved the feeling of security and protection that comes from being encircled. It was like having warm, soothing arms wrapped around you tightly.

Richfield was also very Mormon. I obviously was not. But I had a choice: to hold onto my normal life or throw myself completely into the mix. The sidelines had never been a good place for me—so a deep dive it was. Full Mormon immersion, complete with letting go of my beloved coffee. Despite never converting (much to my family's disappointment), I learnt amazing lessons from my time there—lessons that have stayed with me all my life, particularly the importance of family. If nothing else, I couldn't help but admire and respect the incredibly strong family values of the Mormon faith.

My twelve months there were a crazy blur of a life completely upside down to the one I'd lived at home. It was a life of mountains, hunting, farming, and dragging Main in pickup trucks while drinking Sprite (Coke wasn't allowed). It was rural USA, and I loved it completely. (OK, maybe not the hunting.)

But it had been so long ago. I'd held the memories of my time there so close to my heart that I didn't want to compromise them by returning and finding things weren't as I remembered them. I wanted everything to stay as perfect as it was in my head.

That's what I told myself.

BRAVE ENOUGH TO COME HOME

But the real reason I hadn't been back was that my life over those thirty years had been very different to the life my exchange family lived. Against a world of faith, strong values, and beliefs, I'd lived a life of...well, not exactly that. To the outside world, my life was considered normal—if you count being a deckhand for an arms dealer, being held at gunpoint, or being protected by the South of France mafia "normal" (it's a long story). But it certainly wasn't a "normal" life for Richfield, Utah.

Sure, I'd eventually settled down and done all the right things— gotten married and had beautiful boys—but the life in-between had been—well, *interesting*. It had been so different to the life they'd led, and I wasn't sure how I could explain it to them.

My biggest fear was that they'd be disappointed in me—that somehow, in living a life of "colour," I'd let them down. That I wasn't the daughter they'd loved and cherished thirty years ago.

How much living do we lose when we let fear take hold? How many experiences do we miss when fear stops us in our tracks? How much love do we deny ourselves when fear is in control? About thirty years' worth, is what I discovered.

The minute I stepped off Voodoo—dirty, dishevelled, and drenched—it was like time had stopped. A window had opened, thirty years had slipped out, the window had closed, and everything had changed, but nothing had changed.

As I pulled off my helmet, soaked to the skin and filthy, my beautiful mom hugged me and said all I needed to hear:

"Honey, welcome home. We've missed you so much."

No judgements. No explanations (although some things were better left unsaid). I was home and that was all that mattered.

My time back in Richfield was precious. Together with my family and long-lost friends, we laughed hard at old stories, cried about tough times, and created special new memories to keep us going. We held each other's hands and held each other tight. In the blink of an eye, thirty years were erased.

It's amazing how life opens up when you let go of fear—when you're brave enough to come home.

DAY 65: RICHFIELD TO EVANSTON

Leaving Richfield was hard. It was wonderful to have stepped back into the warmth of that special world and to feel like I'd never left. Sure, some things had changed—like discovering traffic lights on Main for the first time—but people hadn't changed, and I was grateful for the chance to reconnect with my family and friends.

I cried huge, unattractive sobs all of the 200 km to Salt Lake—and managing tears in a helmet at high speed is not easy. It's impossible to open your visor to dry your eyes, so the world is just a massive blur, mile after mile. (I'm not even going to try to explain the mechanics of blowing your nose!)

I'd loved to have stayed longer, but I was on a mission. Jakey had been filming a commercial in Jackson, Wyoming, about 700 km away. If I put my head down and really toughed it out on the interstate, I could ride to Jackson in one day, giving us two days together before he flew back to Vancouver. It would be my longest day ever on Voodoo, but I was desperate to see my boy.

Let no crazy distance get between a momma bear and her cub.

Then again...

PLANS CHANGED

Looking like I'd been peeling onions in my helmet, I pulled over for gas just before Salt Lake to discover Jakey's shoot had been extended and he was delayed.

As devastated as I was to lose some of my time with him, I was secretly relieved. I'd been insane thinking I could plough through 700 km in one hit. In my heart, I knew it was an unrealistic distance and one that I'd be lucky to make safely, but my head had convinced me to push through regardless. My warrior was working overtime!

Riding on the freeway that morning had been a nightmare. In theory, going direct should have been faster, but the winds were so ferocious I had to pull back speed just to stay on the road. And that's before I even mention trucks.

Surprisingly, there are usually large numbers of trucks on the highways, and their impact on a bike can often be terrifying. You're incredibly vulnerable being surrounded by trucks. There's the obvious danger of them not seeing you, but there's also the physical toll they take on your body. Sitting behind them, you're buffeted in a vortex that shoves you from side to side as you try desperately to hold it together long enough to overtake—flying debris adding to the challenge of visibility.

Pulling in after passing also has its moments, as you're often hit with a compression wave from the truck you've passed that throws you sideways. But that's nothing compared to the compression waves you get from trucks travelling the other way, which hit you like a giant slap all over your body.

After three hours of being continually smashed by trucks and the wind, I was totally exhausted and barely able to hold my helmet up as my neck had been snapped around so hard. With Jakey's news, a closer destination was selected: Evanston. It was still another slamming 250 km away, but it meant I could get off the freeway, and it sure as hell beat another 500 km!

The plan was to head for the canyons around Park City and Deer Lake, then cut through the mountains to Wyoming. It was a great plan—back on beautiful roads with incredible mountain scenery, colours galore, twisty tight roads—yep, a great plan. Just a shame about the execution!

WHAT NEXT?

I dropped into the canyons just outside of Salt Lake, and after the soulless interstate, life became instantly vibrant. Autumn had arrived. Overnight, the mountains had burst into flames. I was surrounded by a kaleidoscope of reds, oranges, and yellows as the leaves around me changed colour.

I'd spotted a hidden canyon on the map and decided to find it, but Utah roads rivalled California with the lack of signs, impossible-to-see signs, or signs that don't tell you what you need to know until after you need to know it. Unwilling to get lost, I pulled into a gas station to check directions, where two cheeky trash collectors came to my aid. Or so I thought. They pored over my maps intently—grunting and nodding furiously—before one of them finally admitted:

"I can't see a thing without my glasses. Can I borrow yours?"

Now, my glasses are twenty-dollar magnifiers. I really do need glasses, but I'm too vain to admit it. So my life is surrounded by twenty-dollar specials. They seemed to work for the garbo boys, though, who identified the route and pointed me in the right direction. Or so it seemed.

About 30 km down the road, I realised I was hopelessly lost. Back to the gas station, someone wearing their own glasses pointed me in a very different direction to the route I'd missed two hours ago.

And breathe...

By this stage, the sky looked ominous—dark blue, black, and purple. At some point, I was going to get very, very wet, if I didn't freeze to death first. In my excitement of exploring the canyons, I'd failed to notice we were climbing a mountain pass that went over 3,000 metres—about 2,500 metres too high for me to keep warm. As the heavens opened and the rain turned to ice on my body, I looked up to the Universe and asked, "So what next?"

Sometimes, it's better not to ask.

SO CLOSE AND SO FAR

Just as I reached the top of the pass—soaked and frozen to the bone—I noticed white stuff falling from the sky. *Snow? You've gotta be kidding me!* It was nearly a throw-in-the-towel moment, except I had no towel and nowhere to throw it. I had nothing left to give.

In the middle of a deserted mountain pass, all I could do was keep moving forward. I focused on trying to relax, not letting my teeth chatter uncontrollably, breathing deeply, not grizzling, and watching the beauty of the leaves.

The leaves won out eventually. The more I focused on beauty and concentrated on what I was seeing instead of what I was feeling, the better it got. Marginally, anyway.

Emotional, exhausted, and with my body completely frozen onto Voodoo's tank, I pulled into the first highway hotel in Evanston—the "all you can eat" salad bar being an extra draw card. I barely had enough strength to ease myself off Voodoo and into the shower to defrost. For twenty minutes, I sat on the floor of the shower with hot water pouring all over me as I tried to stop shaking and get warm.

Starving and barely thawed, I wandered over to the salad bar, only to find the "all you can eat" salad had already been eaten. All that remained was lettuce, tomato, and (my all-time favourite) plastic cheese.

Nooo! Seriously? I've had the day from hell. I'm cold, exhausted, miserable, and I need fuel! Really? That's all there is?

Back in my room, I tipped my bags upside down and found a half-eaten raw food bar. It looked and tasted worse for wear, but hey—it was dinner. By that stage, I'd reached my limit. I just wanted it to be over—to sleep away the pain and emotion from such a bone-shattering day.

At least the bed was clean, and tomorrow would be better. All that mattered was getting to Jakey.

I was nearly there.

DAY 66: EVANSTON TO JACKSON

The alarm went off at 0530. There was a thick darkness outside, and inside my tiny ice block cell of a room, I was frozen. It's never a good sign when you see ice forming on the insides of your windows.

But despite the cold, part of me (a very small part) still wanted to run. *Sad but true, you can't take the morning discipline out of the girl.* But damn—if I was getting ice in my room, how cold was it outside?

OK, confession: as much as I like to think of myself as a hard ass, I am a complete baby in the cold. I lose the plot completely when the chill sets in. Especially on a bike—anything under ten degrees and I'm in trouble.

Rolling over to check the temperature, I made a deal with myself. If it was above zero degrees, I'd run. If it was below, I'd bunker in. Don't you love it when nature takes the decision out of your hands? *Thank you, thank you.* At minus one degree Celsius, I had an excuse not to head out into the blackness. I bundled under my thin duvet and tried to sneak a last few moments of cosiness.

I KNOW BEST

But no matter what I did, I couldn't get warm. I headed for the shower, hoping to burn heat into my body, but steam from the hot water set the fire alarm off. So to add insult to injury, wrapped in nothing but a towel, I had to open the front door and let the icy wind in to shut off the alarm.

Slowly, I lumbered around my room, trying to get myself organised. Everything hurt. After the epic ride the day before and no food last night, I could barely hold it together. I was overwhelmingly tired, with fatigue seeping deep into my bones. My body was stiff and aching, and I knew I was right on the edge emotionally.

I was a mess—physically and mentally. But I kept moving. I

knew I'd be better once I was on the road. Everything was always better once you were on the road.

My gear, still damp from the drowning the day before, was draped hopefully over feeble heaters. My jacket and pants weren't too bad, but water was still oozing out of my gloves, despite having shoved a hair dryer inside them to try to dry them out. The hair dryer exploded within minutes. I'm not sure why I was surprised.

Braving the cold, I stepped outside to check on Voodoo, only to find her encased in a thick layer of ice. By this stage, texts were arriving from the bike brotherhood who knew that I was headed to Jackson. They warned me it was too cold to go—that I should stay put until it got warmer and head out after lunch when the sun had had a chance to heat things up a little.

But no, I knew best.

By now, it was two degrees, and according to the fount of all weather wisdom (my iPhone) it was still going to be two degrees at eight o'clock, nine o'clock, ten o'clock…There was no point waiting. I was desperate to see Jakey. I was going. End of story. Besides, it was only going to get warmer, right?

I headed back outside to pour hot water over Voodoo, trying to defrost her, but within seconds of the hot water hitting her, she would turn to ice again.

OK, breathe...it'll be OK...you can do this.

Back inside, I started to gear up. I had so many layers on I could barely move. I figured I was going to need a step ladder to get up onto Voodoo. I struggled into my heated vest—the most critical piece of equipment to get me through the cold—and as I plugged it in, the connector snapped off in my hand.

No, no, no! You've gotta be kidding me! The time I most desperately need my heated vest, it disintegrates? Shit. I'm gonna die out there.

I stared down at the useless connector, willing it to miraculously weld itself together, but the power of positive thinking didn't extend itself to reconnecting metal. To compound the problem, my other potential saviour in the cold—Voodoo's heated hand grips—weren't working. There would be absolutely no source of heat on this leg of the journey.

OK. This is bad—really bad. But I have a choice. Do I stay, or do I go? The words "toughen up, princess" rang in my ears, and taking a deep breath (if only to calm myself), I headed out.

BLUE-EYED TRUCK DRIVER

As I sat on Voodoo while she warmed up, I went through my standard routine of asking the Universe to protect us. To put a bubble of safety around us until we arrived at our destination. If ever I needed the help, it was today.

Nothing felt right. My heart said wait, my head said go. My head was the victor—we went.

I'd been sadly mistaken in believing it would get warmer. Impossibly, it got colder and colder. I lay flat on my tank bag trying to reduce the wind while my legs clung to my tank, desperately squeezing any last ounce of heat from the engine.

Without warning, a dense, thick fog descended and persistently seeped its way through seven layers of clothing—not satisfied until it had reached my bare skin. I was frozen to the bone.

I was so cold my teeth were chattering uncontrollably—my body convulsing as it tried to shake off hypothermia. I tried desperately to breathe deeply and not become overwhelmed by the freezing cold, but taking deep breaths just fogged up my visor on the inside, making it impossible to see. I had a choice—relax or see. I chose vision.

Here's the thing. When you're that cold, your mind freezes as well as your body. Your brain fogs up, your judgement is impaired, and you make bad decisions. Really bad decisions. In my head, I kept hearing, "Stop. Pull over. Get a coffee. Warm up." But no. I was possessed. I was determined to get to Jackson as fast as I could, so I just kept pushing. Even though both my body and brain had almost shut down.

For what seemed like hours (instead of the few minutes it

probably was), I'd been stuck behind a massive eighteen-wheeler—waiting to pass. I was scared. The wind coming off the back of the truck was slamming us all over the road. Having lost all feeling in my hands and legs, I could scarcely grip onto Voodoo as we were tossed violently from side to side. To make it worse, snow and grit were being kicked up all over me, making it almost impossible to see. I had to get past it or I was in grave danger of sliding Voodoo down the road.

Eventually, I lost patience and slid out to check the gap. It looked fine—plenty of space between me and the oncoming truck. I dropped Voodoo down a couple of gears, hammered the throttle to speed past the truck and...nothing.

She was completely flat. No big surge in acceleration at all. In a moment of panic, I realised I'd left her in rain mode from the day before, which meant I had seriously reduced power. Looking up, I was suddenly acutely aware that the oncoming truck was a lot closer than I'd bargained for. My frozen brain hadn't accurately computed the distance between us, and within seconds, it was right on top of me. We were all moving at incredible speeds, and I'd completely misjudged my position.

I've always said that I don't want my last words on the planet to be "Aw, fuck," as I smack into something on the bike—but today it looked like that fear was about to be realised.

I was too far forward to drop back and not far enough forward to make the gap. I was committed. They say moments like this happen in slow motion, and they're right. In a moment of calm, I knew there was only one place for me to go. I tucked in alongside the truck I was passing, breathing in (as if that were going to help) as I prepared to become a slice of cheese in a two-truck sandwich.

Just as I thought I was gone, the truck I was overtaking saw me in the lee of his load and braked just enough for me to slide in front of him and squeeze into safety.

But it was close. Really close. I saw the colour of the other truck driver's eyes. (They were blue.)

As he sliced past me, his compression wave threw me all over the road, and I struggled desperately to get Voodoo under control. But that was nothing compared to trying to get myself under control.

GO FIND JAKEY

I'd made such a rookie mistake. I'd never called it so wrong in all my years of riding. I'd never come so close to killing myself. Others had certainly come close, but this time, I only had myself to blame.

When I finally stopped hyperventilating, I looked up to the sky and whispered, "Thank you" to the Universe. Immediately, I got the message, "Yep, but you didn't do your job." And the Universe was right—cold, physical and emotional exhaustion, and bad judgement had gotten the better of me. I'd screwed up big time.

Still a complete mess, I pulled into the first gas station I could find for the coffee and warmth I'd been ignoring. Huddled over my coffee, still shaking, I felt a massive hand like a bunch of bananas on my shoulder.

"Pretty close out there, Missy. You OK?"

It was the truck driver I'd overtaken. He pulled up a chair alongside me.

We weren't big on conversation. I couldn't speak, and he didn't want to, but he sat with me until the adrenaline and the cold had washed through me and I'd stopped convulsing. He refilled my coffee, and as he left, he gave me an incredibly sage piece of advice:

"Ya might want to think about slowing down a little out there, Missy."

Ya reckon?

As the adrenaline drained out of my body, I was left exhausted and completely spent. I had nothing more to give. It was as if someone had pulled my power cord out. I felt weak, fatigued, and completely drained. Not to mention scared and just the tiniest bit unglued. But I had to let it go. Having just had my life flash before me, I had to get back on Voodoo and finish the job. I still had another 170 km to ride.

Besides, what were my options? I was sitting in a gas station in the middle of nowhere with no one around to rescue me or comfort me. There was no duvet to hide under and only so much coffee that even I could drink. There was no choice but to just keep going, to finish the journey, and to go find Jakey.

With immense gratitude to the Universe, the utmost respect for Voodoo, and a fearfully beating heart, I hesitantly geared up and got moving. A little slower this time, but it was warmer now. The fog had lifted, the sun had broken through, and my confidence—if not entirely regained—got a little stronger. I rode the last 170 km like a nervous geriatric, but under the circumstances, that wasn't such a bad thing. Besides, it gave me the opportunity to absorb the incredible beauty of Jackson and to appreciate one of the most stunning rides I've had. Once I stopped shaking.

Feeling more than a little shattered, I finally pulled into my hotel. After two hours in the shower—which is how long it took me to get my core temperature back to normal—I finally got the call I was waiting for.

"Mum, I'm in reception. What's our room number?"

My son was finally here. Everything would be OK.

DAY 67: JACKSON

Except it wasn't. The night was hard. I struggled with sleep. The minute I closed my eyes, I relived every terrifying second of my very close encounter, again and again and again. The impatience of pulling out from behind the truck, the panic when I realised I didn't have enough power, the fear in the pit of my stomach when I saw the gap closing, and the unnerving calm in my body when I grasped the fact that this wasn't going to end well.

In reality, the whole incident probably took seconds, but when it plays in your head in slow motion, it takes forever. Lying in bed, it was all so vivid in my head—the emotions, the cold, the colours, the smells. Too vivid.

Leaving aside how cavalier I'd been about my own personal safety, one of the things that hit me hardest was the potential danger I'd put other people in. When a motorbike takes on an eighteen-wheeler, the bike is usually going to come off second best. But anything could have happened out there. Trucks could have swerved, gone into ditches to miss me, lost control of their trailers...the prospect was horrific.

It would be bad enough if I'd killed myself, but the thought of endangering others through my own foolhardiness was even worse.

Staring up at the ceiling in the dark, I realised that "The Incident" (as it would now be called) was the perfect analogy of my life. Pushing too hard, not listening to advice, going too fast, ignoring the dangers, and not being prepared to back down until it almost killed me.

What the hell was wrong with me? What was it going to take for me to learn these lessons? How much more danger did I need to put myself and others in before I stopped being such a bloody idiot?

Damn. I thought I'd put down that warrior shield and started to surrender to life. I thought I'd let go or at least released a little of that fanatical need to keep pushing—to ignore the signs. To always be right and be in control.

"Toughen up, princess" had been a taunt, like a red rag to a bull. Once those words entered my consciousness, it was game on. Despite all the warning signs, I chose to push through. That's what warriors do.

Throughout that morning, I'd received great advice—external and internal. Wait till it warms up, don't go when it's so cold, it won't matter if you're late, ride to the conditions, pull over and warm up—all excellent advice that I chose to ignore. Because, of course, the warrior knew best.

The conditions were abysmal, both the road and the weather. My hands were completely frozen, which meant I couldn't feel the throttle, brake, or clutch. The cold also destroyed my ability to think rationally. I knew I was close to the edge. I knew my body was struggling badly. I was tired, undernourished, and emotionally drained.

There's nothing like the silence of the night to shake you to your core. What part of that equation made me think it was OK to go? Nothing but my stupidity. Damn! Has everything I thought I'd gained over the past two months gone? Do I have to go back and start again? Was it like being on a diet where you sneak a cookie and then figure if you've had one you might as well have the whole pack?

Was I always destined to be a warrior? Despite everything I'd learnt over the past months, was that always going to be my default position? Was it impossible for me to ever change?

That was my biggest fear—that I'd seen the light. I'd seen a life where I didn't have to be that ferocious superhero—where I could be vulnerable, I could surrender and trust, and it would be OK. But when it had come to the crunch, I'd stepped right back into it. I'd gone back to the safe option, even though I knew it wasn't safe.

In shock, I realised I was more confronted by the loss of who I thought I was becoming, than the thought of being smeared between two trucks.

A POWERFUL CHOICE

Sleep was never going to be an option. In the end, I gave up. Despite the biting minus five degree Celsius temperature at 3:30 in the morning, I ran. I ran out of town and into the plains towards Yellowstone. The cold numbed my hands, my face, and just about every part of my body. Thankfully, it also numbed my ability to think.

In complete darkness, I could see nothing but my next step. The sound of my feet in the absolute stillness of the night was calming. Eventually, through the meditative rhythm of the run—left foot, right foot, left foot, right foot—I started to let the fear, the pain, the anger, and the shock I was carrying go.

I knew I had to make a choice. I could take the powerful lesson I'd just been given and use it to grow, or I could ignore it and go back to the protection and "safety" of my old world. But either way, I couldn't live in both camps.

In the black of the night, I made a decision. I chose to eat just one cookie and not the whole pack. I chose to accept that although I'd made a monumental mistake, I hadn't blown two months of learning and growth. Even the story I'd fallen back into— that I was still a warrior—I knew I could change. Sure, in that moment, I'd defaulted back to that position. But it wasn't who I was anymore—as long as I chose not to be.

Practice, not perfection, right? If I kept practicing long enough, one day I'd wake up and wouldn't have to practice anymore. I wasn't going back. I wasn't going to be that person. It might have served me in the past, but it didn't serve me any longer. I'd be damned if, having escaped the near-truck catastrophe, I'd let it actually take a victim. It stops here. It stops right now.

Enough...enough now.

CHAPTER TWELVE

Jackson to Spokane, WA

DAY 68: JACKSON TO YELLOWSTONE

Jackson was worth the drama of getting there. (Almost.) Surrounded by the stunning Grand Teton Mountains, it was the Wild West town to end all Wild West towns. I felt a little out of place without a Stetson or a six-shooter, but I loved the boot-scooting, vibrant, bustling explosion of energy everywhere we went. I loved the history, the buzz, the people, and being able to look up from Main Street to see a beautiful ski hill nestled right at the base of town.

It'd been soothing to hang with my son for a few days—to sit talking over coffee for hours and to spend time in his world, chasing through the Tetons looking for the perfect shot. He did fire me, however, for being a useless camera assistant. Next time, I'll just send him to his room.

He'd left at 0430 to head to Vancouver, and again unable to sleep, I wandered into town for coffee. Standing in the queue, I met a guy who'd shot a deer the day before and was headed back into the woods to pick it up. I wasn't sure how to process that information. There's not too much you can say when some-one tells you they've just killed a deer. As much as it horrified me, I had to accept that this was another world. I couldn't be in judgement—it was his journey, not mine. But the wild in the west was certainly alive and kicking.

The coffee queue improved when the guy behind me leaned over and asked what I was drinking—he wanted to treat me.

He explained, "A stranger bought me a coffee yesterday, and I'd like to pass the favour on. Your job is to continue to pass the gift forward." *Love it. I can do that!*

PANIC RISING

Nursing my free coffee, a slow panic began to spread. I'd done a quick map check earlier in the morning and realised I only had another ten days on this journey before I wound up back in Whistler. In deep fear, I recognised I wasn't ready for this adventure to end. I still had so much to learn, so much more to experience and work through. I wasn't sure when enough would be enough, but I knew it wouldn't be enough in ten days.

I understood that the panic was just that—panic. I saw it creeping in, and I'd opened the doors and welcomed it. Now I had to shift it. In the middle of the coffee shop, I closed my eyes and tried to breathe deep into the feeling. The panic was so strong I knew I needed to tackle it right away. It's generally not a good idea to close your eyes on a bike—so it was now or never.

I breathed deeply into the emotion, accepting it until I started to feel it releasing. Eventually I let it go. I had to give it a couple of attempts—I couldn't shift it right away—but eventually it started to ease, and I accepted that when the time came to go home, it would be perfect.

Right now, though, I had to get my head back into the game. If I only had ten days left, they were gonna be the best ten days ever. Not a big stretch, seeing as I was heading to Yellowstone National Park.

SMOOTH AS SILK

Out in the early morning, the golden light bathed the mountainside in rich sunlight while the magnificent Tetons, now peppered with snow, stood in purples and blues in the background. The natural beauty surrounded me—as did big, beautiful, brazen bison. Hundreds of them, just wandering all over the roads like they didn't have a care in the world—which I guess you don't when you're a bison. A couple of times, they wandered right out in front of me. I kept my hand hovering close to the throttle, ready to give Voodoo the beans just in case they charged (which apparently, they do).

The highlight of the day came from two unlikely characters—Earl and Boy—who sauntered over when I pulled in to take a photo of a waterfall. They looked like Texas Rangers. Enormous Stetsons, big turquoise belt buckles, cowboy boots, the works.

In a very slow Texan drawl, Earl said, "Say, girlie," (better than dude, I guess!). "Whereya from?"

When I told him Australia, he let out the biggest whoop. Slapping Boy on the back, he laughed, "See? Didn't I tell you she was from Europe? I was right! You owe me ten bucks!"

Now, at this point I didn't know who to side with—Earl who thought Australia was Austria, or Boy who'd just lost ten dollars. I stuck with Earl. I liked his belt buckle best.

As a very reluctant Boy handed over a ten, Earl continued, "Girlie, you might look like a pimple on a pumpkin riding that there motor-sickle," (Yep, that's exactly what he called it!) "but chicken, you're smooth as silk. I watched you come up from behind me, picking them cars off one at a time, and I just knew you weren't from 'round here. You ride too dang smooth. You're totally glued to that baby. I juz knew you'd be European."

I needed to hear those kind words, because if Earl had seen me five minutes earlier, he'd have watched me lose my footing in the gravel as I pushed Voodoo backwards. Another five centimetres and she would have been on the ground. *So much for smooth.* It's hard to be cool when you've got a 210 kg machine on top of you.

ALWAYS PRESENT

I've decided our children are here to teach us. In Jackson, Jakey had been at pains to remind me to slow down. I thought he meant literally (I hadn't been brave enough to tell him about The Incident), but then he mentioned living in the habit of remembering—slowing down and not forgetting to remember what was important.

As I whisked through Yellowstone, his words haunted me. I'd powered through all the amazing sites—virtually ticking them off. *Hot Springs, tick. Old Faithful, done. Canyon Waterfall, all over it.*

It was a shock to have his words come back to me and realise what I was doing. It was full-speed site absorption with zero appreciation in the process.

So I stopped, right in the middle of Sapphire Hot Springs (OK, not quite in the middle) and calmed myself down. I looked at everything around me. I watched the colours and the textures, I breathed in the smell (OK, that bit wasn't good—there's nothing like the smell of sulphur), and I stepped into my breathtaking environment with my whole heart.

Always the lesson: to be completely present and appreciate everything around me. Let's hope I don't forget to remember.

DAY 69: YELLOWSTONE TO CODY

Some mornings, you just have to laugh. I decided to try to pass the coffee on in Yellowstone. Stealthily, I scoped my unsuspecting victim—standing behind me—and asked him what coffee he'd like so that I could buy him one. I explained someone had very kindly done that to me the other morning, and I'd like to return the favour.

In a very European accent, the sharp retort was, "I don't need you to buy my coffee. I buy my own."

Really? OK, fine then. Buy your own, but I won't be fazed. I'll try it again tomorrow. I'll just double-check to make sure my next victim doesn't have an accent!

My GPS tracking system had died the night before, and with Yellowstone not having Wi-Fi, there'd been a little nervousness—

OK, panic—from my home team concerning my whereabouts. Being unable to contact me fuelled the continual fire about my safety while "wandering around the US" on my own on a motorbike. More than a few people have asked my husband why he "let me do this." (Yep—they really asked that question!) For starters, he was brave enough to know not to try to stop me. But more importantly, he knew this was something I had to do. He and my boys don't always get it, but they stand behind me, knowing it's important.

Conversely, there's a pretty strong belief out there that by potentially putting myself at risk each day and causing concern to my team, I'm being selfish.

It's funny. To the outside world, it might look as if I'm not taking the concerns of others into consideration and that I'm just thinking about myself. In my old life, I would probably have felt guilty and agreed. *Yep, that's selfish.*

But if there's one thing this journey has taught me, it's that I can't possibly take care of others until I've taken care of myself. To heal, hold onto my power, and find validation internally. If I'm to have any chance of being the best person I can for others, I need to be OK first. I need to put me and my healing and my growth first. Is that selfish? Maybe. But I've found a better way to describe it: *self-full.*

I need to fill myself first before I can fill others.

So, self-full though it might be for me to be on this journey, I'm OK with it. And my team will be (once I get new batteries for my tracking device!).

BACK IN THE GAME

The early morning cruise through Yellowstone was beautiful. Riding fast wasn't an option. If nothing else, bison have an amazing ability to slow you down. But it gave me the chance to take in this incredible park—smouldering geysers, boiling mud pots, ferocious waterfalls, and bubbling hot springs. Everywhere I looked, it was a powerhouse of percolation.

As glorious as Yellowstone was, a couple of days of crawling on the tourism trail had made us antsy. It was great to head east and get the chance to ride hard—and ride hard we did. Out through the plains, alongside snaking crystal-clear rivers, through yellow and green tree-lined valleys...Voodoo powered her way effortlessly through the spectacular mountain passes. It was demanding but oh-so-exhilarating.

This had been my first full-on ride since The Incident, and I'd needed to push myself hard to get my head back in the game. There's no such thing as a hesitant, capable rider. You can be one or the other, but you can't be both. After a shaky start, eventually it all started to flow again. Having to fight this breathtaking road gave me my confidence, my fire, and my buzz. I'm not sure who was more relieved—me or Voodoo. We were back! Thank God.

WELCOME HUNTERS

Welcome to Cody: home of Buffalo Bill, the infamous William Cody. Now, I'd done Wild West towns before, but they're just "wannabes" in the Wild West hierarchy. This place was the real deal!

Coming into town, the first thing that greeted me was the "Welcome Hunters" signs throughout Main Street. Call me old-fashioned, but I didn't think this town was going to bode well for a raw foodie. As I checked into my hotel, I noticed that every wall was covered by some poor dead animal's head. If that weren't enough, there were stuffed bears guarding the front doors—grizzly, black, and polar—complete with a sign that said, "Don't touch the animals." *Are they kidding? There's no way I'm even going near the animals!*

They take their Wild West heritage very seriously in Cody. I mentioned to the guy on reception that I was only here for the night, and I asked him what I should see. I'd noticed the Bill Cody Museum on the way in—should I see that? With a look of disdain, he told me it would take at least three days to do justice to the museum. *Really? I'd rather clean the oven with a toothbrush than spend three days in a Wild West museum. But then, I've always had an attention deficit issue.*

I did manage to squeeze in a couple of cool things though. They still had the original town that Bill Cody set up back in the late 1890s, which included the house Butch Cassidy and the

Sundance Kid holed up in. (I'm never going to complain about Motel 6 again!)

The pièce de résistance was the Wild West Gun Shootout, starring Buffalo Bill, Doc Holliday, Annie Oakley, and Wyatt Earp. Yep, they dragged out all the heavies for a great gun-slinging street production. It was five dollars to sit down or free to stand. (I stood just in case I needed to run away.) If nothing else, it was very loud. I was only sorry to have missed the Great Cowboy Musical Review later that night, but a girl can only handle so much excitement in one day.

Finding food in Cody was interesting. The definition of whole foods here was steak, fries, and a bit of tomato to make it a complete meal—protein, carbs, and vegetables. I've seriously struggled to find anything to eat over the past few days that didn't resemble road kill. After not being able to face another bowl of iceberg lettuce and mushy tomatoes, I settled for a packet of raw almonds and a two-week-old banana that had been floating around at the bottom of my bag.

But dinner aside, this wild, wild world was the coolest—even if their definition of green was a pickle, and I needed to check my guns at the door everywhere I went.

I'd heard Cody was small in size but big on attitude. *My kinda town!*

DAY 70: CODY TO DILLON

The next morning, leaving my "Hunter's Haven" hotel with deer and cougar heads sadly hanging on the walls, I headed out for coffee—and for one of the biggest treats of my journey.

Desperate to pay my coffee forward, I chose my victim a little more carefully this time. Standing behind me in the queue was an elderly gentleman, and although he was a bit taken aback, he graciously accepted my offer. Together we sat outside, soaking up the sun, sipping and talking.

His name was Donald, "But you can call me Grandpa Don." Grandpa Don was divine. He was weather beaten—worn and craggy around the edges—but there was a ferocious love of life running through the deep lines etched on his face. His eyes twinkled as he told me he was eighty-seven, "But don't tell anyone in town." With a wink, he added, "They all think I'm eighty. I'd hate for them to know how old I really am."

How could I resist this charmer? Do we ever stop worrying about our age?

He'd been married "to the most beautiful girl in the world" for over sixty-five years, and with a cheeky chuckle, he told me, "She still makes my heart sing. The eternal optimist, I'm still hoping for another ten years with my special girl." How precious to be so loved. A few years earlier, he'd had a stroke, losing sight in one eye and becoming partially paralysed down one side. It had taken him a long time to accept what he'd lost and how his world had changed. But as he said with a smile, "Life is about being thankful for what we have and not worrying about what we don't have."

It reminded me of one of my favourite sayings from WuDe: "A lot of suffering comes from wanting to be what is not, and wanting not to be what is." But I think Grandpa Don probably nailed it a little more succinctly in his slow, Wild West way.

I waited with him until his beautiful bride came to collect him. She laughed as she pinched his cheek and teased, "Really, Donald? Here you are in the sunshine of your life still chatting up women?" As they left, he bear-hugged me tight, thanking me for our time together and saying what a joy it'd been to sit with me. But I'd received the greater gift. As he shuffled away with his special girl, Grandpa Don suddenly stopped. Looking over his shoulder, he smiled and said, "Life is about being thankful and making people happy. That's all there is to it."

In one simple sentence, this precious gentleman had poetically summed up both the reason for life and the reason for my journey.

There was nothing more for me to say other than, "Thank you." Grandpa Don had made me more than happy. He had given me the gift of real joy—another successful mission in the wonderful life of this special man.

With a big smile and a warm heart, Voodoo and I pulled out of Cody and rode back to Yellowstone. We were headed northwest towards Montana—the final leg of my journey.

Home was getting close.

IN THE SADDLE AGAIN

The ride out was a message from the Universe: "You're running out of time. Let's throw everything at you." And it did. Stunning deep canyons, long sweeping roads, tight corners that just begged Voodoo to power through, spooky tunnels carving their way through majestic mountains—the world was ours as we wove our way alongside the Shoshone River, back into Yellowstone, and out into Montana.

Compared to the untamed wildness of Wyoming, Montana felt softer. The snow-capped purple mountains were muted, the background colours were pastel.

It was a big day in the saddle—a 480 km day—and yep, I'd been in the Wild West so long I was starting to feel like a cowboy. It was easy to do out there. Such vast open spaces with nothing but mountains on the horizon, I could almost see Buffalo Bill and his boys coming over the hill. Time to move on before I ordered a steak!

But a big day in the saddle means a big day in the helmet. Time to think, time to contemplate, time to resolve, and—if you're not very careful—time to go around and around in circles.

I ached to realise I had less than ten days left on this incredible journey. I'd bartered hard with my team at home to be able to journey for three months, and staying out longer than that would have pushed the bounds of friendship beyond their tensile strength. But after my precious experience with Grandpa Don, I realised I wasn't even close to ready. There was still so much to learn, to answer, to let go.

I knew it had to end sometime or I'd be ninety-eight and still circling the Rockies (actually, what a cool thought!). At some point, I'd have to go back to being a grown-up, but not now. *Please, not now.*

TRUST THE PROCESS

My riding boots were amazing. I'd had them forever, and they were as comfortable as old slippers—until I started this journey. From day one, my feet had ached badly in my boots. When I probed *You Can Heal Yourself*, I discovered feet issues were caused by fear of stepping forward into the future.

OK, that makes sense.

From the beginning, I'd demanded this journey uncover my future. I was scared of the unknown and wanted immediate answers. I wanted to know where I was going, why I was going, and how I was going to get there.

Not surprisingly, the more I demanded security and safety, the more my feet hurt. When I finally let go of the need to know, my feet stopped aching overnight. They'd been fantastic for weeks—until this morning, when my old fears had come tumbling out and my feet started to throb.

I really thought I'd have the answers by now. I was OK leaving my old life behind because I figured my new life would be revealed on this journey. I'm not quite sure what I was expecting. Maybe a neon flashing banner across a mountain pass saying, "OK, baby, here's the next step for you." *Perfect. Thank you. I can relax now that I know.*

But no, nothing. I had no idea. I have to remind myself that, even though I don't have a bloody clue what will happen after I switch Voodoo off for the very last time, it'll be OK. *Don't worry. Just trust the process.* But on a long day in the saddle with too much time for thoughts to rattle around inside my helmet, the fears started oozing in, slowly at first, and then in big gushing waves.

I needed to stop looping—to regroup and get my act together. At a tranquil mountain lookout, I pulled Voodoo to a standstill, and helmet in hand, I sat on a stone-bricked wall, my feet dangling over the edge of a steep cliff face. I closed my eyes and tried to meditate, to calm myself down and find some peace. To breathe.

When I opened my eyes again, I realised I would kick myself hard if I wasted the last ten days of this redefining journey worrying about what would happen at the end. I couldn't spend my last few days being fearful about the real world kicking in. That would happen soon enough. I still had ten days, and I needed to make sure every one of them counted.

I needed to get back on Voodoo and be grateful and present. No more thinking, no more worrying about the future or the past. I needed to focus on the journey—only the journey—and let go of my fears.

Let go and trust the process for fuck's sake! When am I ever going to learn to do that?

With tears streaming down my face, I got up off the wall—pretty stiffly, by this stage—gave myself a shake, and said four empowering words:

"OK. Let's do this."

DAY 71: DILLON TO MISSOULA

Today, Voodoo and I clicked over 18,000 km. When I started this journey, I figured I'd be out for about three months, but I had no idea the kind of kilometres I would do. (I was gonna have to do some serious booty work when I got home. My rear end looked like an ironing board.)

But how much do I love this big beautiful Voodoo girl? She has my heart completely. The original plan had been to sell her at the end of this journey. But thirty seconds after I'd swung my leg over her, I knew that was never going to happen. It was excitement at first sight and love by third gear. She's been my trusty collaborator, my brave co-conspirator, and my spirited confidante.

She's been my home for nearly three months. There's no way we will ever be separated.

WINDEX FROM THE UNIVERSE

Montana feels like a vast wilderness. It's beautiful with its wide-open spaces, its prairies, and its snow-capped mountains. But today, it felt a little desolate and raw. I felt insignificant—solitary and diminutive riding across the ceaseless expanse.

I wasn't sure I was ever going to fit into the wilds of Montana. Coming down a tight mountain pass, I sat behind a truck with a dead deer in the back. It broke my heart. I had to pull over and let someone overtake me. I accept that it's life here, but it's not the life I choose. Even the bugs are getting to me. They have unique bugs here. After committing suicide on your visor, they leave a thick film that is impossible to clean off. Around the fourth time cleaning my visor that morning, I decided I needed to bring out the big guns in order to see. I needed Windex—except the gas station had none.

So I asked the Universe, and it delivered. Alongside me at the pump, a guy was cleaning his windshield with—yep—Windex. He very kindly wiped my visor, which cleaned the smearing perfectly. (For all of about two minutes.)

Apparently, I needed the same treatment. Later that day, a lady approached me in a coffee shop, and with the slightest of attitudes commented, "Miss, do you know there are dead bugs all over your jacket?"

Really? Ma'am, I've got dead bugs in my teeth—which is why I'm not smiling at you. It looks like I've just eaten a poppy seed bagel! I'm so good in the outdoors!

HEY, BC BABY

Coming through the Bitterroot National Forest, and completely in the middle of nowhere, I came across the teeny tiny town of Wisdom, which boasted little more than a gas station and restaurant.

It was bitterly cold, and Voodoo was empty, so gas and coffee were the first orders of the day. Stepping off Voodoo, I heard a loud shout:

"Hey, BC Baby. Get your ass over here and come and have coffee with folks from home!"

Yep. Three riders from Vancouver, who were really excited to see me until I opened my mouth. There's nothing like an unexpected broad Aussie accent to throw you. Like true gentlemen, they recovered quickly and accepted me as an adopted Canadian.

After they headed out, I stayed in the sun still trying to get warm, when out from the restaurant came three bears. (OK, they were hunters, but they were the size of bears.) Fully decked out in camo gear, they'd been out hunting for three days and had just come back into town for supplies and a decent lunch. So much for being big tough hunters!

When they heard I was just cruising on Voodoo and didn't have a schedule, they asked if I wanted to come back into the mountains with them and hunt(!). I'd been skirting around it all conversation, but at this point, I had to confess:

"You know, guys...actually, I'm vegan." I figured *plant-based* would have been too much of a stretch.

They burst out laughing when they heard that and told me "vegan" was just Native American for "poor shot." They might have been right, but I was OK with that.

NO MORE SHOULDS

After gently but firmly refusing some jerky, "Try this, seriously, you'll never go back to being a vegan"—I pointed Voodoo north to Missoula—a funky, energetic university town bursting with colourful Victorian houses, wide tree-lined streets, coffee shops on every corner—and yes, juice bars! After days of wandering in vegan wilderness, I was desperate for something green that wasn't a pickle!

Sitting on a river bank, an amazing juice finally in my hands, I thought about a conversation I'd just had with a friend who suggested I reframe my question about the future. Instead of, "What am I going to do when I get home?" change the story and ask, "What am I *free* to do when I get home?"

Wow. Talk about a difference in perspective. Put a similar question into a different context and the whole world changes. A wealth of opportunities suddenly appears, all by changing one simple word. It felt like a giant weight had been lifted off my shoulders. I knew I couldn't just ask the question and wait for the answer to be handed to me on a plate. I had to show up, do the work, and keep moving forward.

I had to actively participate to make opportunities happen, but it's a balance—a fine line between surrendering to the process and still doing the work. I can't keep demanding results, but I can't just put my feet up and wait for things to happen.

I'm struggling knowing how to balance on that fine line. The pushy personality that still lurks pretty close to the surface wants answers now, but it knows it needs to take a back seat to trust. *Damn it!*

As the stars started to light up the sky, I felt at peace. I was truly free to do whatever I wanted. I was free to be whoever I chose to be. I was free to change my story and to create anything I wanted. I was free to be me. No more *shoulds*...just freedom.

And, for the first time, I wasn't scared of freedom—and that felt amazing.

DAY 72: MISSOULA TO WHITEFISH

One of the things I've learnt to love on this journey is the power of my daily rituals. They set my energy up for the day, give me purpose, and remind me of who I am. They connect me with the Universe and keep me engaged in the awesomeness of this journey.

I've found that the way I start my day will be the way I live my day.

If I start the day in chaos, funnily enough, it only goes downhill after that. But if I kick off the day with some degree of conscious energy, that's how my day flows. Most days, anyway.

I'd learnt the hard way about being a ritual overachiever. When I first headed out on this journey, I grabbed everything I'd learnt about how to set the energy for the day and being a "more is better" kinda girl, and I tried to do them all at once. At one point, I was so busy first thing in the morning deep breathing, centring myself, being grateful, setting intents, meditating, doing affirmations—blah, blah, blah—that I didn't have time to ride. I was so focused on setting up *for* the day that I didn't have time to *live* the day.

Through more error than trial, I let almost everything go and settled on a routine that gave me a kickass combination of energy and peace, calm and fire. It was a hell of a combination, but exactly what I needed on this journey to really help me frame my day.

The morning ritual that worked best for me was simple. Before my feet hit the floor every morning, I took three deep breaths to get centred and to get my mind to kick in. Then I chose one thing to be grateful for. It could be more than one, but it had to be something that I could carry deeply in my heart. Next was setting the intention for the day—my living masterpiece—then bam!

Outta bed, run, meditate, and gear up. Kiss for Voodoo, ask the Universe to protect us, and we're away.

In the warmth of my snug bed in Missoula, today's intention would be inspiration. I wanted to connect with people and experiences that filled me with energy, that challenged me, and inspired me to be the best I could be. Seemed simple enough. *Over to you, Universe. Let's see what you have in store for me today.*

I really should learn to scale down my intentions. Sometimes they're too much for me to even handle.

IN THE FLOW

Coming back in from a very slow and very cold shuffle along the banks of the Clark Fork River, I decided to delay my departure to Whitefish until it warmed up a little. It was just on freezing, and I was still without a heated vest (although one was en route to Whitefish).

As I waited for the sun to warm my world, I wandered into the lounge of my B&B for coffee. A beautiful elderly gentleman with the most translucent skin I'd ever seen was sitting there with his wife, and he just glowed. I wanted to know his secret!

He'd been the first chemist employed by one of the most successful natural cosmetic companies in the world. He was in his late eighties, but he looked about seventy, with energy, fire, and vigour oozing out of him as he spoke about his work. He told me he dreamt of new products in his sleep and would get up at 2:00 in the morning to work on the formulas. Sometimes he'd be so consumed that he'd work forty-eight hours straight till he got it right.

He said he never got tired when he was creating. He was so engrossed in what he was doing that he lost all concept of time, and he loved knowing that every time he got it wrong, he was closer to getting it right.

Now that's seriously in the flow. At the wellness conference in Telluride, Deepak Chopra had talked about stress and the fact that 67 percent of people hated their jobs. He also mentioned that more deaths occurred on Mondays than any other day of the week. I guess the lesson there is either to find a job you love or don't go to work on Mondays.

But for this amazing man, every day could have been a Monday and it wouldn't have made the slightest bit of difference. How powerful it was to meet someone so passionate, so enlightening, so inspiring!

I could have sat listening to him all day, but Whitefish and a new heated vest called. Although I'd given her a couple of hours to warm up, Voodoo was still covered in ice by the time I loaded up. As brave as I tried to be, the ride out was fiercely cold despite the watery sun giving it its best shot.

Don't ever say I haven't learnt my lesson! At the first, "OK, you need to stop and warm up" thought, for once I did exactly that. I pulled into the next town and headed for coffee. *Wow, look at me! Nothing like needing a sledge hammer to crack a walnut.*

GRATEFUL FOR OPPORTUNITIES

Being the only person in a coffee shop is usually a good indication of what to expect, and sure enough, the coffee was the second worst I'd experienced on the trip (marginally better than Kenny's in Oregon). But the coffee didn't matter. The company did.

The young "barista" came up to my table and asked if she could sit with me. She wanted to know all about my trip and what I was doing. But as we talked, her story emerged.

She was from California, and she'd been an alcoholic and a drug addict. When she'd gotten into trouble with the police, they gave her the option of either cleaning herself up or going to jail. She'd chosen to move to Montana and start a new life. She was living with a relative, had been clean for two years, and had just gotten off probation.

But she had a new challenge: her cousin had been killed a few days ago in a drive-by shooting. She wanted to go back to California for the funeral, but she was terrified about being pulled back into her old life. She didn't feel strong enough to go home, but she desperately wanted to say goodbye to her cousin. I listened while she worked it out by talking. In the end, she decided not to go. What she'd achieved in Montana was too precious to risk.

This incredible girl was just seventeen years of age. *Seventeen.* I have a son who's just two years older than that. How can a child—and she was still a child—have been through so much in such a short lifetime and still come out the other side smiling, positive, and enthusiastic about life? If it'd been me, I'm pretty sure I would still have my head under a pillow. But not this amazing girl.

She told me she was grateful for having such tough lessons

early in life, because now she could really learn from them and make them count.

You're kidding, right? How did this beautiful girl become so insightful?

It's easy to be grateful when you've had the opportunities I've had, when you've had the love and support that I've been given, when despite my perceived "challenges," life had been incredibly good to me. But to live her life and still be grateful? That was a courageous spirit and true inspiration.

After making it to the personality-packed town of Whitefish, I took a stroll and found myself in the midst of a country-and-western sausage sizzle otherwise known as Oktoberfest—complete with yodelling, dancing, steins of beer, and bratwurst. Lots of bratwurst. *Sensational!*

I sat on the grass bemoaning the fact that I hadn't brought my lederhosen, but it didn't stop me feeling part of the community. People chatted, asked me to dance, invited me to join them. If just for an evening, I felt part of something special—not just a stranger wandering through.

Later that night, as I replayed the day in my head, I couldn't help but be in awe of the people today who had inspired me with their courage, determination, and commitment to be part of something bigger than themselves.

Seriously, I'm gonna have to watch this intentions thing. It's starting to scare me.

DAY 73: GOING-TO-THE-SUN

I was in Whitefish specifically to ride a bucket list road for bike riders: the Going-to-the-Sun Road in Glacier Park in northern Montana. It would be an out-and-back ride. I'd leave Whitefish, ride the 130 km highway, then turn around and ride back to Whitefish. A beautiful, easy cruise of a day.

You know when you hear so much about something—about how stunning, spectacular, and awesome a place is—that you really wonder whether it'll live up to your expectations?

This baby was a slam dunk—everything it was cracked up to be and more, if that were possible.

TREACHERY AND BEAUTY

The road was notorious for being an RV graveyard, so being a smart forward planner, I figured I'd get up really early to beat the traffic. Sounds fair enough, except I'd forgotten (God knows how!) how cold it is in the mornings now—but there's always an upside. At least at minus two degrees Celsius, I had the roads to myself.

Within seconds of entering the park, I could see Lake McDonald.

A pristine, crystal clear lake, so perfectly still it was hard to tell which way was up as the stunning mountain backdrop reflected a perfect mirror image on the water. Alongside the lake, the road was shrouded on either side with saffron-coloured trees so thick I had to peek hard to see the lake beyond them.

As we climbed, stunning glaciers revealed themselves, covered head to toe with green, yellow, and orange birch trees setting the mountainside completely aglow. The valleys got sharper and deeper, and the mountain passes became more than a little treacherous. No kidding—they were unbelievably tight and without guardrails, and by now, it was a very, very long way down. Three times, I was almost taken out as cars panicked about going over the edge and came 'round the blind corners seriously wide. I have no idea how two RVs would manage meeting each other on a corner. It was hard enough on Voodoo.

But treachery had its rewards, and it was worth every heart-stopping moment. We climbed over 3,000 metres, so it really did feel like we were going to the sun. By the time we got to the top, it was a blistering twenty-eight degrees! I could feel the heat finally making its way through my seven layers and seeping into my bones for the first time in weeks. At the end of the highway, Voodoo and I turned around and came back down again. Somehow, the same road was completely different riding in the other direction.

I'd certainly come just in time, though. The week before, they'd had three feet of snow, and yet new fires had sprung up over-night. The damage from the summer fires had been catastrophic. It was always eerie riding through fire-razed forests—it was as if the soul of the forest had escaped. It was certainly time for this breathtaking road to close for winter—to recuperate from the ravages of nature. And the RVs.

A QUICK TRANSACTION

Coming back through the park and peacefully minding my own business at the end of a line of traffic, a police car pulled in behind me. I was doing the same speed as everyone else, so I wasn't worried. (Unless he'd seen a fairly interesting RV-overtaking-manoeuvre about twenty minutes earlier?) But sure enough, on came the lights, and I was pulled over.

Are you serious? I'd done nearly three months in the US and hadn't been booked once. I'd spent a lot of time with police and had certainly had some deep and meaningful conversations with them, but so far, my record was impeccable.

Not today. The minute the car door opened, I knew I was in trouble. A policewoman. *Yep, my worst nightmare.* And she wasn't taking prisoners. It appeared I'd been doing two miles per hour over the speed limit.

Mmmm...really? But officer, two miles an hour over? I could have sneezed and gone two miles over. Isn't there any leeway?

Apparently not. I could appeal the citation, but that would mean appearing in court in Montana in six weeks. As if that was going to happen! What really smacked was the way she smiled (or maybe it was wind) when she told me she'd never booked a woman on a bike before. *Great. Glad to be a first!* The bite was ninety dollars, but it was impressively efficient. I gave her my credit card, and we were done in minutes. *Fabulous!*

Although I was a little stung, I figured I owed the US Police Department far more than that for the past ten weeks. It probably served me right for all the fines I'd missed out on. Guess karma finally caught me.

Riding well within the speed limit, I had a gentler ride out of the park. I saw more scenery than usual, I ensured the wildlife were safer, and I enjoyed contributing to the US economy. Mostly, anyway.

DAY 74: WHITEFISH TO MISSOULA

That evening, I'd bravely headed back for round two of Oktoberfest, which was just as wild as it had been the night before. Nothing like a sausage-eating contest to get a raw foodie excited! There is, however only so much yodelling a girl can handle. Who'd have thought?

As I'd walked back to my hotel, I mulled over a message from a good friend who knew me oh too well, and whose judgement I trusted. In love, he mentioned I was still driven by the need to achieve. I was pushing hard just to see if I could hold on, and I was riding to the point of obsession. (It's lucky he hadn't heard about The Incident!)

Ouch! Really? Am I still that person? Didn't I leave her behind in Jackson somewhere? Damn. I thought I'd been making headway. Obviously not—or not enough.

When I first read his email, the air rushed out of my body, shortly followed by two actions: hyperventilation, then anger. I moved onto various stages of anger pretty quickly. Honestly, hyperventilation didn't stand a chance as I crashed into denial, defensiveness, and indignation, followed by just a touch of petulance. (OK—a lot of petulance!)

How dare he? Couldn't he see how far I'd come? Who was he to judge me?

The scary thing was, after I'd finally calmed down, I realised he was right. He'd nailed it. I was still driven by action and execution. Progress had been made for sure, but that compulsion was still alive and kicking, even after The Incident. *Damn, that was irritating. Spare me—just when you think you're making progress.* But that's what good friends are for, right? To tell you the things you don't want to hear? (I still wanted to bite him, though!)

SO MUCH TO LEARN

Not surprisingly, sleep was a waste of time. At about 3:00 a.m., I finally gave up counting backwards from 1,000. I'd already done that five times, and if that hadn't bored me enough to sleep, nothing would. Wrapping myself in a big blanket, I sat looking out into the blackness of the night, contemplating.

Another friend had spoken to me the same afternoon, to remind me I was a human being not a human doing, and I needed to stop pushing. *So, what was that all about? Was this an intervention?* They were on opposite sides of the planet and didn't know each other, so I figured there must have been an important message in there somewhere.

And then it hit me—of course! I was still needing to "do"—to achieve, to push, to strive. My old modus operandi. But in order to grow, what I really needed was to "be"—to be present, to be still, to surrender to the not-knowing. To just be.

Finally, their messages made sense.

Understanding them didn't make it any easier. I had no idea what to do with that flash of insight. *OK, I got it. So now what?*

Sometimes on this journey, the learning was almost too much. It often felt like the enlightenment tap had been turned on full and I was drowning without knowing how to turn it down. I couldn't keep up with it.

When all else fails, breathe and go for a run. Yep, anther action tactic, but hey—I could only be challenged by so much insight at once. Or, so I thought.

I shuffled slowly out into the darkness—my old body was starting to creak and groan every morning like a worn-out chair. I certainly wasn't bouncing back like I used to. I blamed the cold and long hours spent with my knees wrapped around my ears rather than surrendering to just getting old and tired.

A little bruised and battered, I headed out, looking for anything to take my mind off the feeling of failure. I knew in my heart I should be celebrating progress, but that wasn't enough. I figured by now I would have been cured. (Ah, grasshopper—still so many lessons to learn!)

JASON'S STORY AND MINE

My source of inspiration when I run is simple: I listen to podcasts. My podcast of choice today was Rich Roll interviewing Jason Garner, who in his own words was a "streetwise hustler" who'd become the number two executive in the largest music promotion company in the world—before waking up one day and deciding to quit. He walked away from it all. Why? Because he realised it wasn't making him happy. Despite everything he'd accomplished and everything he'd achieved, he still had a giant hole in his life. He was never enough.

He then spent the next six years embarking on a voyage of self-love and self-acceptance—in his words, "changing from a life of matter to a life that matters."

My feet stopped running and the tears poured down my cheeks as Jason told *my* story. He'd been named twice in *Fortune* magazine's list of top earners under forty, and he'd run the world's largest music promotion company. But apart from that (!) our stories were similar. Sitting on a rock in the darkness, I listened. His story and his experience went right to the core of my journey over the last few years, and it was a shock to hear him tell a story that was almost word-for-word (apart from promoting Beyoncé) mine. As he told of his journey—his fears, his warrior behaviour, his patterns, his lack of belief—he told my story.

He'd faltered and occasionally gone backwards, but his commitment to filling the hole in his heart through spirituality, meditation, and breathing had won through. He'd shown up, done the work, and come out the other side. He'd trusted the process and surrendered, and he'd felt peace with what he'd found.

Thank you, Universe. That was just what I needed to hear and exactly when I needed to hear it.

Jason's commitment to self-love—to being kind to himself, giving himself space, honouring himself, and accepting himself exactly as he is—was striking. I have to admit, I'm still struggling a little with self-love. I know you can't truly love others until you love yourself. I know that putting yourself first isn't selfish but self-full—my brilliant new word! I know you have to have compassion for yourself before you can have compassion for others.

And I also know that deep inside, self-love is at the core of all my challenges.

Lack of self-love has let the warrior become powerful—it's stopped me from being vulnerable and left me continually needing external validation. It's driven me to push boundaries beyond their tensile strength, and it has caused me to live in fear and feel like a fraud—and don't even get me started on body image!

Can I now say from my heart that I've reached a position of complete self-love? Nope—far from it. But I'm getting better. After nearly three amazing months on the road, I actually like myself. I like who I am. I like how I'm growing and changing and stretching. And I like how I'm OK about saying that. Whatever I've been through in life has made me the person I am today, and I'm OK with that.

Now, when I wake up in the morning, I like what I see (most days). I'm not there yet, but I know that's the journey, and every day I will keep stepping forward into it.

And stepping forward? That's the real prize.

DAY 75: MISSOULA TO LEWISTON

A brilliant question Jason had asked on the podcast was, "What do you want to build?"

I don't know yet! I need more time! But will there ever be enough time? I guess not. Looks like I'll have to start before I'm ready.

Sometimes the Universe gives you exactly what you want, and sometimes it gives you what you need. The two might not be the same. Yesterday, I needed an easy riding day that gave me the chance to process deep learning and to reflect. And that's exactly what I got.

Today I needed a full-on blistering, burning ride that threw it all down, got back up, and threw it all down again. A ride that brewed and percolated slowly, then burst into life and had me by the scruff of my neck. I wanted fast. I wanted furious. I wanted Voodoo exploding with precision and power.

I needed to be shaken and challenged and (a little) terrified. I needed to be on the edge, no matter what I'd been told. Sometimes you've just gotta break out. It was time!

But as I've learnt on this journey, be very careful what you ask for.

Pulling out of Missoula, the town was deserted. On the previous night, the University of Montana had won an important football game. After celebrating the success till well past four in the morning, the university town had finally collapsed and gone to bed, leaving the town abandoned.

Never fear—there's always a coffee shop open. From my stool at the window, I saw a dishevelled guy circle Voodoo three times before grabbing the locks on the Leaning Tower of Pisa. Now, I have a very intricate and sophisticated locking system with my bags. It's three locks that have either stopped working, changed their own combinations, and/or the guts fell out of them weeks ago. So they do nothing except look like locks, and all I can hope for is that they make someone think twice about going for the bags. But obviously not this guy.

I was out of that shop like a rocket. I "challenged" him calmly (OK, I shouted at him loudly), and he got the message and took off. It was only afterwards that I wondered what I would have done if he hadn't hightailed it. I guess my bloodshot, cross-eyed look had been scary enough.

DANGEROUS AND BEAUTIFUL SURPRISES

Crisis averted, I headed out of town into the wilds of Idaho and onto one of the most electrifying roads I've ever ridden. Highway 12—the infamous Lolo Pass—was 300 km of the most insane, heart-stopping, overwhelming, wildly gorgeous rides Voodoo and I have ever exploded through. Stretching from outside of Missoula, stepping into and then crossing the complete width of Idaho, Lolo Pass was truly magical.

On top of steep turns, tight corners, and ferocious hairpins—for that extra bit of adrenaline first thing in the morning—there was ice. I found myself holding on for dear life as we hit invisible but deadly pockets of frozen water. The challenge with ice is that you can't see it, obviously, but you can certainly feel it. Hopefully, you feel it in time to do something about it rather than when it's too late and your back wheel is sliding out from underneath you halfway through a tight hairpin bend.

Escaping off the mountain, we flew into majestic, imposing pine forests. I've gotta say, I loved the wide-open plains of Wyoming and Montana, but I felt a little lost in their vastness. Give me a tight, all-encompassing pine forest, and I'm a happy girl. And happy I was.

Huge cedars almost blocked the sun, stretching way up the side of the mountain, dense and thickly packed with the occasional sliver of light escaping through. As if to push magnificence to a new level, we scooted along two dazzling rivers all day—the Lochsa and Selway rivers—as they cut their way to the Pacific Ocean. Sometimes they were fast flowing, sometimes they were still. Sometimes narrow, sometimes wide—but always sparkling and always crystal clear. Even from the road, I could see fish swimming near the shallow but visible bottom.

For an extra crowd pleaser, the colours today were better than watching fireworks. Two days ago, yellow had been the top-performing colour, but in no time, it'd been overtaken by orange, with red starting to make up ground. Would the surprising beauty of this journey ever stop?

TO PONDER

Just when I thought life couldn't get any better, it did. As incredible and overwhelming as the ride had been so far, I spied a sign that brings joy to every rider's heart: a small and insignificant sign on the side of the road that said, "Winding road next 99 miles."

Are you kidding me? First, what do you call what I've already gone through, and second, ninety-nine miles of riding heaven? *What have I done to deserve this?*

And heaven it was. It started off easily—gentle, sweeping turns rocked us peacefully and lulled us into a false sense of security. Then suddenly, the road turned into a full-on assault. Within minutes, I was rounding hairpin after hairpin, flying up and down razorbacks, manoeuvring my big, heavy baby through tight radius turns, and frankly, hanging on for all I was worth.

I'd heard that Lolo means *to ponder*. Well, I've gotta say, there was no time for pondering today. The magnificent Lolo Pass had my complete and undivided attention as I wound my way through some of the most demanding twisties I've encountered. Intense focus, total concentration, and pure adrenaline. It was such a gift.

When I finally did have time to ponder—when our glorious ninety-nine miles of exhilaration had come to an end, and we were cruising through flats—I realised Voodoo truly had become a natural extension of me. In a strange way—or maybe it wasn't so strange—being on her represented everything I'd wanted to embrace on this journey.

I'm clear on what and how I want to feel every day. I want to feel happy. I want to experience pure joy. I want to be totally present, and I want wholeheartedly to connect. And that's exactly what I find being on Voodoo every day. With one switch of the ignition, one kick into first gear, and one touch of the throttle—that's where I am. Instantly. And it's pure magic.

But Voodoo is more than just an extension of me. She's my learning in action. The first few corners on the pass were wild. They were tight, tricky, and unpredictable. And because I didn't know the road, I was tense, apprehensive, and wary. (Rightfully so, given some of the hairpins!) But when I settled in—when I relaxed and let go, when I abandoned my need to know what was around the next corner, when I stopped fighting Voodoo and trusted—she just flowed.

GO FOR GROWTH

I'd met a couple driving an RV on the pass today, at one of many stops where it was so cold I had to get off Voodoo and do jumping jacks to get warm. (It's not a pretty picture, seeing the Michelin Man doing star jumps.)

They were fascinated that I was doing this journey on my own. They kept asking me the same question: "But aren't you scared on your own?" I've been asked this question so many times, and perhaps I am naive, but the answer is no. Never. (OK, maybe once at Happy Camp.)

For me, this journey had been about searching for growth, not comfort and safety. (Although technically speaking, I do get the comfort of staying in a hotel with a warm bed every night, so I'm not that hard core.) Instinctively, I'd known I'd never get growth or answers by holding onto my security blanket in the life I'd always lived. Sure, being scared of being alone hadn't been an issue for me, but there had been plenty of other physical and emotional challenges. Finding the energy every day to say, "Let's do this," had often taken courage (OK, and stupidity) on days when all I wanted to do was crawl back into bed and hide under the duvet.

But tonight, as I languished in the comfort of my cosy hotel in the seaport town of Lewiston, Idaho (I'm not sure how they can call it a seaport, seeing it's bang-smack in the middle of the US, but there you go!), I received a text from one of the brotherhood telling me to go outside and watch the lunar eclipse.

When I complained about being too tired to get dressed again and go outside, he berated me for being lazy. (I think he really meant *comfortable*.) So out I went, greeted by the most spectacular blood red moon completely illuminating the sky.

Comfort gets you nowhere, right? Go for growth. Still learning, I guess.

DAY 76: LEWISTON TO WALLA WALLA

It's late September, and I'm sailing close to the wind in terms of making it home before I turn into an ice sculpture. The weather is stunning, for sure—crystal clear blue skies most mornings—but there's very little warmth in that beautiful yellow ball these days. The first few hours of the day are brutal as I rattle and roll all around Voodoo, trying to get warm.

The hardest part is having frozen hands. Within about fifteen minutes most mornings, my hands have turned into blocks of ice. All feeling completely disappears. Being vertically challenged doesn't help my riding position. If I'd chosen a touring bike, I'd be sitting upright all day, but no—I wanted a superbike, remember? That means I ride completely stretched out across my tank, with the full weight of my body taken on my hands. I'm literally leaning on my hands the entire day.

While my body can usually handle the pain, my hands suffer. After they've fallen asleep, I spend the next seven hours shaking them violently to get both blood and feeling back into them.

Given that hands are the most important factors in throttling and braking, when you add "frostbite" to the equation, you get a little more adrenaline than what is recommended for the average day.

A VERY PATIENT BUSTER

Within ten minutes of leaving Lewiston, at a chilly three degrees Celsius, my hands were already in bad shape. The first coffee of the day was in order. Pulling into Starbucks, I manoeuvred Voodoo alongside a car with its window open, where sitting in the passenger seat—completely motionless—was the cutest, ugliest dog I'd ever seen.

He was a bulldog named Buster, and he waited patiently in the passenger seat every morning while his owner had his coffee hit. He sat there without moving for hours at a time. I discovered this because I met Buster's owner—Steve—at the coffee shop and ended up chatting to him for a couple of hours. Spike didn't move a muscle once.

Steve was a fellow superbike rider, and his eyes lit up when I told him I was heading to Hell's Canyon. After scouring my maps, he gave me a blow-by-blow snapshot of the road in about 100-metre increments. Seeing it was a 65 km road, it took us a while to get through where to expect ice, where to watch for gravel, and where to expect my old nemesis: logging trucks. (*Nooo!*)

But then it got a little crazy. As we bunkered into two big chairs, he told me his story. He'd been a heavy-hitting IT guru in Silicon Valley, then woke up one morning feeling completely empty. He realised he liked his job marginally less than he liked himself, so he'd quit. Without a plan, he moved to Squamish, British Columbia—about 50 km from Whistler—to get his head straight.

He'd felt his whole career had been built on "luck." That he was a fraud, and the fear of being found out kept him under incredible pressure. His need for control had been so great he hadn't taken a holiday in seven years. Yet no matter what he'd achieved, it was never enough.

He'd chosen Squamish because he liked the name—always an important selection criteria when choosing your home—and for six months, he climbed, hiked, wandered around in nature, and worked on getting to like himself.

Our conversation was painfully raw. Steve shared stories about the emptiness of his soul, and what it had taken to reclaim his life. And with a complete stranger (OK, he was brotherhood) I spoke from the heart about what it felt like to have been in a sarcophagus for so long, unable to break free. But finally, I had, and now there was nowhere to go but forward. I just needed to work out what to do with all the leftover bandages.

Hey, Universe—this is the second time you've sent me this compelling message in the space of a few days. What are you trying to tell me?

Where do I start? So many lessons about changing my story, about stepping out of fear, about letting go, finding peace within, and being loved for who I am and not what I do. Lessons this journey has continually reinforced for me.

But my biggest lesson this morning was far simpler: it was about realising it would be OK. I would be OK. No matter what, I would come out the other side—maybe a little battered, maybe with the odd scar or two, maybe with some bruising and the odd flesh wound, but I was going to be OK. I was healing. I was growing. I was finding joy. And no matter what, I was finding the real me. And she was going to be just fine in this brave new world.

As I pulled out, Steve threw out a final challenge to sum up our conversation:

"...and if you see any Harley riders up there in the canyon, you've gotta totally smoke 'em, OK? Leave no Harley standing. We have a reputation to uphold!"

Gotta love a man who has his priories right. And Buster? He never moved a muscle!

THE DEVIL'S DECISION

Even the name "Hell's Canyon" inspired fear and trepidation, and five minutes into it, I knew it had been aptly named. Hugging the borders of Idaho and Oregon and straddling both sides of the spectacular Snake River, it's a massive 16 km wide. It's the deepest gorge in North America at nearly 3,000 metres deep—over 600 metres deeper than the Grand Canyon.

Combining a phenomenal change of elevation with ominous canyon rims, gnarly mountain passes, rockslides, ice, majestic vistas, and ice—did I mention ice?—you have one hell of an adventure on your hands. And for extra excitement? Maybe it was the Devil's decision, but there wasn't a guardrail in sight.

On the map, the road looked impossibly contorted—like a large intestine that had turned back into, onto, and around itself. I figured the Google-mappers had made a mistake. Their camera must have fallen off the bench and they'd given it a shake before they got it working again. But no. It was definitely a large intestine, with a small intestine thrown in for good measure.

Despite Steve's intricate and detailed explanation of the canyon, he'd failed to warn me there were still moose around. *Really? It's fall. Shouldn't they be hibernating or something?*

Midway through a corner, I looked up and there was a giant moose standing right in front of me.

As always, wildlife never stands in the road at a straight, where you've got plenty of time to see them. For some reason, they choose to stand directly on the apex or exit of a corner, which was where this big boy was today. Luckily for the moose—and me—Voodoo and her incredible Brembo brakes handled it like a pro.

A TETHERED BALLOON

Settling into the funky little town of Walla Walla in the vineyard region in the southeast corner of Washington, I was buzzed about it being a three-state day. I'd started in Idaho, had flown through Oregon, and was now in Washington.

As much as I loved Washington, even saying the name put a small bit of foreboding in me. Washington—the state just below British Columbia. The last US state I'll hit before I head home. It was hard not to think about all the work that still needed to be done. *Don't think, don't think, don't think...I'm not ready! I'm not cooked yet!*

Despite my anxiety, after nearly twelve weeks on the road, I can feel the hole in my heart starting to heal. I can feel the edges slowly coming together.

In a gas station conversation, I'd told someone I felt like a beautiful, bright, hot air balloon that wanted to be free, but I was tethered to the ground by a confusion of ropes and ties. Now, after nearly twelve weeks, I could slowly feel those ropes being cut, one by one. This bright big balloon—appropriately full of hot air—was getting ready to truly fly.

Sometimes, I feel a little guilty about having so much. About everything this journey has given me. But I know if you truly believe you deserve a good life—to fly free—then it'll come. The trick is to truly believe.

I'm starting to believe. I just need to cut a few more ropes.

DAY 77: WALLA WALLA TO SPOKANE

As a university town, Walla Walla was an eclectic mix of buzz and chill. Importantly, it held a place of prominence in the US as the capital of sweet onions. Go figure! I'm not sure that's something I'd like to be famous for, but I learnt this distinguishing fact when I was served some Walla Walla sweet onions at breakfast this morning. An interesting choice at any time, let alone for breakfast. But because it was a "vegetable," the owners thought they'd hit the jackpot for me. *Bless them!*

But do you have any idea what it's like in your helmet after eating onions? It's really not a good way to start the day. Onions and garlic: two things to avoid when your face is enclosed tightly for hours. I managed to avoid the taste test for breakfast but couldn't refuse the kindly donated bottle of preserved onions that now rattled around in my bags. I needed to find someone to donate them to.

RUGGED BEAUTY

Today was girls' pamper day—Voodoo later in the afternoon

for her 20,000 km service in Spokane, but first, me. After all this time on the road, I was starting to look like the Yeti. Time for something radical—time for a haircut.

For guys, that's no big deal, but we girls would rather have root canal therapy than find a new hairdresser. Especially in a new town. Even more so in a town famous for onions. I chose the most upmarket place I could find and challenged them to do their best.

I've obviously been on the road for so long I'd forgotten what a sight I was in dusty boots, worn and faded Kevlar pants, and a disgustingly filthy bike jacket. Even in a small town, the "uber" stylists were dressed in black and gave attitude. As I walked in, they all stopped and stared as if I'd just stepped out of a Mad Max movie. I got the, "Are you serious? We're good, but we're not that good," look—the one most stylists have perfected.

Suddenly, I was acutely conscious of how "rugged" I looked. *Big breath. It's OK. They may all be beautiful and cool, but I'm an adventurer, right? I'm a free-spirited, wild woman of the road. I just wish I didn't look like one!*

Luckily, I'd let go of perfection somewhere south of Death Valley.

The only concession I'd made to femininity on this journey was my jewellery. Almost zero makeup, minimal cosmetics, minimal clothes—most of my space is taken up with wet-weather and cold gear, plus running shoes. Despite the heels and a little black dress still languishing forlornly at the bottom of my bag, (what was I thinking?) there hadn't been a lot of "girly" on this trip—and today, I felt it.

The stylists looked at me as if they'd prefer to spray me down with disinfectant before they touched me (probably not a bad idea), and with complete disdain added, "You could certainly do with a manicure as well..."

Are you for real? It's gonna take more than a manicure to get me back into shape. For right now, just cut my damn hair!

Yep, great to see the warrior could still sharpen her sword when she needed to.

Realistically, my jewellery wasn't a girly concession. There was a reason for everything I wore, and it was to remind me of who I am, what I choose and intend, and what's important to me. Every morning, I put it all on—kind of like my armour—and affirm what it all stands for.

There's a heart necklace from Leavenworth that reminds me I'm loved. That's layered with a shell necklace I discovered with the Brazilian boys in Monticello, to remind me the energy I receive is directly proportional to the energy I put out in the world. That's been such a powerful lesson for me on this trip. I remind myself every morning to make sure I'm consciously putting energy into everything and everyone around me.

Then, my tie bracelets—picked up in Nevada City after a tough day on the road. There's a black shiny one that reminds me I'm vibrant, dynamic, and sparkling (yep, you can't take the diva out of the girl!), and there's a camouflage one to remind me I'm of the earth and grounded. *Take that, stylists!*

THE LAST LEG

With visibility through the fringe finally achieved, it was onto Spokane. For most of the day, we rode through stubbles of harvested wheat. It felt like being on a parched moon. Not a tree in sight—just the last of the crops. It was desolate. For the whole day, I rolled through, around, and over giant yellow folds that stretched as far as the eye could see, with nothing in between.

In some areas, they'd pulled the stubble out in preparation for planting, and the brown cuts turned the hills into giant tiramisu cakes with chocolate and yellow layers. The highlight of the ride was watching the wind ripple like waves through the last of the wheat.

On top of the hills coming out of Walla Walla, giant wind farms controlled the skies, as well as my ride. As awesome and impressive as these massive structures were, with wind farms came wind and lots of it. Funnily enough. It became a real "hang onto your hats" ride for about 100 km, where Voodoo decided she wanted to choose exactly where she wanted to be on the road, regardless of where I had her pointed. *Gotta love it when your bike fights back!*

And fight back she did. Today, she almost threw me off to make her point as we rode sideways through yet another mini tornado. She snapped, she bit, she slid, and she bucked. If nothing else, she's telling me she needs new tires.

Our first stop in Spokane was the BMW dealer for Voodoo's well-deserved and much-needed service. Despite the challenges I'd had with her today, I was devastated to be leaving Voodoo. We were joined at the hip. It felt like leaving my child at pre-school for the first time (I didn't handle that well, either). The service guys were pretty understanding, despite me checking four times that they were clear on what she needed to get ready for our final leg.

Eventually, their patience wore thin. When my cab still hadn't arrived, they decided that driving me into town themselves was a better option than having me watch them pull Voodoo apart. (Or maybe they just wanted to throw away the onions I'd given them!)

Spokane was a city, and not where I wanted to be. I could feel the tension and agitation seeping in already. With a week left on this journey, I don't want noise and traffic and concrete. I don't want city streets and shopping malls and traffic lights. I don't want soulless hotels and office blocks—people not making eye contact with me as they scurry past. I don't want to be invisible. *I don't want to be here.*

But it doesn't matter what I want. This is where I have to be. I have to be here for a reason: to take care of my partner in crime, my one and only Voodoo.

Toughen up, princess. Change your story and breathe. Be grateful and enjoy a very different ride for the next few days.

DAY 78: SPOKANE

Despite everything I'd told myself the night before, I still woke up in my hotel room agitated and unable to settle down. I felt like a caged tiger. I paced my hotel room in the early morning light, frustrated about being in a holding pattern. There was little time left, and I was desperate to be on the road, desperate to be back in nature, desperate to be back on my Big Girl.

And so I ran. Along the riverfront on the outskirts of the city, over bridges and viaducts high above the Spokane River—complete with waterfalls, fast white-water rushes, and whirlpools. Along the riverbank, vibrant trees of red, orange, and yellow lit up the fore-shores, bringing a warmth of colour to the morning.

As I ran, I explored my restlessness and tried to dig in deep to understand it once and for all.

LET IT EVOLVE

My friend's comments about pushing hard still stung, no matter how right he was. Why did I struggle with being still and quiet, with slowing down? Why—after all these weeks on the road—was I still finding it hard to just be? Whatever happened to my beautiful quote from WuDe, "If we can't find the joy right here, right now, in this present moment, then nothing we do or plan in the future will be enough."

Whatever happened to just breathing? To celebrating the simple? To being a human being, not a human doing?

Sometimes, going deep is like peeling an onion. You can't just stop at the first layer. You have to keep asking, "But why?" as you peel back every layer to really get to the core. And yes, that would mean tears. But it was the only way to get to the heart of the truth. With my onion goggles on, I started to pull back the layers.

For sure, I knew I was restless because I was out of my routine. I actually loved my daily routine—it had become a meditative practice. There was a security in knowing each choreographed step in my day. A calm that came from being present in my action, and a comfort in knowing what came next and how the day would flow.

But—and here's the bite—the routine kept me busy. It gave me a place to hide. In moving seamlessly from one routine to another, there were no blank spaces to fill. No silence to listen to or questions to answer. Perpetual motion: my favourite safe place.

Knowing that didn't answer the question: why can't I be still?

I didn't even know where to start to look for answers. But I'd heard a great comment the other day: "Don't try to solve; let it evolve." Again, a challenge for someone who needs immediate answers.

With my head spinning, I decided to walk the streets of Spokane and see what evolved. It wasn't quite the glorious nature of Baker or Shasta, but still beautiful in its own way.

WALKING SPOKANE

As my high heels clicked (yep, I'd frocked up for the city in heels), I pondered. Maybe I was running away from myself. I knew I'd scared lots of people in the past. Maybe I was actually scared of...myself.

So much of my past life had been about avoiding me. Even when tough questions crept in, by staying manic, I could actively hide from doing the confronting work needed to find the answers. This was different.

When you're on a bike for seven hours a day, there's no escape from yourself. There's just you and your helmet, and no matter how much you try to avoid the provoking questions that continually snap at you, sooner or later—once you've finished the hairpins—they find their way back into your head.

So I knew I'd finally stopped running from myself. I sure as hell didn't have all the answers, and maybe I never would. But during this journey, I'd finally tackled the work I needed to do to at least shake out the tough stuff.

OK, fair enough...but why?

As I walked, a quiet word bubbled up: control. *What—really? Control?*

There it was. Staring me in the face. It had been hiding quietly in my tank bag for thousands of kilometres, just waiting to jump out. I'd been putting my maps on top of it every day and squishing it down, but it'd finally found its way to the top. Better late than never, I guess!

I've always had a strong need for control (hotly denied, but sadly true). I've always needed to be running the show and to be in charge. By being busy—by continually moving forward and having a strong routine—I was still in charge. Reality was so far from the truth, of course, but in my head, framework, structure, and action, I was still in command. *How had that been working out for me so far?*

WHAT STAYS AND WHAT GOES

I was scared to let go of control because I still struggled with the concept of surrender. It wasn't a word that sat easily with a warrior, funnily enough.

But surrender had been redefined for me along this journey. Surrender didn't mean giving in or not being in action. It simply meant acceptance. And acceptance didn't mean submissiveness—it meant going *with*, not against.

I'd embraced the new definition, so why was surrender still causing me pain?

Finally. The last layer of the onion: I'd struggled with surrender because I thought it meant giving up me. This journey had been about finding me—the real me. The spiritual me that somehow got lost in all the years of needing to prove and achieve.

But embracing the essential me didn't mean denying who I was at the core. Rolling hard and rolling fast are fundamental to who I am. I will always be moving forward—and usually at speed. There's a feistiness—an energy and a drive at the heart of me, and I think that's OK, most of the time. (I might need to check in with a few people. I'm sure there's some feedback there just waiting to be given!)

But somehow, spirituality had gotten a little lost in translation for me. On this journey, I'd mistakenly tried to fit myself in a still, calm, serene box. *That's how you embrace spirituality, right? Being calm and serene?*

Wrong. You embrace it by celebrating who you are at the core. Although I love being able to be still and I love the joy I get when I'm in the moment, it doesn't mean squashing the energy that is integral to who I am. It just means I'm conscious of when and how I use that energy or that fire or that warrior. It's about conscious decisions instead of default positions. That's the difference.

Being still doesn't mean stopping or doing less. It's potentially about doing more—but doing it with intent. It's about doing it with thought, being totally engaged and being totally present. Ideally, it's about doing one thing at a time so I can really give it my total focus. It's more about *how* I do things, not *what* I do.

After walking the streets of Spokane for hours, I settled down. I remembered a teaching that my spiritual guide had given me: the longer we stay in judgement of ourselves, the longer the hell we create.

I'd been in judgement of myself all day. It was time to let it go.

I was OK with me. I didn't need to change the real me to fill the hole in my heart. I could stay true to who I was and still be able to move forward into the light. I could be the crazy, wild, unpredictable, feisty spirit—and still grow.

I had to let go of the stories I'd told myself. I had to let go of the protections I'd put around me. I had to let go of fear. But that person right at the core of me? She's OK. She can stay.

I didn't need to let go of her. She was doing just fine.

CHAPTER THIRTEEN

Spokane to Whistler, BC

DAY 79: SPOKANE TO CHELAN

I was so excited to see Voodoo all shiny and clean inside and out, resplendent with two new tires. As I went through her diagnostics, Pete—the head mechanic—looked up from his notes and quietly asked, "So, what are you going to do when you step off Voodoo?" (Even to the mechanics, she had her own personality.) "How are you going to cope? She is so much a part of you."

Please don't ask me that.

I can't imagine what it's going to be like to get up every morning and not have my routine. I can't imagine what it's going to feel like to not be stepping onto my amazing Big Girl every morning—kicking her into gear and making the call: left or right. I know it's going to hurt, and I know it's going to be hard. I always figured stopping would be tough. I just had no idea how devastating it would actually be.

It is what it is. And when the time comes, I'll deal with it—and just cry!

For right now? Breathe. Don't waste a second of your last days thinking that the final destination is hurtling towards you like a speeding bullet. Don't be anxious about the future. Hold onto the present and squeeze everything you can out of it.

THE DOUGHNUT HOLE

Wiping away a couple of tears that managed to find their way out of my eyes, I pulled out my maps. I had to travel clear across Washington today—from east to west—and everything on my map looked desolate. Figuring the Beemer guys would have a special scenic route up their sleeve, I asked the experts for their advice.

I'm not sure laughing was advice, but that was about all I got.

"Dude," (Yep, I was back in the bloke's world) "there's only one way across to the west, and that's through the Hole."

The Hole?

"Yeah, the Doughnut Hole. There's nothing in the middle. Just put your head down and get it over and done with. You're gonna wanna stick needles in your eyes, it's so boring."

Maybe, but then they weren't riding Voodoo. Sure, technically the scenery didn't make my hair stand on end with excitement— it was completely flat with nothing on the horizon other than yellow wheat stubble and scrub land. Not a tree in sight. Just flat, yellow fields for miles.

But I loved it.

A little desolate for sure, but I didn't care. I was buzzing to be back on Voodoo. I could have been riding through gravel, and I would still have been happy. (OK, maybe not.)

GRATEFUL FOR GLASSES

For once, I stopped looking at the landscape and completely stepped my whole body, heart, and energy into being back on my Big Girl. I was achingly present, with every square centimetre of my body in tune with my bike.

I could feel the balls of my feet pushing down on my pegs, my knees through to my thighs gripping the tank and holding me in position. My arms were dropped at the elbows, perfectly relaxed and fluid, my first two fingers hovering lightly above the clutch and the brake. My ribs were ever-so-slightly on the tank. I was completely moulded to Voodoo and at one in her world.

We were so in sync that I didn't want this day to end. I pulled into a gas station and checked my maps. The guys had told me to just go straight and get the tough riding over and done with, but I didn't care what I was riding through. I just wanted to stay on Voodoo.

With the aid of my twenty-dollar magnifier glasses, I spotted the tiniest, thinnest, twistiest road alongside a river. It was a big deviation from my original route, but what the hell. The sun was out, Voodoo was flying, and besides—it was alongside a river.

You can never go wrong with a river.

Thank goodness for twenty-dollar glasses—without them, I would never have spotted one of the most incredible roads of my journey. There we were, on roads of straight, yellow stubble before suddenly dropping into what can only be described as Washington's answer to the Grand Canyon and Utah's Lake Powell all rolled into one. It wasn't quite as audaciously spectacular, but it was incredibly gorgeous nonetheless.

On we wound through the bottom of heroic canyons, until the Universe said, "OK, you've had your fun. We've opened up these beautiful canyons, and now we're going to close them again."

Within minutes, we were back to yellow stubble. Not that it mattered. Everything today was a gift.

THE GRATEFUL TREE

As we headed further west, the landscape started to change again. Bit-by-bit, small patches of green started to appear. They gradually grew until finally I was in the midst of massive orchards and vineyards stretching for miles. Acres and acres of apple and pear trees and grapes hanging on the vine.

Pulling into Chelan late in the afternoon, I decided to sit by the river and watch the sun go down. As I meandered through a park, I discovered something amazing.

It was a Grateful Tree. A beautiful big oak tree where people had taken cards, written down what they were grateful for, and then attached them to ribbons hanging on the tree. The tree was completely covered in brightly coloured cards, all with tender messages of thanks and appreciation: the sunrise, the challenges, the nosy neighbour, the love of their family, the heartbreak, Aunty May's apple pie...there was so much to be thankful for.

Later that night, I found myself thinking about the Grateful Tree. Learning to practice gratitude had been such an important lesson for me throughout this whole trip. I'd lost count of the amount of times I'd had to remind myself, "When all else fails, step back into gratitude."

I went back over notes I'd written in my journal after listening to a Rich Roll podcast with WuDe just days before I'd left on this journey. As I was flicking through my notes, a comment from WuDe hit me like a lightning bolt:

"Gratitude is about being thankful for the way things are."

I must have read that sentence about twenty times previously, but suddenly the depth of its meaning hit me with such clarity. All this time, I'd been focused in being grateful for the things around me—mainly, the good and positive things. My journey, my experiences, my family, my connections, breathtaking nature—all incredible things to be grateful for, for sure. But I'd missed the point.

Gratitude was about being thankful for the way things are—not the way they were or might be. Not the way you'd like them to be, but for exactly the way they are, no matter what "are" looks like. Gratitude is being thankful for the "good," of course, but it's also about being thankful for the tough stuff—the things that don't work out, the challenges that we don't want, the things that hurt. Being thankful for the way things are, because the way things are is perfect. It's the way it's supposed to be.

That was such a powerful shift for me. I realised that, when I step into being grateful for the way things are, I can stop fighting. It's an acceptance—a surrender (there's that word again!)—to everything exactly as it is.

It's realising that even in tough times, there is still an opportunity. There's a purpose—a reason—for everything you're experiencing in your life right now, no matter what it is.

The last few days have been a little crazy—lessons are coming through thick and fast. It's as if the Universe is saying, "OK, you missed the lesson five times. Your days are numbered—you'd better start getting this stuff soon!" It would really help if I wasn't such a slow learner!

Despite the fact that it takes me twenty times to get a lesson, I'm grateful for that—and everything—as it is. Exactly as it is.

DAY 80: CHELAN TO WINTHROP

The ache in my heart woke me up well before dawn. How does your heart know to hurt while you're asleep? Does it start to ache gently the minute your eyes close? I think it does. I think it knows your pain and slowly builds on it while you sleep until it's strong enough to wake you so you can share it.

The pain of leaving my journey behind was so intense, I needed to run it out. I needed to push myself and to feel a physical pain that matched my heart. This was the safe place in my old world—punishing my body to escape turmoil—but I figured just this once it would be OK. At least now I could see the evil tactic and choose to use it, rather than it using me.

Out into the darkness, I ran along the banks of beautiful Lake Chelan, breathing hard as I tried to power over the trails. I was slowing up after weeks on Voodoo, but I had to get it all out. I wanted to leave nothing behind.

With my body seriously complaining, I finally made it home—just on sunrise—and the morning decided to reward me for all my hard work. The sky was alight with pink flashes of cloud, purple mountains reflecting perfect mirror images on the still water, and a warm orange sun making its way upward. The ache had stopped, and my heart was smiling. It was a hell of a way to start the day, and it wasn't even 7:00 in the morning.

BALLASTS FOR TOOTS

I'd planned to grab a quick coffee before heading out, though I'd come to realise there was no such thing as a quick coffee on this journey. Sitting fully loaded and ready to go, outside the coffee shop, a feisty old-timer came out to inspect Voodoo. He mentioned we were expecting 60 kph winds today, and after circling Voodoo a couple of times and feeling the weight of my bags in his hands, he came to the solemn conclusion:

"Listen, Toots." (Yep, he called me Toots and lived.) "You're gonna need some ballasts today in these winds. You're seriously gonna need some help to keep this baby on the ground. She's too big for you, by the way." (Really? Now I find that out?)

I forgave him. He worked for the local aviation company and told me to swing by on my way out of town, so he could fix me up with some lead.

It was a beautiful offer, but seriously? OK, two things: first, I don't think he'd counted on the extra ten kilograms of ingrained dirt I'm carrying in my jacket. That thing gets heavier and harder to put on every day. And second, I can barely push Voodoo around at the best of times, let alone with another ten to twenty kilograms on her.

I'm not fearful of riding her anywhere, and I'm OK in most conditions. My only fear is manoeuvring her when I'm stopped. That's the closest I ever come to dropping her. I just need longer legs! (OK, I needed a lot of things, but longer legs would certainly be a start.) Needless to say, we went ballast-free.

I'd made the call to double back a little for my last leg home. I could have gone straight north towards Vancouver through Seattle, but I was headed to Winthrop again—ostensibly to be able to come back to Whistler through Lillooet and the Duffey Road. After all these weeks, it was still one of my top five roads. But the real reason was that Winthrop was the jumping off point to Highway 20—the number one bike road in Washington. I'd done it before in summer, and it was just too amazing not to do it one more time before this journey came to an end. *Bring it on!*

Oh, be very careful what you wish for.

The Universe certainly did bring it on. Rain, hail, more rain, freezing cold—and yep, of course those 60 kph winds. Forget what I've said about not being fearful of riding Voodoo in tough conditions. As we flew, skated, and were thrown all over the road, I was scared.

When the wind picked us up, I had zero control over Voodoo. I had no idea where she was going to land or how she was going to land, and in my complete and total terror, I had but one thought:

"Where's the fucking ballast, you goose?"

DIFFERENT THIS TIME 'ROUND

Highway 20 is an incredible mountain pass that has you climbing, dipping, diving, riding through canyons and over peaks—twisting, turning, curve ball after curve ball. It keeps you on your toes and keeps you hanging on. Every magnificent inch of it has you on fire, and it is incredibly, breathtakingly beautiful.

It was very different from when I'd ridden it in the summer.

Back then, there were giant, deep-green pine forests as far as the eye could see. But today, the mountains were ablaze with bright yellows, deep oranges, and flaming reds—it was simply spectacular. And more than a little wild. The wind furiously whipped leaves from the trees and sent them everywhere. I either had leaves floating down on me like rain onto my helmet, or I was kicking them up from the ground like a leaf blower.

I rode like there was no tomorrow—and although there will be a tomorrow, there won't be a day like today.

There was absolutely no thinking—just feeling and being. Feeling every corner, every bump, every canyon, every incline. Feeling the rain and the wind, feeling the sun for just a brief moment, feeling the weight of Voodoo as we powered out of corners. Just *being*. Completely in the moment, being so present it actually hurt.

I couldn't stop the tears from rolling down my face, knowing this was my last big ride—my last big push of my journey. And although there were tears (and there were always going to be tears), I was just so happy—so grateful, so full of real joy—to have had this ride today.

ROADSIDE CONNECTIONS

I was also grateful to be staying in Winthrop—just about my favourite town, with its funky, cheeky energy. I couldn't put my finger on it, but it felt so powerful and positive. I was glad to be spending my last night in the US in this amazing little town. As if to give me a final farewell to the States, the Universe had one more crazy connection for me.

As I cut through a field to head into town for dinner, out of the corner of my eye, I saw a guy ride past on a beautiful antique BMW motorbike. It was a stunning bike. By the time I'd reached the road, the bike reappeared. Pulling up right in front of me, the rider jumped off and raced to hug me.

Now, I know I'm a friendly kinda girl, but finding myself being hugged by an absolute stranger did take me aback just a little. Luckily for him—because I was just about to get a little antsy—he lifted me right off the ground and, using my Instagram handle, exclaimed, "Sueperlife! Wow! It's really you! The guys and I were just talking about you and wondering how you were getting on—and here you are!"

OK, he got a brief pass because he knew my name. But once he'd taken his helmet off, I'd recognised him—he was one of the three British Columbian guys I'd met in the middle of Wisdom, Montana, a couple of weeks ago—the guys of the "Hey BC, get your ass over here" fame!

My new buddy—Chris—lived in Winthrop a few months of the year, and he'd recognised me as I'd walked past. Half an hour later, three hugs, and a promise to meet him for coffee the next morning, I'd finally made it to dinner.

There's such a crazy, wild bond that comes from being on the road. You can't explain it, and you don't need to. And tonight— tonight of all nights—it was almost unbearably special.

Back in my cabin, the owners of my beautiful B&B had generously upgraded me to my own personal chalet. I watched a doe and a fawn hesitantly grazing close to me as the sun slowly disappeared.

I felt like I had a split personality today (just today?)—one part of me busting out of my skin, totally psyched and buzzing after the most spectacular day of riding, but the other part was chilled and at peace knowing today had been a gift. No matter what, I knew if this all ended tomorrow (or in a couple of days), I could truly hang my helmet up with a smile.

My last day in the US. It will be etched in my memory for a long, long time—this precious, exquisite, extraordinary day.

DAY 81: WINTHROP TO OSOYOOS

At the crack of dawn, I ran. Out into the hills, past the local fish hatchery, past the yellow fields of wheat stubble, and onto the small settlement of Wolf Creek—a collection of barns and houses standing quietly and peacefully alongside a slow, winding river.

I'd run there at the start of my journey, and it was soothing to run through familiar territory and see things I'd seen before—a well-loved tree house sitting snugly on the banks of the river, deer drinking by the edge of the water, fence posts covered with waving US flags.

Today, nature was as confused as I was. The sun was on my shoulder, but the sky was growing darker and darker, with ominous black rain clouds building. For nature, the confusion was a mixture of sun and rain. For me, it was the jumble of peace and apprehension.

There was no holding back now. This was it. We were crossing the line today—or at least the border.

TITANIUM BONDS AND WINDY ROADS

After a quick shower, it was into town for coffee with my new best friend, Chris. I seriously loved the brotherhood. Chris and I had probably spent about forty-three minutes together previously, but right now he was my very best friend. It was an instantaneous bond. It might be thin, but on the road, it's titanium.

I stalled leaving Winthrop. I loved it here—that crazy, quirky, gun-slinging town with its boarded sidewalks and feisty saloons. I loved the amazing B&B I'd stayed at. I had a great farewell chat with the owners, who'd given me a beautiful picture of the inn to take with me.

They'd wanted to give me a set of glasses to remember them by, but they figured I wouldn't have room. They were right. I'd struggle getting an extra pair of undies in my bags—we were still packed to the max. But they gave me an even bigger present as we were pulling out.

With a hug, they mentioned how excited they'd been to have me back—that my energy just radiated and made people feel good.

In nearly three months on the road, that was one of the most powerful and beautiful things anyone had said to me. It was the intention I'd set on this journey—to connect, to put the energy out there, and to help people feel valued. I wasn't sure I'd even come close to that, but nevertheless, I was overwhelmed—and yep, there were tears with the hugs.

But the main reason for me dragging my heels out of town was the wind. Big wind. Heavy duty wind. The wind was reaching 60 kph throughout the region, and I started to worry that Alzheimer's must be starting to kick in. Did I not remember how the wind had almost beaten me raw the day before? Obviously not, or I was just plain insane!

I'd spoken to Jakey who, in his infinite wisdom, told me not to ride. To take cover until the wind had died down. But nah. I figured if I stayed another day I might not ever leave. And besides, I didn't have far to go. It'd be over in no time.

Remind me to listen to my son next time.

It felt like I was in a combine harvester. It was unbelievable. I was absolutely churned and thrown about in the wind and completely encased in dust. The dust, sadly, was a legacy of the forest fires. There'd been horrific fires throughout the region all summer. Winthrop had them before I arrived the first time, and Osoyoos had them after I left. The landscape decimation had been devastating.

Fires had ripped through wheat fields, vineyards, and fruit-growing areas, leaving the hillsides completely charred with nothing to hold back the dust and erosion. The combination of exposed earth and unbelievably high winds created something out of the Thunderdome.

I had dust lodged in the back of my eyeballs. Despite being covered head to toe in countless layers of clothing, when I finally hit the showers later that day, I found dust in places that defied logic.

And I got to ride through it! That's what happens when you ask to max out your last few days. We were being flicked all over the road on the straights, but the corners opened up a whole new world of entertainment. I had absolutely no idea where we were going to end up as my ever-trusty Voodoo decided to run her own race and disobey me completely. (Again, where was the ballast when I needed it?)

It was tough. As the wind grabbed us, I'd fight hard to take a line and get Voodoo under control. I'd get the chance to breathe for just seconds before the wind would change direction again, and we'd be picked up and thrown to the opposite side of the road.

There was only one conversation loop in my head: *Hold on. You've got this. OK, bring her back, bring her back. Hold on. You've got this. OK, bring her back, bring her back...*

I'd probably been through worse and come out the other side, right? Maybe—I just couldn't remember when! As I sat at a set of traffic lights in Omak, quietly minding my own business, I suddenly felt a "thwack" as a massive cross-breeze hit me, sending Voodoo sideways.

Just before she hit the ground, I managed to catch her.

Another couple of centimetres and we would both have been on the road. Crisis averted—but what I wouldn't give for longer legs. (Maybe I *should* just ride a scooter!) This was not what I wanted on the home straight.

Life in the wind tunnel quietened down marginally as I headed west to Tonasket then gently picked my way to Loomis, which hugged the border close to Nighthawk. The road was as inhospitable on the way out as it had been on the way in—all gravel and no tar.

But it was amazing what 21,000 km under your belt could do to reduce your level of agitation at being in the middle of nowhere with just the desert, harsh craggy mountains, and a huge eagle to keep you company. I loved it. My last real time of being completely in the wilderness. And though by now the wind had picked up right where it left off and Voodoo had gone back to dancing a solo tango, I just smiled—happy, happy in my helmet.

And slowly, slowly, I headed towards the border.

WELCOME TO CANADA

Confession: just short of the line, I pulled up to sit for a few minutes and reflect. I remember having come that way eleven weeks and almost a lifetime ago. I remember leaving Canada and rolling into the States with just the tiniest bit of apprehension.

I'd had nearly three weeks on the road by then, in BC and Alberta, and I was so at home in Canada. The US had seemed daunting, and part of me had wanted to stay in Canada. Now, I didn't want to cross back. Funny. Or crazy. Or maybe both.

I'd had such a kerfuffle crossing into the States that I was expecting the worst coming back into Canada. But there was a blessing in the wind as it hurtled us over the border. The guard didn't want to leave his hut to come out to me. I was expecting the usual wrangle, but he just grabbed my passport, ran inside, stamped it, and thrust it back at me, shouting, "Welcome to Canada," as he ran back to the security of his hut.

That's it? Oh, OK then. I guess I'm free to go. So much for the welcome committee!

After settling into Osoyoos, I pulled out my trusty, worn, hole-infested, scribbled-on, coffee-stained maps for the very last time. I could have made it back to Whistler in one day, but I was stalling. Big time. As I looked at them, I started to compute...

"Mmmm...I could head up to Picton, go up to Revelstoke, move onto Kelowna...I could, I could..."

But I couldn't. It was time to go home. It was time. *Enough now.*

As the sun went down across the stunning Osoyoos Lake, I found the most sheltered spot out of the tornado that was still hurtling around me, and I closed my eyes—savouring every last minute, every last drop, every last emotion and experience.

The wild wind, the wilder characters, the unexpected, the uncomfortable, the beautiful, the stark, the joyous—I was hanging on by my fingernails. Hanging on and loving it all, right to the end.

DAY 82: OSOYOOS TO HOPE

My last full day on the road. Osoyoos was where I began this journey, and now it was where the end would start.

Jealously protecting my routine to the very end, I ran in the cold morning light along the banks of Lake Okanagan. The air hurt my lungs as I tried to get my body moving, and it was a struggle. My legs didn't want to run, and for once, my head didn't try to make them.

I stopped on the side of the lake and looked over its gentle calmness—a pink-purple light starting to emerge behind the mountains. In the stillness, I thought about how far I'd travelled—in so many ways—since I was here at the start. Slowly, the tears started to fall (yep, there were bound to be tears) as I thought about the wonder of my life over the past three months.

I cried for everything. I cried that things were closing, that things were changing, that things were opening. I cried for the way things were. In my wildest dreams, could I have ever envisaged this staggering, wild adventure? Never in a million years.

It had been quite the ride.

Back at my hotel, I geared Voodoo up slowly and deliberately. It was amazing how I'd struggled to slow down this whole trip, but now, facing the inevitable, I was trying to hold onto every last moment. Any slower and I'd stall.

As I backed Voodoo into a car park outside my favourite coffee shop in Osoyoos, a group of young guys came up to talk to me about my bike and the journey. With a heavy heart, I realised this would be one of the last times I'd share that conversation and heart-felt connection. After tomorrow, there would be no journey.

The ache in my chest at this realisation was excruciating. Eventually, I pulled myself away from them. Sitting outside with the sun on my back and my hands warming around my coffee, I tried to breathe.

MOUNT UP

There was absolutely no hope of me "noticing" my emotions this morning and just letting them go. First, there were too many of them flowing in from everywhere, and second, I was on such a roller-coaster that I couldn't tell whether I was up or down, happy or sad.

I was anxious, buzzing, apprehensive, agitated, exhilarated—all at once. It was almost too much to handle. Instead of trying to dissolve them, I let every emotion stay as long as it wanted, and I smiled through my ever-present tears.

Although my heart felt like it was breaking, I was at peace. There was anticipation in my belly and excitement in my heart. After the last few crazy days, today there was no wind and the sun was ablaze. I dried my eyes—for the moment anyway—and reminded myself that I wasn't finishing this journey with a whimper but with strength and power, love and gratitude.

Toughen up, princess. Time to mount up.

LARGE AMERICANO

It wasn't a long ride to Hope—about 200 km direct—so I decided to push the day out as far as I could by taking a couple of wild detours. I had time for just one more adventure. Or maybe two.

Instead of heading directly to Hope, I took a deserted backroad that travelled along the vineyard ridges right into the heart of nowhere—and I mean nowhere. For nearly an hour, there was nothing. Not a town, not a house, not a sign, not a car...nothing. Figuring I'd missed a turn somewhere and gotten horribly lost (over 20,000 km under my belt and today is the day I get lost?) I had two choices: retrace my steps or just go along for the ride. I had nothing better to do today, so I'd just go where the road took me.

The road took me all over the place. It was skinny, twisty, and windy—filled with potholes, cracks too big for me to jump over, and edges that completely fell away. It was bumpy and lumpy, with a surface as slippery as glass that cambered badly and threw me up in the air and nearly off Voodoo more times than I could count. Yep, I loved it! And I loved it even more when I realised it was actually the right road and I wasn't going to be lost without a trace in the wilderness on my last day.

As wild as the road was, it was exactly what the doctor ordered for my last full day. Instead of racing at breakneck speed to the finishing line (as if I'd ever do that), this demented road left me no choice but to go slowly—to focus on the road and what was going on around me, to be present and to sit back (or in this case, hold on) and enjoy the ride.

The vineyards eventually spat me out, and I was back to the main road to Princeton—my last gas stop before Hope. It had been about five degrees Celsius when I'd left Osoyoos. The further west I went, the colder it got. I completely missed the stunning beauty of the canyons coming into town as I huddled over Voodoo's tank, trying in vain to squeeze whatever warmth I could out of her engine.

Pulling in for coffee, my body was so numb with cold that I couldn't get off Voodoo. My legs had frozen in a forty-five-degree angle, and it was impossible to swing my right leg over the back of the bike. I put Voodoo on her side stand and sat, slowly waiting for my legs to defrost before I could dismount. (Thank God, the streets were empty when I finally managed to get off. It wasn't pretty!)

As I walked into a familiar coffee shop, I was greeted with, "Hey, you're back! How was the trip? Large Americano?" Now, I'd like to think it was my wit and sparkling personality that made the cute barista remember me, but I think it was probably that he didn't get too many dirty, scruffy, Aussie girl bikers in need of a good haircut and a wash coming through town.

SURRENDERING TO THE INEVITABLE

I decided to cruise the last 100 km. I'd been tempted to give Voodoo the beans one last time, but nah. Today, I would ease her in gently on her last day—a slow, smooth, seamless ride. One to savour—one to remember.

Well, that and the fact that the faster I rode, the colder I got. The age-old conundrum: go slow and take longer but stay warm, or go fast and get there quicker but be an ice block. Today, I chose slow.

But there was one more detour to be taken before we hit Hope. On the outskirts of Manning Park, I discovered a tight mountain pass—a narrow, treacherous road of switchbacks that turned and twisted its way to the top of the peak.

With the wind my only companion, I looked out at the valley below. Snow-covered mountains stood in the distance in layers of purple and blue stretching out towards the horizon. Beneath me, the world was a riot of yellow, orange, and red as the fall leaves lit up the valley. I couldn't have been in a more beautiful place to sit silently in the sun and consider the enormity of this profound journey.

So many thoughts, so many emotions, so many memories— everything came flooding through me like a tsunami. I was in grave danger of drowning in emotion at the top of this glorious mountain peak. Struggling for air, I did what this journey has taught me to do: I breathed. And as I breathed, all was well.

Carefully, I rewound my way down the feisty hairpins, then as slowly as I could, I eased myself into the gentleness of Hope one last time. As I filled up at the gas station where I'd boogied badly with my Harley-riding mate, I realised: just one more tank of gas and I'd be home.

Emotions had oozed out of every pore all day—they'd managed to find every nook and cranny of my body—and as I bunkered in for my last night, I braced myself for the worst. I was expecting pain, sorrow, and heartache (never one to shy away from drama or heavy-duty emotions). Strangely, it didn't come.

Once I'd finally surrendered to the inevitable, two unexpected emotions emerged: calm, and peace. I pulled up the duvet in a strange bedroom for the very last time and breathed deeply.

In my heart, I know. It's time.

DAY 83: HOPE TO WHISTLER

I'm up at 0500, rubbing my eyes as I tell myself the bags underneath them give my face character. It's a stretch, but it's going to have to do today. Besides, I'm hoping the excitement of my last ride will make my face glow. (Still hoping for miracles, even on my last day.)

Sleep evaded me completely last night. In Hope, you have a choice of a hotel on the main road, near the railway, or sometimes both. I went for the "romantic" option of being close to the railway. But—as I'd discovered on my first night in Spences Bridge—when freight trains continually blast their way through your bedroom all night, the romance wears off just a little. Still, it made me smile to finish as I'd started, serenaded by the dulcet tones of a freight train's howling.

Sleep was never going to be an option anyway. I was too wired, too excited, too anxious, too nervous to let darkness quiet my mind. There were so many questions I couldn't answer, so many things I still didn't know. The one thing I did know for sure: today, it was really over. No more stalling, no more holding back, no more dragging my dusty old boots. Today, I was done. I was moving forward.

For the very last time, I sit in my room, bags packed and ready to go. But I can't move. The sunlight filters through the blinds—dust particles flickering in the air while the sun warms my face and encourages me on. *Time to go, baby. Time to bring this Big*

Girl home. I close my eyes, take a deep breath for courage and head out onto the road one last time.

It's cold—very, very cold. It's another hot-water-to-melt-frost-off-Voodoo kinda morning. Frozen mornings have not boded well for us in the past. I know today will be different, but I'm nervous.

HOLD ON

After 21,000 km, I am so very close to home. I'm so near the finishing line—this is not the time to drop Voodoo or slide her down the road.

Hold on, hold on, hold on. Be good to me for one last day, Big Girl. Let's finish this with style and grace. Let's come in proud and strong.

Although, why am I asking Voodoo? I'm the one who could potentially make a mistake. Voodoo will do just fine, as always. She will be brilliant and spectacular, and she will give me the ride of my life. I know this within every ounce of my body. As do my amazing friends and the brotherhood who've sent messages all night wishing my Big Girl well on her journey home. She is far more than an extension of me—my brilliant partner in crime. She has a life, an energy, and a personality all her own. And, it seems my friends are more concerned about her big finish than they are about mine. (Lucky I've got thick skin!)

It feels surreal to gear up. For eighty-two mornings, I've come out to Voodoo and carefully, meticulously loaded my gear. Loading my infamous Leaning Tower of Pisa has been an art form—a serious zen experience every day. After today? No more.

Packed and ready for action, with a kiss on the tank for Voodoo, I breathe my prayer to the Universe: "Please keep us safe. Hold us in a bubble and protect us just one more time on this journey."

With a growl, my Big Girl fires up and we head out onto the road—full of excitement and awe. We've been given the most perfect day. Brilliant sunshine, crystal blue skies, not a sign of a cloud for miles. It's bloody freezing, for sure, but it's the most glorious day imaginable. The most stunning day to come home.

NO TEARS, JUST CHEERS

The road between Hope and Whistler is like three completely different worlds all rolled into one. I sometimes wonder whether I should have just spent three months going up and down this road a zillion times. It's hard to beat.

The spectacular Fraser Canyon runs for about 84 km along the impressive but ferocious Fraser River. As I hit the canyon, the Universe had just one thing to say: "OK, you want breathtaking nature? Here you go—just one last time."

I'm bombarded with deep canyons, narrow rock gorges, water-falls, steep craggy rock faces, rivers, spooky tunnels (I still don't like tunnels), and majestic mountains so tall I can't see the peaks. Without a doubt, it's one of the most stunning sights I've seen this trip. Such an incredible send-off. The lush green pine trees are surrounded by bright yellow, orange, and red autumn leaves—my own personal fireworks display.

As I burst out of the canyon, my world turns into desert as I head towards the old gold-mining town of Lillooet. The road is harsh, dusty, and dry—a powerful contrast to the lushness of the canyons.

There's a compelling beauty in its starkness, but it's not for the fainthearted. From out of the canyon, I slowly and carefully pick my way up a climbing, treacherous mountain pass. The tiny, narrow road weaves its way up and down the mountains while I cling to Voodoo as if my life depended on it. In some places on this road, it did!

Remember the first rule of riding a motorbike? The bike will always go where you look? Well, it looks pretty damn steep and foreboding from where I'm sitting, so today, I will not be checking out the scenery below. But I'm exhilarated. Nothing like the heady combination of adrenaline and fear.

I pull into a gas station just after Lillooet. My last tank. My last chance for a gas station encounter—and sure enough, I find one. Sitting at a picnic table on the side of the gas station, trying to warm up and get my head together for the last push home, I meet a group of Harley riders—ex-policemen out for a four-day spin together. They tell me they want to stay out longer, but their wives won't let them.

I tell them I've been out on my own for nearly three months, and they decide collectively that they're all leaving their wives for me. Really? Now, one of them I could maybe handle, but four of them?

They ask me to ride with them back to Whistler, but I graciously decline. I know I have to do this by myself. I *want* to do this by myself. Just me and my Big Girl.

After 21,000 km, this was my last leg. I thought the big finish through Duffey Lake might just finish me off. Heaven knows there have been so many tears over the past few days—so much raw emotion. Strangely, I'm calm. I'm strong.

As a friend reminded me last night: no tears, just cheers. Grab every last minute, savour every last taste, capture every last emotion. I'm totally, exquisitely present. I'm not thinking about the past three months, I'm not trying to look into the future, I'm just here, right now, experiencing one of the most beautiful places in the world.

After everything I've seen, this is still just about my favourite road. Sublime mountains, a glimmering green lake that sparkles like an emerald, snappy streams, mountain passes that defy gravity, and twisty, windy roads just perfect for Voodoo to fly through.

At the edge of Duffey Lake, I pull over for one last breath. I'm stalling the inevitable. A guy on a Beemer drops in behind me and slowly saunters over to check out Voodoo and to chat in the sun.

"Been on the road long?"

I smile. "Yeah. A little while."

"Looks like it's been fun."

Oh, you have no idea...

With joy escaping from every part of my body, I climb onto Voodoo one last time as we peacefully wind our way back home to Whistler. No land speed records will be broken today. Let me make it home in one piece and let me make it last just as long as I can.

YOU DID IT, MUMMA

Breathing deeply, I pull into Jakey's office—where this incredible adventure began a mere eighty-three days ago—I'm glad I don't wobble coming in like I did heading out. After nearly three months, I finally have this Big Girl under control—well, kind of.

My beautiful boy comes out—hair still escaping from the man bun—and gives me the biggest bear hug as I struggle off Voodoo. He whispers quietly, "I love you, Mumma. I am so proud of you."

I hold his words like a warm stone in my heart. I can barely breathe with the emotion as I bury my face into his shoulder.

"You did it, Mumma. You did it. I'm so proud of you. It's so good to have you home."

I need nothing more. My heart is full, my destination has been reached. My journey is complete. Eighty-three days, two countries, twelve states, and 21,373 km later, I'm home.

I hug my son tightly, not trusting myself to speak. It's perfect. Everything is perfect. Everything is as it's meant to be.

THERE WILL BE NO MORE

Heading back to the apartment, I'm surprisingly calm. I expected tears, but strangely, there are none. I'm together. I'm collected. I'm completely in control.

But not for long.

Pulling into the underground car park, my hands start to shake, and the pain in my heart starts to sear. I reach over and switch Voodoo off for the very last time. Swinging my leg over her, I can barely get my tank bag off before it hits. A wave of emotion so strong, it punches me in my chest and knocks me to the ground.

Huddled on the concrete floor, my back against a warm Voodoo, my heart opens up and the tears start to fall. I cry until I'm beyond crying. Huge, gasping sobs refuse to stop. I have a choice: I can weep, or I can breathe. Weeping wins.

I'm weeping because it's nothing but it's everything. It's small but it's immense. It's insignificant but it's pivotal.

The journey is over. There will be no more. And that's OK. It will all be OK.

The tears eventually subside, and I breathe. Big, deep breaths till the pain starts to release its grip. When all else fails—sitting in the middle of the grease and the dirt, the oil and the stains on the car park floor—I go back to gratitude.

I'm grateful for this powerful, heart-exploding experience. For everything it has taught me. For everything it has blessed me with. For everything it has planted in me to help me grow. I'm grateful that without me knowing how or when or even why, it has healed me. It has filled the hole that had burnt empty and bright inside my chest.

I'm grateful for the not-knowing. For stepping into this journey in complete trust and total darkness, never understanding how the final destination would evolve, but surrendering nonetheless. I knew it all, but I knew nothing. It called, and I followed blindly.

As it unfolded, as the journey pushed and tested and challenged, I embraced it—often not knowing the answers or sometimes even the questions—safe in the knowledge that somewhere, deep inside me, that it would be OK. That I would be ok. That I was more than enough.

I'm grateful to understand, finally, that it's not me but us. It's not alone but together. To be raw and exposed and bare is to be connected. In that special place of connection, souls soar.

I'm grateful that although this journey is over, it will never end. This is just the beginning. I'm being pulled forward into an adventure—into a life—that is wider, brighter, deeper, and richer than I could ever have imagined.

A life that is still yet loud, that explores and opens and sometimes closes, that is strong yet vulnerable. A life full of energy, passion, and joy. A life that's my own.

And I'm grateful—from the bottom of my heart—for the way things have been and the way things will be. But mostly, I'm thankful for the way things *are*. Just as they are. Right here and now. It is as it should be, and it is perfect.

As I loosen the final gear straps on my breathtaking Big Girl, I feel the last rope tethering my brilliant, vibrant hot air balloon being cut.

Letting it float gently into the sky, I am free. And I fly.

Thank You

Where would I be in this world without the love and support of my incredible family, friends, and backup team? Without you, my journey would have been very different! And so...my heartfelt thanks...

To my long-suffering Mum and Dad: I'm sure there were moments (OK, there were quite a few!) but thanks for holding on for the ride and believing in me anyway!

To my Guides Ross Kerr and Michelle Capper-Fay: you've irrevocably changed my life. Thanks for never asking, "WHEN is she going to get this lesson?"

To my mentors, coaches and teachers Sandra McPhee, Kevin Lawrence, Caralyn Taylor, and Ricardo Riskalla: your guidance, support, encouragement, and infinite patience have known no bounds!

To the Best Business Partner in the World Grant Wilson: together we've made magic. Thanks for our amazing journey and for everything we've created together.

To Very Special People in my life: my very Bestie Myrine Soul for always having my back no matter where in the world that back was located; Mirae Campbell for whispering encouragement and shouting acknowledgement; and Lesley Usiskin for so beautifully holding "our baby" until she was ready to go solo. We did this together.

To the Book in a Box Team: to Tucker, Zach, John, Andrew, Hal, thank you for bravely letting me work outside the box! And of course, thank you to the incredible Brannan Sirratt who fearlessly went on the editing ride of her life with me. You're the best!

And to all the amazing people who welcomed me into their world with open hearts and blistering smiles on this ride—I'm so grateful for our breathtaking connections. Thank you.

About the Author

Sue Hollis has been a corporate heavy hitter in the aviation industry, as well as an entrepreneur helming a multimillion-dollar company (and voted one of Australia's Top 10 Women Entrepreneurs).

She currently embraces the role of Adventurepreneur—following her passions, building communities, exploring the world by motorbike, and helping people create lives of epic proportions!

She spends her time between Canada and Sydney where she is a coach, writer, speaker, and the occasional seeker of adrenaline.

suehollis.com

Facebook: Sue Hollis

Instagram: suehollis_

84981519R00285

Made in the USA
San Bernardino, CA
15 August 2018